PRAISE FOR **LOVE WARS: CLASH OF THE PARENTS**

"A most moving story. The narrator's courage is memorable and will surely inspire many to read this remarkable book."
Alexander McCall Smith, Author of the New York Times *Best-Selling* No.1 Ladies' Detective Agency *Series*

"A timeless classic! From the moment I started reading, I was riveted. I will forever be its biggest cheerleader."
Linda Sivertsen, Award-Winning Author of Beautiful Writers *and* Generation Green

"LOVE WARS captivated me from start to finish! This real-life cautionary tale touched me personally."
Rob Reger, Creator of Emily the Strange

"LOVE WARS is awesome! I want to read it over and over."
Amri Gray, young reader

"On a scale of 1 to 10, I would rate LOVE WARS an 11! I couldn't put it down."
Danny Hernandez, young reader

"LOVE WARS is my favorite book! I love how Matthew evolves throughout the story."
Max Hauser, young reader

"LOVE WARS is the best book I've ever read! It's the only book I've read in which I could relate to the story."
Shatonya Amerson, young reader

"I stayed up past midnight finishing it. Fantastic!"
Stephanie Berger, middle school English teacher

"LOVE WARS is perfect for young adults. It's a mature story with real, grown-up issues seen through the eyes of a child."
Philip Halpern, high school English teacher

"I'm going to share LOVE WARS with friends and family!"
Morgan Mason, young reader

"After reading LOVE WARS, I realized I'm not alone, and I felt empowered. The writing is amazing!"
Sophia Olaya-Hermes, young reader

"I love LOVE WARS, especially the way the hero grows up."
Isaac Kenin, young reader

"LOVE WARS will make you laugh, make you cry, and compel you to do everything in your power to stop the divorce wars of everyone you know!"
Bill Eddy, President of the High Conflict Institute

"Matthew A. Tower has captured the essence of what it's like to grow up in a chronically conflicted divorce."
Janet R. Johnston Ph.D., Co-Author of In the Name of the Child

"It's a must-read for parents. This is a beautiful, well-written story of a boy who uses amazing courage and creativity to survive and overcome."
Meridel Tobias, MFT

CLASH OF THE PARENTS

A TRUE DIVORCE STORY

LOVE WARS

CLASH OF THE PARENTS

A TRUE DIVORCE STORY

MATTHEW A. TOWER

ILLUSTRATED by
TSUNEO SANDA

RAJA MEDIA
YOUNGLING EMPOWERMENT

For Chelsea, My Angel

Dramatized Audiobook and eBook versions are available, visit: LoveWars.com

PUBLISHED BY RAJA MEDIA LLC
San Francisco, California

Text copyright © 2025 Matthew A. Tower and Raja Media LLC.
Illustrations copyright © 2025 Raja Media LLC. All rights reserved.
LOVE WARS, RAJA MEDIA, YOUNGLING EMPOWERMENT,
and the RAJA MEDIA logo are trademarks of Raja Media LLC.

To order bulk copies at a discount, email: LoveWars.Contact@gmail.com or visit LoveWars.com. Special editions for educational or professional use are available upon request, including with customized book covers.

No part of this book may be used or reproduced in any matter whatsoever without written permission except in the case of brief quotations embodied in critical articles or reviews. For information, email: LoveWars.Contact@gmail.com

Love Wars: Clash of the Parents, A True Divorce Story / Matthew A. Tower
Edited by Chelsea Page
Cover and Interior Illustrations by Tsuneo Sanda
Jacket Design, Interior Design, and Typography by Marcelo Anciano
Art Direction by E.B. Lewis, Marcelo Anciano, and Matthew A. Tower

Summary: When young Matthew's parents put him in the middle of their divorce custody battle, he must imitate his hero Luke Skywalker and put an end to their fighting.

ISBN 979-8-9995038-0-0 (hardcover) | ISBN 979-8-9995038-1-7 (ePub ebook)
ISBN 979-8-9995038-2-4 (audiobook)
Library of Congress Control Number: 2025914779
Record available at: https://lccn.loc.gov/2025914779

Subjects: 1. Divorce; 2. Custody Battle; 3. Growing Up and Facts of Life; 4. Parenting; 5. Broken Families; 6. Adolescence; 7. Homage to Star Wars; 8. 1980s American Culture; 9. Stepparents; 10. Bullying; 11. Adult Children of Divorce; 12. Romantic Conflict; 13. Middle Grade; 14. Young Adult; 15. Memoir; 16. Nonfiction

BISAC Subject Headings: JNF019020 - Juvenile Nonfiction / Family / Marriage & Divorce;
YAN018340 - Young Adult Nonfiction / Family / Marriage & Divorce;
BIO026000 - Biography & Autobiography / Memoirs;
FAM015000 - Family & Relationships / Divorce & Separation;
FAM039000 - Family & Relationships / Life Stages / School Age

First American edition, October 2025

Contents

PART I: THE NUCLEAR DIVORCE
1. Goodbye to My Hundred Acre Wood — 17
2. How the Divorce Stole Christmas — 35
3. Drafted — 55
4. The Shrink — 81
5. Who's the Real Parent? — 99
6. My New Daddy — 115
7. Escape from the Parking Lot — 145

PART II: THE REBELLION
8. Tuning the Violin — 161
9. The Ten Plagues — 189
10. Hebrew Lessons…*Or Else!* — 205
11. Mother and Child Reunion — 227
12. Here Comes the Bride — 255
13. Quality Time — 287
14. The Trial — 309

EPILOGUE
A Conversation with Grandma Libby — 339
Last Dance — 345
Where Are They Now? — 355

Key to Illustrations — 358
Artist's Afterword — 363
Acknowledgments — 365
About the Author and Illustrator — 368

All of the experiences in this memoir are true,
based on my memories, interviews with family members,
and family history research.

Names, dates, locations, and a few minor details
have been changed.

LOVE WARS

PART I:

THE NUCLEAR DIVORCE

Chapter One
GOODBYE TO MY HUNDRED ACRE WOOD
Age 6 • 1980 • First Grade

As I listened to my father read my favorite bedtime story, I curled up against his chest and felt the comforting rise and fall of his breathing. His big scratchy beard snuggled my cheek.

"Once upon a time, a long time ago, there lived two happy people called Tim and Maggie with their two children, John and Lucy," Dad read out loud to me from *The Warm Fuzzy Tale*. "To understand how happy they were, you have to understand how things were in those days."

We heard footsteps on the stairwell, and Dad's voice trailed off with his finger still on the page pointing at colorful pictures.

Love Wars

Suddenly, my mother burst into the room, her face bright red.

"Nate! It's *my turn* to spend the night with Matthew!" she yelled.

My father shut the book and glared at her.

"You're wrong, Vanessa! *It's my turn!*"

I hid my face in Dad's chest and put my hands over my ears. I curled up into a tiny ball.

My mother dashed over, yanked my arm, and pulled me out of the bed. As I staggered to my feet, my father sprang up and grabbed my other arm.

"*LET GO OF HIM*, NATE!"

"NO VANESSA, *YOU LET GO!*"

My parents were pulling my arms out of their sockets. My shoulders hurt. My head hurt. My heart hurt.

While my parents fought and pulled, I screamed at the top of my lungs, desperate for them to let go. For long, unbearable moments, I was the rope in their tug-of-war. Why couldn't they stop fighting and love each other again? It hadn't always been this way...

* * *

We used to be a happy family. I remembered being two years old and strapped into the kiddie seat of my parents' yellow Volvo station wagon, clutching my Winnie-the-Pooh. The car was filled with the smells of sticky spilled apple juice and soggy yummy animal crackers. My silly old bear was even dirtier than the car. His once soft yellow fur was dingy, faded, and coarse. He had one ear hanging by a thread and a black button eye drooping from its socket.

Love Wars

Mom and Dad were taking Pooh Bear and me to Sears—hooray! The car's tape deck played a familiar story:

> Deep in the Hundred Acre Wood,
> where Christopher Robin plays,
> you'll find the enchanted neighborhood
> of Christopher's childhood days.

The tape came to an abrupt end in the Sears parking lot. I kicked my feet madly, straining against the kiddie seat harness. The moment Mommy unstrapped me, I burst forth, squirmed through her arms and legs, and tumbled out of the car into the sweltering North Carolina summer. Blinking my eyes against the bright sun, I raced into the store and made a beeline to the kids' section.

Piled onto each other and overflowing the shelves were Eeyore, Tigger, Kanga, Roo, Owl, Rabbit, Piglet . . . but the only one I wanted was Winnie. I grabbed him and hugged him tight to my chest. His velvety fur felt like the biggest, happiest smile in the world. My old Winnie would soon retire to a huge plastic box in the corner of my room where I kept all my stuffed animals, including half a dozen old Winnies I refused to throw out.

My parents finally caught up and escorted me to the cash register. "Thank you, Mommy, thank you, Daddy," I laughed as I jumped up and down.

When we arrived at our cozy brick house on Blueway Road, it was bath time.

"Come on, Mr. Smiles, time for a bath," Dad announced.

Clutching my new old friend, I made a run for it to escape his grasp—I loved playing this game with him. As always, Dad

Goodbye to My Hundred Acre Wood

caught me, wrestled off my blue cord pants and green T-shirt, and threw me into the tub. I held tight to Winnie and giggled while Mom and Dad sang one of their favorite show tunes. They were such bad singers.

"They couldn't pick a better time to start in life," Mom sang as she shampooed my fine hair. Her long, flowing black hair fell around her shoulders, and thick glasses framed her eyes.

"It ain't too early, and it ain't too late," Dad sang as he scrubbed me with a brush, his arm muscles rippling beneath the sleeves of his plaid shirt.

"Startin' as a farmer with a brand-new wife," Mom sang.

"Soon be living in a brand-new state," Dad sang.

And then they sang together: "O-O-O-Oklahoma! Every night my honey lamb and I sit alone and talk, and watch a hawk makin' lazy circles in the sky!"

Mom reached into the tub and moved my arms and legs as if I were dancing on a slippery, bubble-filled stage, the sole performer in their off-Broadway, off-key musical.

"Mommy, where's Oklahoma? Are we moving to Oklahoma, Daddy? Are you gonna be a farmer? Are you getting a new wife?" I asked, splashing my drenched Winnie.

They both laughed.

"No, pumpkin. I've told you before, I'll tell you again: we just like the song. I'm not getting a new wife, but you might get a new brother before too long." Dad grinned and kissed Mom on the cheek.

"Or a new sister," Mom added.

"I love you, Vanessa," Dad said, gazing into her eyes with adoration.

"I love you, Nate," Mom said, enraptured by her co-star.

Love Wars

Dad pulled me out of the tub and held me close. His big bushy beard scratched my face as he toweled me dry. He kissed me on the head and said, "I love you, pumpkin. Don't worry, we're staying right here in Chapel Hill. We're not going anywhere!"

* * *

My parents met in college in New York in the 1960s, and they settled down in North Carolina. My mother was a doctor, and my father was a professor of genetic engineering. I never saw my parents fight during the first few years of my life, and they were overjoyed when my baby brother, Thomas, joined the family just before I turned three.

Shortly after he was born, the greatest movie ever came to a theater near me: *Star Wars*! For my third birthday, in June of 1977, my mother left my baby brother at home with Dad so the two of us could go see it together. I made her stay with me in the theater to watch it three times in a row. The next weekend, they traded off, and I made Dad watch it with me three times in a row *again*.

Around that time, I started noticing that Mom and Dad didn't seem to like each other as much as they did before. They never kissed. Sometimes they fought, their voices as loud as air-raid sirens and their faces twisted like monsters.

By the time I was four, family activities rarely involved Mom anymore. It was just the three boys—playing catch, watering Dad's vegetable garden, running around catching fireflies, mowing the lawn, watching fireworks on the Fourth of July.

Goodbye to My Hundred Acre Wood

When I was five years old, Dad took Thomas and me to the animal shelter to play with dogs. As much as I loved my stuffed animals, I loved real animals even more. I was in love with every single dog there, but I wanted a little doggie just like *Happy Scrappy Hero Pup* from my favorite Saturday morning cartoon.

Soon I settled on my Hero Pup—a bouncy, friendly white puppy with a tail that wagged faster than an airplane propeller. The moment we met, she crawled all over me and licked my face. If she'd been a boy, I would have named her Tigger. Instead I named her Carrie, after the most excitable and energetic little girl in my preschool class. Sometimes Carrie the Wild Child hit other kids and screamed at them. I told myself I hated her, but secretly I had a crush on her.

After we adopted Carrie, I brought her to preschool for show-and-tell. When my classmates heard her name, they accused me of being in love with my dog's namesake. "Of course not, no way, I don't like *her*," I told them. "My dog just reminds me of her." I turned bright red in the face of their teasing.

When I started kindergarten, Mom seemed more flustered than ever about work, her problems with Dad, my bad behavior, and especially my dog. She'd never liked Carrie, and soon she was announcing her frustrations at the dinner table every night.

"Nate, why do I have to work so hard all the time? I'm raising two kids and seeing patients and I have to clean up after Matthew's *stupid little dog*."

She glared at me. "Matthew, when we adopted the dog you said you'd take care of it, but you haven't been taking it out enough. It's pooping on the carpet all the time! When are you going to potty train that nuisance?"

My father looked away and said nothing.

Love Wars

"Yes, Mommy," I said, then ran to find Carrie so I could cuddle with her. She licked my face, and then I took her to play in the backyard, leaving behind Mom's anger for as long as I could.

* * *

My mother and father's fighting escalated over the summer between kindergarten and first grade. During one showdown, Mom screamed from the top of the stairwell and Dad yelled back at her from the bottom. I sat in the middle, curled up on the cold wooden steps with my eyes shut tight, but they didn't stop. They shouted over me as if I wasn't even there.

"Nate, you're never available! You never have time for me!"

"Vanessa, I'm under so much pressure at work, I have to publish papers. You don't understand what it's like in a competitive university research environment!"

"You think I don't know, Nate? I fought my way through medical school! I was the only woman in my class! All the men gave me crap! I know damn well what it's like. Don't patronize me!"

They kept screaming at each other, and I feared their anger would blow up the whole house. I had to make them stop. I tried telling them what they always ordered me to do when I misbehaved.

"Go to your room." My voice was choked as I looked at each of them in turn. They paid no attention and kept on yelling, their voices growing louder, their gazes focused like lasers on each other, not seeing me at all.

"VANESSA, YOU DON'T SPEND ENOUGH TIME WITH THE KIDS! IT'S LIKE YOU EXPECT ME TO BE THEIR MOTHER! *THEY'RE DEPRIVED!*"

Goodbye to My Hundred Acre Wood

"Go to your room!" I commanded, louder. No response.

"NATE, YOU STINK! YOU LEAVE YOUR DIRTY SWEAT SOCKS ALL OVER THE FLOOR. YOU'RE A NEANDERTHAL! YOU NEVER TAKE ME OUT ANYMORE! *YOU'D RATHER RUN IN YOUR STUPID MARATHONS THAN . . .*"

"GO TO YOUR ROOM! GO TO YOUR ROOM! *GO TO YOUR ROOM!*" I screamed at the top of my lungs, aiming my proton torpedoes at their fighting, hoping against hope I would get through to them.

The guns . . . they stopped. Mom and Dad fell silent and looked at me. Then, as if they'd reached an unspoken agreement, they walked toward their bedroom, where they resumed their arguing but in quieter voices. I could still hear them, but they weren't shaking the walls with their screams anymore.

I waited a few moments, listening, then went to my bedroom and pulled out my *Star Wars* toys. Had I done it? Could I stop my parents from fighting? I held Luke Skywalker, my truest hero, proudly in my hands. I extended his glowing blue lightsaber and moved him around in a phantom dance, his electric blade slicing through all the anger that was consuming my parents' marriage.

I had to be a Jedi. I had to use the Force and get Mom and Dad to stop fighting. Maybe I could learn the Jedi mind trick like Obi-Wan Kenobi.

I imagined myself in a scene from a movie, talking to my parents, who were wearing white stormtrooper uniforms.

"These are not the droids you're looking for," I said.

"These are not the droids we're looking for," the weak-minded stormtroopers echoed in unison.

Goodbye to My Hundred Acre Wood

"Your children don't like it when you fight," I said, waving my hand. In my mind's eye, my brown Jedi robe half-covered my mysterious face.

"Our children don't like it when we fight," they replied together.

"Let's all be a happy family," I said.

"Let's all be a happy family," they mimicked.

I had them now.

"Matthew's life will be complete if you buy him a *Millennium Falcon*," I said.

"We already bought you Luke's landspeeder for your birthday. What part of *no* don't you understand?" they responded.

What? This was *my* movie!

I called for a retake: "Matthew's life will be complete if you buy him a *Millennium Falcon*."

"We will take you to the toy store and buy you a *Millennium Falcon*."

Good, good. Everything was unfolding according to my plan.

Just then, I heard the door open, and my little blond-haired brother waddled in. He always came into my room when he wanted to play. He picked up a TIE fighter from my toy pile and said "Whoosh!" as he flew it through the air. I grabbed Luke's X-wing and made laser sounds, imagining myself defeating a whole swarm of enemy spaceships, and tried to ignore the sounds of fighting still seeping through the walls.

That summer, shortly after my sixth birthday, my father took Thomas and me to see the new *Star Wars* film—*The Empire Strikes Back*. Dad loved it and couldn't stop cracking jokes about his favorite lines, like "I'd just as soon kiss a Wookiee."

Love Wars

But I kept thinking about the ending scene. Was Darth Vader truly Luke's father? Could a parent really become so twisted and mean?

* * *

When school started again, Dad told me we were going to move over Christmas vacation.

"Are we moving to Oklahoma?" I asked.

"No, kiddo, I've told you once, I'll tell you again: I just like the song. We're moving to the country."

"So you're going to be a farmer, Daddy?"

"No, pumpkin, we just want more space for you and Thomas to play, and I want more land for a bigger garden, and your mother wants to get away from the city." Under his breath, he said, "And maybe it will help your mother and me get along better..."

"Am I going to have to go to a new school?"

"No, your mother and I will drive you to your old school on the way to work. Nothing's going to change other than we'll live in a bigger, better house. I promise."

At the start of my first grade winter break, we moved into our huge new country home on Stonehouse Road, about twenty miles outside Chapel Hill. We left behind the small brick house with the tiny backyard near the university and arrived in a new neighborhood with long, muddy dirt roads, houses spaced far apart from one another, and spooky woods everywhere. Dad called the place Mud Flats.

While my parents unpacked moving boxes, their fighting grew ferocious. I knew they were screaming terrible things at each other, but I didn't allow myself to listen to the words. I

Goodbye to My Hundred Acre Wood

spent as much time as possible outside. Bundled up in my fuzzy yellow-and-black Pittsburgh Steelers winter coat, I tromped around Mud Flats with new friends I met on my rambles. But whenever I was home, my stomach tightened like a vise as my hopes for a better life in our new home fell apart.

Mom and Dad traded off between yelling at each other and giving each other the silent treatment. Family dinners were unbearable. They didn't even look at each other anymore, and even my usually bubbly three-year-old brother kept his head down.

One night, I got out of bed long after my parents thought I was asleep. I padded softly down the hallway to my parents' room, trying not to make the wood floor creak, and pressed my ear to the door. I heard them talking in agitated voices, saying lots of adult things. Most of it was muffled, but there was one word I could make out clearly because they kept repeating it over and over: divorce, divorce, divorce.

The next day, after my father got home from work, I asked him, "What's divorce mean?" He looked at me, an eyebrow raised. If he figured out that I'd been listening in on him and Mom, he said nothing about it. He seemed to have bigger things on his mind than to scold me for spying.

"Pumpkin, sit down, I need to talk to you. Your mother and I haven't been getting along, and sometimes when mommies and daddies don't get along, they have to separate."

"Separate? Separate what?" I asked.

"Well, Matthew, it's like this," he said, looking confused. Finally he said, "Your mother and I can't live together anymore."

It started to sink in. My stomach churned, like I wanted to vomit, crap, scream, cry, and hurl the insides of my body out of me all at once.

Love Wars

"No no *no!* Why can't you and Mommy love each other?"

He stared back and said nothing.

I remembered the stories my father had told me about his childhood, so normal and happy with his mom and dad and brother and dog, and everyone loving each other. Why did my whole world have to fall apart like this?

"There, there, Matthew," he said, patting my back. I collapsed into his arms, crying, the tears staining his powder-blue Tar Heels sweatshirt. "Look, Matthew, I know this is going to be hard for you. It'll be hard for me too. But it's not the end of the world. You'll still have your mommy, you'll still have your daddy, and we will be happier not living together. You see how much we fight. It'll be better this way, I promise. Trust me, pumpkin, this is for the best."

Mostly I didn't believe him, but I had no energy to argue. If I couldn't get them to stop fighting, I didn't see how I could stop them from getting divorced. My Luke Skywalker powers had failed! I had no control over the Force after all.

"What's going to happen, Daddy? What's going to happen?" I asked, stuck inside the worst worst worst movie ever, dreading the next scene. "Are you moving out? Is Mommy moving out? Where will me and Thomas live?" I sniffled through my sobs.

"I don't know, pumpkin. We haven't figured it out. We're still talking about everything. It took us two years to get this house built, we just moved in, and it's all so complicated . . ." His voice trailed off as he gazed into the distance. "Matthew, you know I didn't want this to happen. I asked your mother to go to marriage counseling with me, but she refused. She's determined to separate as soon as possible. When we get it all sorted out, I'll let you know what the plan is."

Goodbye to My Hundred Acre Wood

That night, my parents stopped sleeping together in their bedroom. Mom told me I would sleep with her in my parents' former bedroom while my father stayed with Thomas in his bedroom. I crawled into bed with Mom and said nothing. She tickled me and told me she loved me and everything was going to be fine. Her long black hair whipped around her face and seemed to suffocate me as it fell into my eyes and mouth.

"Mommy, are you sure?" I asked.

"Yes, Matthew, I'm doing the best I can, and I promise I still love you and Thomas." The unspoken words hanging in the air were that she didn't love my father anymore. I put my head facedown on the pillow, not wanting to look at her. She kept tickling me, trying to get me to respond. I just lay still.

"Give me a hug," she said. I did as she asked.

"Can we go to sleep now, Mommy, please?" She relented. Sleep came at last.

* * *

Mom and Dad began trading off and told Thomas and me we had to take turns spending nights with them. On the nights Thomas slept in Mom's room, Dad stayed with me and read bedtime stories. I tried not to think about the divorce.

Mom left town for a few days to visit her parents. When she came back late one night, Thomas was asleep in his bedroom, and my father was reading *The Warm Fuzzy Tale* to me. My irate mother burst into my bedroom, grabbed my wrist, and they started their tug-of-war.

As my parents pulled me apart, tears clouded my eyes,

and memories of my early years flashed past, like one of my father's family slide shows at warp speed. I was desperate to rewind and return to my Hundred Acre Wood. But it was gone, charred to cinders.

They pulled, and pulled, and pulled. Their hateful screams sounded like Darth Vader's theme song.

"STOP TRYING TO STEAL MY SON AWAY FROM ME! YOU'RE A TERRIBLE FATHER!"

"I'LL SEE YOU IN COURT, *YOU LUNATIC!*"

Which half of me did they want?

Finally, something shifted and my father let go. *Thank God he let go.* My mother pulled my sore, sobbing body furiously toward her, dragged me off to her bedroom, and slammed the door behind us. She sat me down on the bed and wiped the tears from my face.

"Everything is going to be okay. Everything will be all right," she said.

I stared off into space. There was a ringing sound in my ears, like a dial tone, only higher pitched, whinier, more annoying. It almost drowned out her words.

Almost. But not quite.

"Your father's a miserable bastard and I'm sorry he did that to you, but it was my turn to spend the night with you and he's trying to steal you away from me and—ARE YOU LISTENING TO ME?"

I turned to look at my mother, blinking back the stream of tears to see her blurry, angry face.

"Matthew, I've tried so hard with him. I've done everything I can, but he's leaving me no choice. I have to divorce him. Do you understand what that means?"

Love Wars

I buried my face in the pillow, refused to look at her, and sobbed. Snot ran out of my nose, mixing with spit and tears, making the pillow soggy. She tried to read a Winnie-the-Pooh story to me, but I refused to look up or listen. I cried myself to sleep.

The next morning, my mother shook my shoulder. My face was plastered to the sheets, and I refused to move. She pulled my head off the pillow and rolled me over. I didn't open my eyes and tried to stay silent. But suddenly a strange voice emerged from my throat, as if some other kid was talking, a pathetic little weakling who had given up on everything.

"Mommy, I want to stick a knife into my heart."

I heard a gasp. Then her words floated down at me.

"Matthew, I promise, it's going to be okay. It's going to be okay. It's going to be okay."

Chapter Two
HOW THE DIVORCE STOLE CHRISTMAS
Age 6 • 1980 • First Grade

"Take everything—yes, everything. And don't forget the Christmas tree." Mom pointed at the bare plastic tree in the corner of the living room, still waiting for decorations and Santa. Like many of our Jewish friends, my family celebrated both Hanukkah and American Christmas, minus the religious parts.

"What's going on?" I asked as strange men began loading all our furniture into a big truck. It was the morning of Christmas Eve, a few days after the tug-of-war, and Dad was at work.

"We're moving out. Your father is a cretin and we're done with him. Come on." She grabbed my hand.

Love Wars

I didn't even bother to ask her what a "cretin" was; I knew it was just another way for Mom to say, "I hate your father." An icy chill ran up my spine.

"I'm going to go play with my friends," I said, wriggling to escape her grasp. Her grip tightened and held me fast.

"No, you're coming with me. You'll make new friends where we're going."

Part of me wanted to sob and scream and pull back, but I knew it was useless. I went limp and allowed her to trundle me off to the yellow Volvo station wagon.

I sat in the car all by myself, waiting for her to collect Thomas. I stared out the frost-coated window into gray clouds, numbing my eyes until it was all a hazy fog, and listened to the car's relentless clock go "*Click. Click. Click.*" The loud *clicks* thudded in my soul like the stiff boots of millions of stormtroopers marching to war, and I was the only one on earth who could hear them. I wished with all my heart for the clock to run backwards so Mom and Dad would love each other again. The car still smelled of apple juice and animal crackers, a cloying stench of helpless children who can't get grown-ups to do anything right.

My mother strapped Thomas into the kiddie seat, and we pulled out of the driveway onto Stonehouse Road. I took one last look at my parents' massive, empty dream home in Mud Flats.

Just then, hail pelted the car, the icy chunks rattling the windshield. Mom drove for about twenty minutes, then pulled into the parking lot of a rundown motel. With peeling yellow paint, detached gutters swinging in the wind, and the numbers on the doors hanging sideways, the motel looked like it was straight out of a scary movie.

Love Wars

"Martha's going to look after you boys for a few days," my mother said as she deposited us into a dimly lit, smelly room that contained a wrinkled, gray-haired woman I'd never met before. I wasn't sure which smelled worse, the cigarette odors or the old maid.

"I have a lot of errands to run," Mom said. "I have to go meet with my lawyer to prepare the divorce papers, I have patients to see at the hospital, and I have to finish moving all of my furniture into our new home. I'll be back later tonight to check up on you two. I'm leaving some board games to keep you happy." Then she left, pulling the door hastily behind her.

We were alone in the motel room for hours. Martha fed us graham crackers with peanut butter and jelly. I refused to say a word to her. Thomas played quietly with his stuffed rabbits. He was so little, I wasn't sure if he understood what was happening to us. And I couldn't talk to him about it. He was too small and too clueless to be a friend in my hour of despair. I played Sorry! The Game of Sweet Revenge in complete silence with Martha. Thomas drifted off to sleep, clutching his bunnies.

In that moment, I hated both Martha and my little brother. Neither of them was my daddy. All I wanted was my daddy.

I flicked on the TV and watched the Christmas Eve special, *How the Grinch Stole Christmas*. Unlike my mom, the green monster didn't need a whole bunch of burly men to help him clean out the Whos' presents and furniture. He pulled it off with just an overworked pooch posing as a reindeer. In the end, the Grinch's heart grew three sizes and he returned all the stolen goods to the Whos and carved the roast beast with them. How much bigger would my mother's heart have to grow for her to bring us home for Christmas?

How the Divorce Stole Christmas

Mom finally returned late at night, blowing into the motel room like the arrival of another hailstorm. Her long, flowing black hair had disappeared, replaced by short curls that clung tightly to her head.

"I've had a horrible day. I had to see so many patients at the hospital, and getting all the furniture moved was a nightmare. This is all your father's fault, you know. He's such a miserable cretin. He was never there for me. He stank like a Neanderthal and left his smelly clothes everywhere and—Are you listening to me?"

I looked out the darkened motel window partially covered by mini-blinds. I couldn't actually see outside, but I pretended I could. On the other side were my new friends from Mud Flats, a grassy field, a soccer ball, my father . . .

"MATTHEW, *PAY ATTENTION!* I'm telling you something very important about your father and . . ."

I didn't want to hear what she was saying. I wanted to leave, to fly away, to be gone from her and that motel room and that stupid old hag Martha and the stupid board games.

I silently walked over to the board game and picked up the pieces to set up a new game. Maybe she'd play with me in silence so I wouldn't have to listen to her talk bad about my father.

"DO *NOT* DISRESPECT YOUR MOTHER!" she thundered. She flung Sorry! from the coffee table. Little green, yellow, and red plastic pieces scattered onto the carpet, and the dice rolled under the bed.

"You can play the game later, but right now you need to listen to me. You need to understand who your father is and what he did to me and what he did to you and your brother."

I gave up. I sat on the corner of the bed and looked at my

mother's face, smeared with makeup. Her haggard brown eyes drilled into me.

"Matthew, I *tried*. I tried so hard with your father," she said. "I offered to go to marriage counseling, but he refused. I put up with his self-absorbed crap for eleven years. It was always about him, about his research, about winning the Nobel Prize. That's all he cared about—his science. It was never about me, never about our relationship. He only wanted fame and glory. He's just like his father. He delusionally thinks he's the greatest scientist on earth. Getting him to pay attention to me was like pulling teeth. He'd rather run his stupid marathons than spend any romantic time with me. He'd rather watch barbaric wrestling matches at the university than take me out on a date."

Now I was listening intently. Even though I hated hearing her say bad things about Dad, I wanted to know why they were getting divorced. But it was hard to follow all the adult stuff. Mom spoke in a continuous flow, her words coming one after another, like a pent-up river of sludge bursting through a crumbling, bitter dam. She held my gaze and I didn't dare look away for fear of angering her.

"Your father's a horrible human being. Do you know that he was awful to you and Thomas? He used to hit both of you until I made him stop. And he made you both run around the racetrack until Thomas collapsed from heat exhaustion. Thank God your brother didn't die. But the worst part is he's been trying to steal you away from me for years. Imagine *the nerve* of that man, trying to break a son's love for his mother. There is no worse crime. *Matthew, your father is worse than Adolf Hitler!*"

The words hit me in slow motion, like bricks casually lobbed at my forehead. Worse than Adolf Hitler? *Worse?* I remembered

my first day at Jewish Sunday school, when the teacher had lit six candles. "Do you know why we are lighting six candles, Matthew? We are remembering the six million Jews who died in the Holocaust." The teacher had told us all about the Nazi dictator with the mustache, the concentration camps, the gas chambers, the ovens. Was Dad really the worst Nazi of all time?

My mother was twisting a wrench deep inside my head. She was in total control, and there was no escape. I tried not to listen, but the wrench kept twisting.

I went numb. I allowed my eyes to glaze over, just like when I'd looked out the car's window that morning. Fortunately, she didn't notice that I'd stopped listening. She rambled on and on and on.

Mom spewed her torrential poison onto me and I had to swallow it. She droned on for over an hour, and I felt like vomiting. Finally, when she ran out of angry things to say, I sucked up every bit of courage in my little Luke Skywalker body and asked her the only question that mattered to me, even though I dreaded the answer.

"Mommy, when will I see Daddy again?"

My mother sucked in her breath, her cheeks taut like an overinflated balloon that was ready to pop.

"WHAT? How could you ask such a question? Didn't you listen to a single word I just said? *NEVER!* I'm done with him, and so are you, and so is your brother. You never have to see that Neanderthal ever again. I won't let him hit you or make you run in races anymore. He's never going to steal you away from me again."

If I'd been bigger, I would have wanted to hit, to throw, to attack. But I just cried and flung myself onto the bed facedown.

How the Divorce Stole Christmas

"It's okay, Matthew," my mother said as she patted my back. "Don't worry, you'll get over it. We're moving into a new house, where you'll make new friends. Everything will be fine, and Martha and I will take care of you and your brother. I don't need a man. We don't need a man. Most men are full of crap anyway."

Through my tears, I turned my head to look over at Thomas, who was snoring, curled up with his rabbits in the other bed. It must be blissful to be so little and so unaware. Maybe if I fell asleep too, the real-life nightmare would be gone when I woke up.

In my dreams, barbed wire surrounded me. It was gray and bleak and cold, and everyone wore uniforms with black-and-white stripes. Then I saw Anne Frank, who I had heard about in Jewish Sunday school. She was cute, writing in her little notebook. She paused for a moment, and looked me right in the eye.

"Matthew, be brave and write about what's happening to you *no matter what*." Then the angel with the pen shimmered and disappeared.

Two people ran the camp: my mother and my father, who had grown an Adolf Hitler mustache. Just as they were telling me, "Matthew, you need to take a shower *for your own good*," I woke up with pee running down my leg.

"Aren't you past the bed-wetting age yet?" Mom said the next morning.

I wanted to write it all down, to keep a diary like Anne Frank, but I didn't dare. I was too afraid Mom would find it and scold me for telling stories about the family.

* * *

Love Wars

Christmas came and went. After several boring, lonely days with Martha, Mom moved us into a new home in the countryside on Lark Lane. The house had faded orange paint, a big backyard, and a creek running through the nearby woods. It was smaller than the one in Mud Flats but still big enough that Thomas and I both got our own bedrooms.

On our first morning at the new house, we woke up to a belated Christmas celebration. Loads of presents waited for us under the plastic tree. I unwrapped Hardy Boys books, stuffed animals, and *Star Wars* toys—even a *Millennium Falcon*! Later, when I went up to my bedroom, I set up my toys and lost myself in visions of intergalactic battles between the Rebels and the Empire. But then the spaceships turned into my parents fighting, their heads the size of twin Death Stars with screams powerful enough to destroy an entire planet.

At least there were plenty of kids in the new neighborhood. The ground was covered with snow, and I went sledding with my new pals Jonathan Callaghan and Daniel Griswell, who were also six years old. Afterwards, Mom fed us hot chocolate, donuts, and ice cream. I ate lots and lots, more than all my friends. Anytime I got sad and thought about how much I missed my father, I went to the refrigerator and helped myself.

Soon after we moved in, Mom bought us a color television set. I was so excited; we'd only ever had a black-and-white TV before. As the cable guy flipped through the channels to make sure everything was set up right, he landed on the crime-solving canine Scooby-Doo. I told him to stop right there. I watched Scooby, Woody Woodpecker, and Bugs Bunny for hours every day.

Johnny Callaghan had an Atari video game system, and I

How the Divorce Stole Christmas

wanted an Atari, too. I kicked and screamed and begged. Mom refused, saying she had to save money for her custody battle with my father. "You aren't the center of the universe, Matthew. You can't have everything you want. Santa Claus gave you and your brother all those toys for Christmas. Isn't that enough?"

One day I got really sad and didn't get out of bed. I cried and stared up at the wooden slats above my bunk bed. Mom asked me over and over again, "Matthew, what do you want? Why are you so sad? What can I do to make you happy?"

What I wished I could say was, "I want you and Daddy to love each other again and get back together" and "Let me see my daddy," but I was too scared to say either one of these things because I knew she would get angry at me. Crying continuously, I said, "I want Atari, Mommy, I want Atari."

There was a long pause, and I knew I was about to win. If I couldn't see my father, video games were better than nothing.

* * *

The next day, my mother took Thomas and me down to the local electronics store and bought us an Atari with *Space Invaders* and *Pac-Man*. Back home, she disappeared into her bedroom while we played.

A few hours later, Mom went out into the cold afternoon to collect the mail, then pranced back into the living room to make an Important Announcement.

"Matthew, Thomas, guess what?"

"What?" I asked, my eyes transfixed on Pac-Man.

"We're going to be rich!" She sounded like a girl playing with her first My Little Pony.

Love Wars

"What do you mean, Mommy?" I asked, moving the joystick furiously as I tried to escape the ghosts that were closing in on me.

"Let me show you," she said.

"Just a minute." I gobbled down a power pellet so I could munch on ghost lunch.

"We're going to win a million dollars," she said.

I looked up at her. My mother was holding a huge, overstuffed brown envelope with slips of paper bursting out of it. A million dollars! How many video games would that buy? I handed the controller to Thomas. "You take over."

My mother emptied the envelope's contents onto the glass coffee table, arranging the colorful papers as if they were the last will and testament of a wealthy relative who'd left her a fortune. The envelope was addressed to "Current Resident."

"What is it?" I asked.

"Ed McMahon's giving away one million dollars every year for life to one lucky winner. But that's not all—we could win a car, a new home, a private Learjet, even our own tropical island." My mother squealed with glee. "All we have to do is put these stamps on these squares here, see?" I started pasting in the stamps just like she showed me.

"Are you sure we're going to win?" I asked, slowly reading the "Dear lucky winner" letter from Publishers Clearing House.

"Oh, who knows, but it's fun to think about, right? We've got as good a chance as anyone. Plus, it's free to enter."

"What about all these magazines? If we buy them, do we have a better chance of winning?" I asked.

"No purchase required for entry. But is there one you want?" she asked.

How the Divorce Stole Christmas

"*Sports Illustrated* and *Boys' Life*."

She pulled out her checkbook.

Somehow I knew we weren't going to win, but I loved playing this game with her. At least I got some cool magazines out of it, and for a few minutes, I forgot how much I missed my father.

* * *

When winter break came to an end, I had to go to a new school, George Armstrong Custer Elementary. I cried and told Mom I wanted to go back to my old school in the city like Dad had promised, but she said it was too far away. At Custer Elementary, the other kids teased me for being fat, and I had no friends except Johnny and Danny.

After my first day of school, I came home to find my little brother reading his favorite Peter Rabbit book. He was so cute with his stringy blond hair and face full of a thousand freckles. He clutched at least three stuffed bunnies in his lap, maybe four. Mom was busy in the kitchen cooking dinner and couldn't see what we were doing.

"Thomas, wanna play a game?" I asked.

"Okay. Which one?"

"How about *Punch-Out*?" It was our favorite arcade video game, but I wanted to show him how to play for real.

"Okay." Thomas adored me and did anything I wanted. He put aside his bunnies and stood up. "How are we going to play?"

"I'll be Little Mac and you can be Glass Joe," I said. Glass Joe was the easiest boxer to fight. You could press buttons randomly and still beat him.

"Jab, jab, hook, uppercut, mighty blow!" I called out, just

Love Wars

like the ringside commentator, and threw soft, slow punches at Thomas's hands. He blocked them easily.

Suddenly, rage burned inside my heart. I thought to myself, *Mom and Dad loved each other before Thomas was born. They never fought. It's all my brother's fault!*

I started punching for real. I hit Thomas in the face and chest, again and again, and he cried. My tummy curdled into knots as I saw the tears in his face, reminding me of how much I had cried when my parents had pulled me apart.

"Whoops, I went too far," I told him. "Don't cry." I looked around nervously, worried Mom would hear.

After that, everything about Thomas irritated me. I teased him, spit on him, insulted him, played tricks on him, and ordered him to do things for me. I hated him and wanted him to be my slave. I wondered why I despised him, and couldn't figure it out.

* * *

One day, my mother's parents, Gramma Libby and Grampa Avi, came into town to visit. I loved it when they showed up because Gramma always took Thomas and me to the toy store, and this time I loaded up on video games. Thomas picked out an enormous stuffed bunny with a blue bowtie.

"Anything for my gorgeous grandsons," Gramma Libby said as her wrinkled face turned into a huge smile, exposing teeth browner than tree bark. I had to hold my nose around her because she smoked a pack a day and her clothing smelled like nasty cigarettes.

When we got home from the toy store, I waited until she

How the Divorce Stole Christmas

wasn't looking, then stole her death sticks out of her purse and threw them into the trash. I didn't want her to die of lung cancer like my great-grandfather and namesake had. But Gramma Libby was onto me, and she fished the cigarettes out of the trash and disappeared into the bathroom.

"You're so precious, my sweet grandson! Trying to save me from myself," Gramma Libby proclaimed as she came back out, little wisps of smoke trailing after her. "This is the last pack of my life, promise." I knew she was lying.

Grampa Avi winked at me and gave me a thumbs up. He'd been trying to convince Libby to quit smoking for years. She was the one person on earth he couldn't control.

My grandfather had been a trial lawyer for the Army before he retired. He had a disease that made his head nod in a slow, continuous, rhythmic motion. His liver-spot-coated chrome dome reflected lights like a mirror, with only two small tufts of white hair above his ears. He walked with a cane and had a crook in his back that made him look like the Hunchback of Notre Dame's grandfather.

"Matthew, you're a real fighter, a warrior. You're going to be a powerful attorney someday, just like me."

I ran away from Grampa Avi, crying. I didn't want to have to fight grown-ups, especially not in a courtroom.

Before they left for their vacation home in Florida, I went to talk with Gramma Libby privately. I wanted her to know how much I missed my dad and how sad and confused I felt about the divorce. But I couldn't say anything. I knew she and Grampa were on Mom's side. I'd overheard my grandparents talking with my mother about "that bastard Nate."

"What is it, my darling?" Gramma Libby asked me.

How the Divorce Stole Christmas

All I could say to her was, "I hate Thomas and wish he was dead."

"You don't mean that," Gramma said, shocked.

"No, no, I really do. *I really do*," I cried. "We were all happy before Thomas was born!"

"Shhhhh, Matthew. Your mother will take care of you. You'll get over it," Gramma Libby said, reaching out to comfort me. She held me close, and I cried into her blouse, inhaling the stench of cigarettes.

* * *

I tried not to think about how much I missed my father, but I cried at night when my mother wasn't looking. Even if she hated him, I promised myself I would never ever forget him, the way I'd tried to forget about my dog, Carrie. In my nightmares, I didn't see my father again until I was all grown up and he was as old and wrinkled as my grandparents.

"I miss Daddy too," Thomas told me when Mom wasn't around.

One day after school, my mother walked through the door with her shoulders slumped. She didn't look at me, and just stared at the floor. Something bad must have happened.

"Mommy, what's wrong? Did we lose the Publishers Clearing House contest?"

"No, Matthew. Much worse than that. The judge ruled that you have to go see your father. Our lawyers drafted a separation contract, and unfortunately he's got visitation rights every Wednesday, Friday, and every other weekend."

She sighed, sat down on the stairwell next to me, and continued.

Love Wars

"He's coming to pick you up tomorrow. But don't worry, I still have primary custody. And this isn't a permanent arrangement. When the final hearing happens, I promise I'll fight to keep you away from him. I don't want you to have to suffer through any more of his crap than necessary."

I bit my lip, trying not to smile. "Can I go play with my friends?"

I buckled on my rubber galoshes so fast my fingers shook. I shot out the front door, then dashed across the snowy yard, screaming and laughing. As I scampered onto the street, my feet slipped on an icy patch and I tumbled forward, catching myself on the hard gravel. I scraped the skin through my gloves and skinned my knee, but I didn't care. I bounced up to my feet and ran next door to the Callaghans' house, sucking on a handful of snow until my tongue went numb.

I pushed the doorbell again and again, sending loud rings that echoed from inside the house. The door opened and Ms. Callaghan said, "You're in a hurry, little Matthew. Are you looking for my Jonathan?"

I didn't even look up at her and scooted around the folds of her rumpled purple dress into the warm confines of my new best friend's home, remembering only too late to take off my boots.

"Look at this mess, Matthew," Ms. Callaghan chided. I turned around to see that I'd left a trail of dirty snow melting on her orange carpet.

"Sorry," I said sheepishly, removing my galoshes and placing them near the door next to Johnny's. The smell of fresh-baked chocolate chip cookies wafted through the house, but not even that could distract me.

How the Divorce Stole Christmas

"Johnny! Johnny! Johnny!" I found him in his usual spot in the living room, commanding both sides of yet another epic battle of plastic army men. A roaring fire blazed in their wood-burning stove.

"Hold on a second, I'm concentrating," Johnny said as he held a long red rubber band between his thumb and forefinger, one eye closed and the other focused unerringly on his target. *Twang!* went the rubber band as Johnny's aim found its mark, knocking over three green soldiers, who joined the ever-growing pile of plastic bodies. "A triple score!" he cried, pleased with his destructive talents. "What's up?" he asked, finally turning to me.

"Johnny, Johnny, guess what? I'm going to see my daddy! I'm going to see my daddy!"

"Really? That's great." My thin, wiry friend's voice sounded a little flat, like roadkill. He paused for a moment, and a tear appeared in one eye, rolling slowly down his pinched face.

My breath caught, and shame consumed my heart. Johnny hadn't seen his own father since his dad ditched him, preoccupied with a new wife. Johnny's mother had moved him and his brothers with her from Ireland to America two years ago, and now his father was an ocean away. Though he never talked about it, Johnny missed his dad terribly. What a jerk I was.

"Here, come over and help me set up the rest of the reinforcements," he sniffed, choking it back. "This war's only just begun. Go draft the soldiers in that coffee can." Johnny put on a drill-sergeant voice as he set to work propping up little camouflaged men on the carpet battlefield.

I couldn't bring myself to apologize or say anything at all. I silently helped Johnny arrange the troops, hoping my assistance

Love Wars

in his war would prove my loyalty.

"You be the brown guys. I'll be the green." He handed me a pile of rubber band ammunition. "You go first," he said smugly, knowing what would happen next.

I took aim and, as usual, missed my target. I wasn't very good at this war.

Chapter Three
Drafted
Age 6 • 1981 • First Grade

I pressed my face to the frosty window, staring out for any sign of my father.

"When is Daddy coming over to pick us up?"

"Four o'clock," Mom said. Thomas sat on the stairs, playing with his stuffed rabbits.

At 3:45, a beat-up green car pulled up in front of the house. Dad emerged from the car smiling and clean-shaven. He walked slowly down the snowy embankment in his huge red winter jacket, his boots disappearing into the fresh snow. When he knocked on the door, my mother went to look through the peephole.

"NATE! IT'S NOT FOUR O'CLOCK YET! OBEY THE CONTRACT! COME BACK AT FOUR." Red-faced, my

Love Wars

mother screamed so loudly the door seemed to shake. Thomas started crying.

"VANESSA! WHAT THE HELL IS YOUR PROBLEM?" my father yelled back. His face tightened into a scowl. He turned around and walked up the embankment back to his car.

"Shhhh, Thomas," Mom said, patting him on the head. "It's going to be okay. Don't cry. You don't have to cry."

Thomas kept on crying.

"Mommy, what's going on? I thought you said we could see Daddy today." I knew what the answer was going to be, but I wanted to make sure she wasn't going to use Dad's early arrival as an excuse to keep us away from him.

"Matthew, I *told you* you would be able to see him today, but your father must respect The Contract. You'll see him at four o'clock when it's his time, *not during my time!*"

Thomas kept crying. I looked out the window for a few more minutes, afraid Dad might drive away. When I saw the green car stay put, I moved back from the window and sat on the edge of the stairwell next to my bawling brother with my eyes fixated on my Snoopy watch. I willed the hand to move: 3:51. . . 3:52 . . . 3:53 . . . I shook with nervousness. No one said anything. My mother kept trying to comfort Thomas.

Finally, just as Thomas calmed down, there was a knock at the door.

"*Is it four?*" my exasperated mother asked.

I showed her Snoopy's hands.

Mom flung open the door and stood to the side, refusing to make eye contact with Dad. I ran into his arms, and his hug felt like the happiest Warm Fuzzy in the world.

Dad strapped Thomas into the kiddie seat in the back of

Drafted

the rundown green sedan. "Matthew, before you say anything, I know the car sucks, but it's all I could afford. Your mother cleaned out the bank account. So, how are you boys doing? What's new? How's school?"

"It's okay," I said. "I miss my old school but this one's okay too. I've made some new friends who live near Mommy. But, Daddy, I thought we'd never see you. Mommy said we'd never see you again."

"Really, *is that what that lunatic said?*" He started the car, causing a crashing sound and a cloud of smoke. I imagined the car would blow up or break down.

I sat in the front seat next to Dad. I'd never done that before and felt like I was his co-pilot. I kept looking for the flashing green button that would make the car fly like Chitty Chitty Bang Bang.

"Daddy, you have a green car and you're wearing green socks. Did you know green is my favorite color?"

My father grinned. "I'd forgotten. But maybe I chose green just for you."

"I'm so happy to see you, Daddy," I said.

"Me too, pumpkin. Me too."

"What happened to your beard?" I asked.

"The day your mother's lawyer served me with the divorce papers, I went to the barber."

I missed his comforting, bushy beard.

It had been nearly two months since Mom had taken us away from the family home in Mud Flats. On the way back there, my father was all questions: "How's school? What are you learning? Who are your teachers? What's your favorite subject? Are they challenging you? What's your homework? Are you playing any sports?"

Love Wars

And *lots* of questions about Mom: "What else did your mother say about me? What did she say about the divorce? Is she dating anyone? What did she say about the custody hearing?"

I answered his questions as best I could. And I had questions for him, too, like "What's 'dating' mean?"

When we pulled up to the big house on Stonehouse Road, Dad's eyebrows furrowed as he helped Thomas out of the kiddie seat. "When we go inside, I'm wondering if you boys will notice anything," he said, with a glint in his eye.

"What is it? Do you have a new Big Wheel for me?"

"No, nothing like that, just . . . You'll see . . ."

We entered the house and I looked around anxiously. Nothing. The house was big and cold and empty, both familiar and lonely.

"I don't see anything."

"Really? Keep looking."

"But, Daddy, I don't see anything."

He sighed, a big, aching, dramatic sigh that announced his disappointment louder than words ever could.

"Matthew, don't you see? Your crazy mother stole all the furniture out of the house."

I felt ashamed. So that's what he meant. I thought about saying, *But Daddy, I said I didn't see anything*, but I kept quiet.

He pointed at a tiny little box of a fridge in the kitchen. "You see that? It's all I could afford." Then he pointed at three bare mattresses on the floor of the living room. "And that's where we're sleeping tonight. When you see your mother, you can thank her for not having a bed here." Other than the mattresses, the only thing in the living room was a tiny black-and-white television with crooked antennas.

Drafted

Dad loved to tell stories about his childhood. Like the time he and his brother wrestled so hard, they broke their parents' bed, and then they tried to prop the bed back together to hide the damage. It didn't work; the next time Gramma Miriam and Grampa Stanley sat on the bed, it fell apart right under them. Or the time he and his brother ate all of Gramma's cupcakes that were supposed to be for a dinner party. Or how Grampa used to club him and his brother with his fist, "The Meathook," if they were rowdy on long car rides.

He always concluded his tales with his famous tagline, "It's a true story, and you can look it up."

Now Dad had a new set of true stories to tell: What Vanessa Had Done To Him. His new favorite story revolved around how Vanessa Stole All The Furniture Out Of The House, and how he had arrived home on Christmas Eve to find it all gone. The fact that Vanessa had also stolen the kids out of the house seemed less important in the telling.

* * *

The next morning, Dad took us down to the park, where we played on swings and jungle gyms and rolled around inside gigantic wooden barrels until we got dizzy. If we'd been with Mom, I might have hit Thomas or spit on him, but I didn't feel like doing that as much now that we were with my father. I helped Thomas get unstuck when he got his mitten caught inside one of the barrels.

While we played, Dad leaned against a forlorn cherry tree without any blossoms. He stared off into space and quietly sang to himself. Thomas went off to play with a soccer ball, so

Love Wars

I walked over to hear what Dad was singing.

"Where have all the flowers gone? Long time passing. Where have all the flowers gone? Long time ago..."

"What are you singing about, Daddy?"

"Shhh, Matthew, just listen." He carried on singing.

"Where have all the flowers gone? Young girls have picked them every one. Oh when will they ever learn? Oh when will they ever learn..."

I looked at him quizzically. "Are you sad because all the flowers are gone? They'll come back in spring. I promise."

He looked at me through teary eyes and chuckled in spite of himself.

"Kiddo, you're wise beyond your years," he said. "But that's not what the song is about. Listen."

He sang the rest of the song, about young girls who marry husbands who become soldiers, end up in graveyards, and turn into flowers.

"Is it a song about war?" I asked.

"Yes, kiddo. How'd you know?"

"Because of the soldiers and the graveyards. Which war?"

"It's timeless, but if I had to pick one, Vietnam," he said.

"Why does the song start over with more flowers?"

"Because it never ends, kiddo, it just goes on forever. *They never learn, dammit!*"

"Daddy, didn't you tell me the Vietnam War is over?"

"Yes, but I'm sad about all my friends who died over there for no reason. All the Vietnamese who had to die, too... But to tell you the God's honest truth, right now, I feel sad about what happened between me and your mother."

When he looked down at me, I saw a tear rolling down his cheek.

Drafted

"You know I loved her. I really loved her, kiddo, and I just don't understand why we ended up this way," he said. "You saw how it's been over the past few years. We fought so much. I never understood why we fought. Sometimes it was over the stupidest little things. I wanted it to stop, but I didn't know how to make it stop. We had your brother because we thought it would save our marriage, but after he was born, things only got worse. I didn't want to lose her and didn't want our family to break apart. It's so painful."

He sighed. "And now your mother blames me for everything. She wants revenge. But I won't let her interfere with me being your father."

He stood up straighter, his eyes blinking away the dampness. "That's enough of that. It's not your concern, tiger. Let's play catch." And with that he pulled out the baseball gloves from the gym bag we had brought. I loved the way the creased leather felt against my hands, the way the laces smelled like fun on a bright summer afternoon. "Keep your eye on the ball," he said in a coach's voice.

As we tossed the wiffle ball back and forth, my imagination wandered to the song about the flowers and the soldiers. I thought of my parents screaming at each other and wondered: *When will they ever learn?*

On the way home from the park, Dad told us he'd started dating a biologist from his laboratory. "She's coming over tonight, and she's bringing dinner."

I felt nervous the rest of the afternoon until the doorbell rang and a blue-eyed woman with wavy red hair stood at our door. She was holding a casserole dish in one arm and something that smelled like dessert in another arm.

Love Wars

"Hi, Matthew, I'm Holly. I'm a friend of your father's." She extended her hand to me. I shook it, but looked down at my shoes. I still wanted Mom and Dad to get back together.

Dad set up a folding card table with a ripped vinyl cover and brought out a set of paper plates and plastic silverware. He lit candles and we all sat around the table in folding chairs.

Holly's beef noodle casserole was warm and yummy, and I had seconds and thirds. Then she brought out dessert bowls. "It's called Pompadour Pudding," Holly said. I wolfed down the flaky, chocolaty crust and creamy filling and asked for more. Holly gave me seconds.

"Haven't you had enough yet?" my father asked. He'd pointed out to me several times how chubby I'd gotten since he'd last seen me.

I excused myself from the table and wandered outside to the back patio to stargaze by myself. I looked through Dad's telescope at the vast canvas of lights that showered the night sky. A long time ago, in a galaxy far, far away, did the parents of young Jedi ever get divorced—just like mine?

* * *

On Sunday, a few minutes before four o'clock, my mother pulled up to Stonehouse Road in the yellow Volvo station wagon. I watched through the window as she walked briskly up the driveway wearing dark sunglasses and her white doctor's robe. Her heels clicked on the gravel and she stumbled once, but then pulled herself upright and kept marching forward. When she reached the front door, she did not knock but pounded on the door—*Bam! Bam! Bam!*

Love Wars

"NATE, LET THE KIDS OUT!" she yelled.

"VANESSA, YOU'RE THREE MINUTES EARLY! YOU'LL HAVE TO WAIT!" my father yelled back.

Thomas started crying.

She waited out front for three minutes until Dad opened the door. Thomas ran into her arms, and she scooped him up.

"Don't worry, boys, I'll see you on Wednesday," Dad said.

On the drive back to Mom's house, she bombarded me with questions.

"What did your father say about me?"

"He said he doesn't like it when you two fight."

"THE FIGHTING'S ALL HIS FAULT!" she screamed at me. "He started it! He was a miserable husband, he was a cretin of a father, and he tried to steal you and Thomas away from me!"

"I'm just telling you what he said. Why are you yelling at me?"

"BECAUSE YOU SHOULDN'T LISTEN TO THAT BASTARD!" Her fingers gripped the steering wheel. "What else did your father say about me?"

"Nothing," I lied, deciding it would be unwise to mention that he'd called her a lunatic.

My mother was silent for a few minutes, staring intently at the road. Then she continued the interrogation.

"Is he dating anyone? Is he sleeping with anyone?"

I started playing with the handle on the car door, moving it up and down. Then I set to jiggling the lock, locking and unlocking the door. My mother reached over and grabbed my hand.

"Well?" She refused to let the questions go unanswered.

"He had a new friend over. Her name is Holly."

"HOLLY? Who the hell is she?"

Drafted

"I don't know, Mommy. Someone from his lab." I looked out the window, feeling nauseous.

She was taking the scenic way home on a road called Twenty-Nine Curves. Every time we whipped around one of those curves, I felt more and more carsick. I counted the number of curves, hoping it would be over soon, but we were only up to number eight.

"Tell me everything you know about her," Mom said.

"I don't know much. I only met her once. I didn't really talk to her, because . . . well . . ." I wanted to say "because I want you and Daddy to get back together and love each other," but I didn't.

"Well?"

"I don't know. She's a good cook. Her food tastes good."

"Better than mine?"

"No, Mommy," I lied. My mother was the worst cook on earth. I'd rather eat school cafeteria food. But I'd never ever say that.

"Whose cooking is better?" she asked.

"I dunno. Maybe it's a tie," I said.

She scowled.

"Are they sleeping together?"

"What do you mean?"

"Did she spend the night?"

"Yeah, I guess she did."

"THEY ARE SLEEPING TOGETHER!" my mother thundered.

"Mommy, can you stop the car?"

"What?" She looked over at me.

"I don't want to make a mess." I clutched my stomach.

She pulled over to the side of the road. I struggled with the seatbelt and got it loose just in time to open the door and vomit up Holly's Pompadour Pudding.

Love Wars

Mom waited until I was done. "Are you sure you got it all out of you?" she asked and wiped my face with her lipstick-stained handkerchief.

"Yeah, I think so." I felt a mix of relief and disgust, hoping she hadn't left red lipstick marks on my face.

"Can we not take Twenty-Nine Curves anymore? I hate this road," I said.

"I'll try to go a different way next time."

When I got back in the car and buckled my seatbelt, my mother launched back into her tirade.

"Your father's a sick bastard and he's going to burn in hell."

I imagined Dad falling down a dark hole into the center of the earth, where flames burned and consumed him, his screams of "I'm sorry!" not good enough to save him from his fate.

"What do you mean? Why will Daddy burn in hell?"

"Because he's sleeping with another woman. You know it's illegal. He could go to jail for it. But more important, it's against God's law. You go to Sunday school, you know the Ten Commandments, don't you?"

"Yes, I know them."

"Do you remember commandment number seven?"

"Ummm . . . Thou shall not steal?"

"No, it's *Thou shall not commit adultery*."

"What's adultery?" I figured it meant pretending to be an adult when you're not.

"Adultery means sleeping with another woman when you're married. The divorce isn't finalized yet, so technically your father is still married. That sinner is breaking man's laws *and* he's breaking God's laws."

Drafted

I fell quiet. My mother was really angry, and maybe she had a point. I was scared of God and knew breaking any of the Ten Commandments was the worst thing in the world any Jew could ever do. My father said he didn't believe in God, but he was still a Jew. If you weren't allowed to sleep with another woman while you were still married, why was he doing it?

When we got home, Mom made us a dinner of hard, rubbery green beans and stiff, dry chicken. I poked at my meal and said nothing about how it tasted.

* * *

"Let's play hide-and-go-seek!" my mom announced after dinner.

This was my favorite game to play with her. Thomas was terrible at it; when it was his turn, he'd hide somewhere really obvious and we'd find him in about one minute. My mother wasn't much better. She was so big it was easy to find her no matter where she hid.

But I was really good. When it came my turn, I snuck up into her bedroom, went into her huge walk-in closet filled with dresses and business suits and doctor's robes, crawled inside one of her huge plaid suit bags, and pulled the zipper shut so there was only a little hole for air. I stood still inside the stuffy suit bag for over an hour, sweaty, quiet, and proud of my genius hiding spot. I listened to them look for me. They came into the closet several times, but didn't find me. I could hear her getting frantic in her search. After an hour, I heard her on the phone.

"Ms. Callaghan? Yes, this is Dr. Tower next door. I was playing a game with my son, Matthew, and he seems to have

Love Wars

disappeared. Did he turn up at your house? No? Well if he does, please call me. I'm worried about him, and I might call the police."

I waited until I heard her hang up, then I unzipped the suit bag and quietly climbed out and padded across the carpet of her bedroom. She was holding the phone to her ear, her head hunched against her shoulder, her back turned to me. The phone went *click—click—click* as she worriedly dialed the numbers.

"Boo!" I said.

She dropped the phone and screamed out in delight, like a little girl who'd stumbled across a misplaced favorite doll.

"Matthew!" She rushed over to hug me. "I'm so glad you're okay. I was so worried about you. What happened? Where were you hiding?"

"Wouldn't you like to know," I said smugly, hugging her back. I loved this game.

Thomas jumped up and down, grinning. He didn't seem particularly worried.

Mom hoisted me up and flung me onto her bed, then put Thomas on the bed and started tickling both of us.

I laughed uncontrollably. It wasn't funny, but my armpits were sensitive and she was forcing me to laugh.

Then she tickled Thomas, then me, then Thomas, then me.

I tickled her back, and she tickled me back. I played the game with her because she wanted me to, but secretly I always wanted it to stop.

After we were worn out from tickling, Mom's face misted over as she looked at both of us lying on her bed.

"Matthew," she said—she always talked at me, not at little Thomas—"do you know how much work it is to be a mother? Of course you don't, how could you? All the pain, the agony of childbirth, and you were upside down, you know that? So I had to have a C-section."

"What's a C-section?"

"When they cut you open and pull out the baby because it's pointed the wrong way in the mommy's tummy."

Eeeeewwwww. That sounded gross. And painful.

"I wish you appreciated me more, Matthew. I've done so much for you. I put myself through so much agony to bring you into this world."

"I love you, Mommy," I said, knowing she expected me to say it.

"I know you do. I love you too. Do you know you should have had a sister?"

"What do you mean?"

"I had two—no, not two—*three* miscarriages while I was married to your father. At least one of them definitely was supposed to be a girl." She gazed off. "I don't think your father even knew. He never said anything. He was never there for me during my miscarriages. I always wanted a girl, with all my heart. It was my greatest wish..."

She looked at me with disappointment in her eyes.

"I wish you'd been a girl."

Her words landed like a tidal wave. I felt the rush of the crash coming down, and my heart went numb.

I wriggled free of her grasp. "I'm going to play Atari." I bolted downstairs to find my true friends, Pac-Man and the ghosts. I didn't want to think about what I'd just heard.

Mom let me go and kept tickling little Thomas.

* * *

Love Wars

When my father came to pick us up three days later, I noticed he was wearing my favorite color once again.

"Daddy, you're wearing your green socks."

"Yes, pumpkin, I am. They're my special lucky socks and I've decided to wear them every time I pick up you and Thomas."

"Really? But will you ever wash them?"

"No way, kiddo, they'll lose their good luck," he joked.

"Ewww!" I was delighted and grossed out all at once.

This time, I didn't wait for Dad to bring up Mom. I wanted to know if he was a lawbreaker.

"Daddy, Mommy said you're breaking man's laws and God's laws because you're sleeping with Holly."

My father gave me a funny look. "What *the hell* are you talking about, Matthew?"

"She says you're breaking the Ten Commandments and committing adult—adultery."

He looked at me again and sighed.

"Your crazy mother is just angry and bitter because she thinks the failure of our marriage was my fault, so she's trying to find any way she can to get back at me," Dad said. "She was the one who refused to go to marriage counseling. She was the one who ended the marriage. There's no good reason I can't date another woman. If your mother wanted me to be faithful to her, she shouldn't have left. I don't care what man's laws or God's laws say. It's just a technicality."

"What's a technicality?"

"It means it's small potatoes."

"What do potatoes have to do with who you're dating?"

Dad laughed.

Drafted

"You're so smart," he said. "You're right, potatoes have nothing to do with it. Ask your mother why she's so upset about me sleeping with another woman when she was the one who moved out. And ask her why she stole all the furniture out of the house!"

* * *

The next time we were at Mom's house, I did as Dad asked.

"Daddy wants to know why you're upset about him sleeping with another woman. If you didn't want him to do that, why did you leave him? And why did you steal all the furniture out of the house?"

Only in *Bugs Bunny* cartoons had I ever seen a person's face change to bright red so fast.

"YOU STUPID LITTLE BRAT, DO *NOT* QUESTION ME LIKE THAT! IT'S MY FURNITURE! DO *NOT* TAKE YOUR FATHER'S SIDE AGAINST ME! FROM NOW ON, *YOUR NAME IS MUD!*"

My mother scared me, and I burst into tears.

She lowered her voice. "Matthew, you don't need to cry. They're just words. Sticks and stones can break my bones, but words can never harm me. Call me this and call me that, and call yourself a dirty rat."

I kept crying.

"Come on, say it with me."

I snuffled and did as she said.

"Sticks and stones can break my bones, but words can never harm me. Call me this and call me that, and call yourself a dirty rat."

Love Wars

My mother laughed. She was pleased with herself.

"Oh, Matthew, this isn't your fault, now is it? Your father's trying to brainwash you."

I imagined my father sawing my head open with a hacksaw, leaving a crack in my skull just like the plastic skeleton at school. He pulled out my nice, dry brain and threw it into the washing machine. Over and over the machine turned, filling my brain with soapy suds. Then he inserted my soggy brain back into my skull.

"Matthew, are you paying attention? Listen to your mother when she's talking!"

I snapped out of the vision, feeling confused.

"What else did he say?" she asked.

Choking back tears, I said, "I told him what you said about how he's going to hell for sleeping with another woman."

"Yes, and?"

"He said it was a tech— a technic—"

"A technic-what?" Mom said.

"A technicality. That's it!" I smiled.

"*What?* GOD'S LAW IS NOT A TECHNICALITY!" my mother screamed.

I buried my tears and looked out the window, wanting to go ride bicycles with my friends.

"Your father has no integrity. Zero. He's a lying slime, and a coward, too."

"What do you mean? What does he lie about? Why are you calling him a coward?"

"Before we were married, he told me that if there was ever another war like World War II, he would fight. But then he was drafted and he refused to go to Vietnam. Your father is a draft-dodging, lying coward. *Ask him about that!*"

Drafted

Just then, the doorbell rang. When my mother opened the door, I saw Johnny and Daniel tossing a tennis ball back and forth.

"Matthew, come on, we're going to pet the horses," Johnny said.

Perfect. The horses! Desperate to escape, I looked up at my mother, eyes pleading.

"All right, go on with your friends," she said.

I dashed outside to freedom, leaving behind my mother and her anger.

I timed my run perfectly and snatched the tennis ball in midair. With my two friends chasing hot at my heels, we scampered up the road to the dead-end turnabout and the horse stables, our sneakers kicking up clumps of dirt and hay.

A dappled brown mare snorted with pleasure and trotted out to greet us, accompanied by a white stallion. I dropped the tennis ball, put my head against the mare's neck, and buried my face in her warm fur, smelling the fragrance of galloping joy. While we fed grass to the beasts and petted their snouts, off in the distance I saw my mother standing in the doorway, watching. When she turned her back, I told my friends, "The coast is clear."

We bid goodbye to the horses and ran off into the brambles and up a gravel side road to our true destination: a construction site. The half-finished, seemingly abandoned house was littered with rusty nails, saws, boards, rolls of insulation sitting on exposed wooden floors, and windows waiting to be installed into gaping holes. In short, it was a vagabond boy's dream playhouse—and, I imagined, every parent's worst nightmare.

Love Wars

Thor-like, Johnny picked up a hammer and held it aloft. "When I grow up, I'm going to come back here and finish this house. It'll be my castle." Although I had the same fantasies, I didn't say a word. Johnny could kick my butt in rubber band war games, and I knew he'd pulverize me if I ever physically challenged him as King of the Mountain.

"Are you sure about that, He-Man?" Danny asked. He was the biggest of us. "I found it first."

"Nah-uh! I found it *way* before you did!" Johnny retorted, smacking his bubble gum.

"But I live closer to it than either of you, it should be mine!" I jumped in, encouraged by Danny's brazenness.

"A castle can have only one master. There's only one way to settle this," Johnny said, eyes glinting. "Broken glass war!"

He picked up a rock, and chucked it right through one of the derelict windows.

I hesitated. "Uh, Johnny, are you sure about—?"

Ker-chink! A second window burst into a shower of shards. "One to one to *nothing*," Danny proclaimed.

That did it. I picked up a rock and joined in the whooping, hollering window carnage. Then we heard a truck pull up the driveway.

"Damn!" Johnny shouted, and we clambered down the back of the wooden frame. We heard heavy boots crush gravel. We disappeared into the brambly woods, trying to ignore the vengeful cursing behind us. "By the way," Johnny whispered loudly as we ran like hell, "I won! Five to four to four. When I grow up, it's all mine!" We circled back toward home through the woods and I crept back into my room without my mother noticing.

Love Wars

* * *

The next Friday evening, my mother announced that we needed to learn more about God's law—apparently Sunday school wasn't doing the job. I feared she'd found out about my window-shattering shenanigans. She made Thomas and me dress in our matching stiff blue suits and took us to Shabbat services at the temple, a huge brick building with colorful stained-glass windows in downtown Chapel Hill. We had to wear funny little hats that were constantly slipping off and "be on our best behavior," whatever that was.

Dad was there, too, and he sat on the other side of the temple, which was filled with grown-ups and kids all wearing their best clothes. Most of the other kids looked just as fidgety as we were. My father waved at us, and we waved at him. Mom glared at him, then scolded us.

"Ignore that bastard. He'll get his turn with you two when the service is over."

The service was long and boring. It was mostly in Hebrew, so I couldn't understand anything. I kept asking Mom, "When will it be over?" During the Moment of Silence, I prayed for God to make Mom and Dad stop fighting, love each other, and get back together.

After the service, my father came to get us, and my mother spun on her heel and strode out of the synagogue.

"I was supposed to pick you boys up at four o'clock," Dad said on the ride home. "I hate wasting time in that place, but I had to show up to make sure she didn't kidnap you for the entire weekend."

Drafted

I waited a few minutes for the bulging veins in his neck to disappear. Then I asked about what Mom had said. I knew he'd probably get upset, but I wanted to know his side of the story.

"Daddy, Mommy says you're a coward and a liar because you refused to fight in Vietnam."

My father looked so angry, I was afraid his head would explode. But he kept it bottled up and just said in a quiet, razor-sharp voice: "If I had gone to Vietnam, I would be dead, and you wouldn't be here."

Deep in my heart, I knew what he said was true.

"Your mother's a closet Republican," Dad said. "She told me she was going to vote for Carter, but secretly I think she voted for Reagan, that idiot. If it were up to her, all the good American boys would go right back to Vietnam and keep on dying for nothing. What else did your mother say about me?"

"She said you're brainwashing me . . ."

He cut loose a huge, crazy laugh. I wasn't sure if he was laughing for real or putting on a show.

"Me? Brainwashing you? Oh, give it a rest. Your mother is the one who is brainwashing you. She wants you to hate me."

Both of you want me to hate each other, I thought.

"Seriously, your mother is crazy. I don't know what I was thinking when I married her. I don't know how I survived eleven years of her madness—*eleven years!* But I'm lucky. You and Thomas still have to deal with her. Her attorney claims I've been plotting to steal the two of you away from her for the past two years. I don't know where she gets these lunatic ideas. *Matthew, your mother is sick and she belongs in a mental institution!*"

* * *

Drafted

"Your father is worse than Adolf Hitler."

"Your mother belongs in a mental institution."

Which of these statements was true? Both? Neither? Who could I trust? Nothing made sense.

When Dad forced me to work in his garden, was that *worse* than being in a concentration camp?

If Mom was sick, why was she a doctor and not a patient?

I didn't want to carry their insults back and forth, but I felt a compulsion to ask questions and figure it all out. I hoped I'd eventually learn the truth.

And so it went—back and forth, back and forth. I listened attentively to what each said, then asked the other parent if what had been said was true. I was the dutiful little postal carrier, delivering hate mail.

After drop-offs, each parent would question me at great length. Were you well fed? Did he help you with your homework? How many times did she stick you with a babysitter? Aren't you mad at her because she did this to you? Don't you hate him for doing that to me? Don't you wish you could see me more?

Each parent thought I was on their team. I was a double double double agent. I spied on Mom for Dad; I spied on Dad for Mom. My mother frequently said, "Don't tell your father I said this, but . . ." And Dad often told me, "I don't want this getting back to your mother, but you should know . . ." Whenever I messed up and told a secret I wasn't supposed to, I'd feel so much shame, like I was the worst son in the world.

I hated being in the middle. I wanted to be on both sides, and I wanted to be on neither side. I wanted to love my mom and my dad, and secretly I wanted them to love each other again. But the battles never seemed to end.

Love Wars

The Divorce War Death Star's tractor beam was pulling me in, and there was no escape.

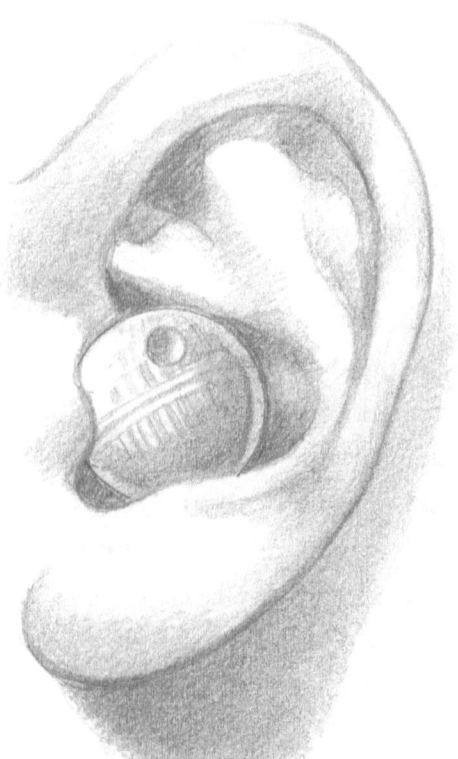

Chapter Four
THE SHRINK
Age 6 • 1981 • First Grade

"Matthew, you're sick, do you know that? You need counseling," my mother declared one Tuesday afternoon, her face flushed from rushing home from work.

"What's counseling?"

"Counseling is for people who are sick."

"But I feel fine."

"Not your body—your head."

"But my head doesn't hurt."

"Your mind, Matthew, your mind. Your father is brainwashing you. He's trying to turn you against me, so I'm taking you to a shrink."

Love Wars

"What's a shrink?"

"A shrink is a doctor for the head."

"You mean like a *headshrinker*?" I liked my head exactly the size it was.

"Yes, I told you, I'm taking you to a shrink. Now enough questions; we're going."

"But I was about to go play soccer with Johnny."

"You can play with him some other time. We're going. *Now*, young man! *Get into the car!*"

My mother practically threw me into the station wagon. I couldn't understand why I was the only one who needed to see a shrink—why not Thomas? He got to stay home with a babysitter. I kept my mouth shut all the way to the University of North Carolina Hospital. Mom parked in the garage of a tall brick office building.

"Can I push the elevator button?"

"Sure."

"What floor?"

"Eighth floor."

I stood on my tiptoes and pushed the button. I loved pushing elevator buttons.

The elevator ride was long and scary. Not because I was afraid of elevators, but because I dreaded seeing the shrink. I'd seen plenty of *Bugs Bunny* cartoons in which white-coated head doctors used shock machines to zap people. Steam would pour out of the ears of the victim, smoke engulfing his hair, singeing it black. I didn't want to get shocked, and I definitely didn't want my head to get shrunk.

When we arrived at the top floor, a tall woman with a British accent greeted us.

Love Wars

"Hi, I'm Dr. McCrantock. I'll be your therapist." She bent down to extend a hand, and waves of her flowery perfume washed over me.

I darted behind my mother, clutching her dress. I'd never felt so scared in my life. I was even more scared than when she took me to the pediatrician's office for a shot in the arm. Mom filled out some forms and chatted with Dr. McCrantock for a minute or two.

"Matthew, it's time for your session to begin. I'll be back in an hour," my mother told me. She started to walk toward the elevator, but realized she wasn't going to make any progress with me clinging to her dress, shaking with fear.

"Matthew, let go. You need help, and Dr. McCrantock is going to help you."

"No, Mommy. *No!* I don't want it. I'm coming with you."

"YOUNG MAN, LET GO OF MY DRESS!" my mother yelled.

She peeled my hands off and walked briskly toward the elevator.

I chased after her, and when the elevator door opened, I followed.

"Matthew! Get out of this elevator, now! *You are staying with Dr. McCrantock!*"

But my finger was already on the button marked "1." I waved bye-bye to Dr. Shrink as the doors closed.

My mother turned on me, furious. Her face was red, and she stopped speaking. As the elevator descended, I thought I'd won. When the doors opened on the first floor, I saw freedom ahead: The parking garage. The yellow station wagon. A ride home. Playing soccer with Johnny.

The Shrink

But then, out of the corner of my eye, I saw her reach to push the button for floor eight. *No!* She was taking me right back to the shrink's office. I dashed forward and slid through the elevator door just before it closed. I heard my mother scream, but the sound was cut short as the elevator carried her up. I ran through the parking garage and found the car. I grabbed at the handle, praying the door was open. I was in luck. I climbed into the car, dug a Hardy Boys book out from underneath the front seat, and tried to focus on it, hoping against hope that when Mom came back down, she'd give up and drive me home.

No such luck. She reappeared a few minutes later. Saying nothing, she grabbed my wrist and pulled *hard*.

"Owww!" I cried as she dragged me across the parking lot toward the elevator. I tried to resist for a minute, but when that didn't work, I gave up and went limp. This time, I didn't try to escape.

When we got to the eighth floor, I made one last stand by refusing to get out of the elevator. My mother picked me up. I kicked my legs and screamed. She handed me to the doctor and said, "I'll be back in forty minutes. Thanks for putting up with his *baby crap!*" She yelled the last part at me.

The elevator door closed behind her and again I went limp. The shrink set me down and said, "Matthew, I know you're scared, but this won't be so bad. I promise."

I turned away, refusing to look at her, and cried. I didn't want her to see me cry.

She stood there for a few minutes then said, "I have toys. Do you want to see my toys?"

I didn't believe her. *Toys?* She had to be lying.

"Look. See?" She opened the door to her office.

Love Wars

I couldn't believe it. She had a sandbox filled with plastic buckets, shovels, and little action figures. *It has to be a trap*, I thought.

"Do you want to play with the toys?" She walked to the sandbox, picked up a shovel, and scooped sand into a bucket.

Her back was turned to me. *Now's my chance. Go!* I ran back to the elevator and hit the button.

Before the elevator arrived, though, Dr. McCrantock grabbed me and spun me around.

"Matthew, I can't have you running away on me. Your mother would be very upset when she comes back to get you. She'll be back soon. Why are you so afraid? What do you think could happen to you?"

At first I said nothing. Then I asked, "Are you going to shrink my head?"

She laughed. "No, no. That's not why we're called shrinks." She smiled broadly.

I stared down at my shoes.

She bent down to my level, looked into my eyes as best she could, and said, "Matthew, I'm not going to hurt you. You can play in the sandbox until your mother gets back, and I'm going to ask you some questions. You can answer me if you want, but no one will force you."

"Promise?"

"Promise," she said.

"Cross your heart, hope to die, stick a needle in your eye?" I asked.

"Yes."

I wasn't sure if I believed her, especially about the dying part, but I decided I'd rather play than stand around doing nothing.

The Shrink

I climbed inside her sandbox and dug in the sand until I had made three big holes. I placed one action figure in a hole on one side, another in the hole on the opposite side, then two smaller figures in a hole in the middle. Then I covered the figures with sand, burying them.

"How's your school going, Matthew?"

"Fine," I said, not looking up.

"What are you learning in school?"

"Stuff." I continued to dig.

"What's your favorite subject? Math, science, English?"

"English," I said.

"Why?"

"Because I want to be a writer some day."

"A writer? Really? What are you going to write about?"

"I don't know. Probably dragons, wizards, Luke Skywalker, the Hardy Boys, Atari games, and soccer," I said.

"Do you have a lot of friends?"

"Yeah, I've got a few friends who live near Mommy and a few who live near Daddy."

"So you spend time with both your mommy and your daddy?"

"Yeah." So far, this wasn't too bad. I didn't exactly like Dr. McCrantock, but I wasn't feeling quite as afraid of her.

"How do you feel about your mommy?"

"I dunno. She's a good mommy," I said.

"What about your daddy? How do you feel about him?"

"I dunno. He's a good daddy," I said.

"Tell me more about your daddy. What do you like about him?"

"I like it when he plays soccer with me, and when he plays baseball with me, and when he tells ghost stories," I said.

"What kinds of stories does he tell?" she asked.

Love Wars

"His favorite one is about the dead guy who wants his liver back and comes after the kids for it," I said.

"What don't you like about your father?"

"I don't like it when he forces me to work in the garden, and . . ."

Dr. McCrantock's pen scribbled furiously.

I stopped cold. As I looked up at the shrink, my mother's words came rushing into my ears: *"Your father is brainwashing you. He's trying to turn you against me, so I'm taking you to a shrink."*

I said nothing else.

"And? What else don't you like about him?" Dr. McCrackpot asked.

I stared at her, shooting laser beams out of my eyes. *I'm not going to talk bad about my daddy.* I said nothing. I turned back to my project in the sandbox and refused to look at her.

For the next five minutes, as I waited for my mother to pick me up, I silently played in the sandbox and finished burying the plastic figures.

* * *

When I told my father that Mom was making me see a shrink, I was surprised that he thought it was a good idea.

"You're going through a hard time. Shrinks can help you feel better, you know. Is she helping you?"

"No! I hate her, Daddy, I don't ever want to see her again."

"Why do you hate her so much?"

"I don't want to talk to her about you, or about Mommy. She keeps asking all these questions, and it's none of her beeswax," I said.

The Shrink

My father got a worried look on his face.

"What is it, Daddy?"

"This is too adult for you to understand."

"No, it's not. What is it?"

Finally he responded. "I didn't want to tell you this, but one of the reasons you have to see the shrink is so she can make a recommendation to the court about custody arrangements."

"What does that mean?" I asked.

He sighed. "If the shrink tells the judge I'm an unfit father..."

"I might not get to see you anymore?"

"You got it, kiddo. You're wise beyond your years."

"Don't worry, Daddy, I wouldn't say bad things about you."

* * *

My mother took me for counseling every Tuesday afternoon. I played the elevator game every time, and when Dr. McCrantock took me by the hand and led me to the sandbox, I said nothing. The only time I talked was to tell her that I hated her and didn't want to be there.

Finally, at the end of one of my sessions with Dr. McCrackpot, the shrink said she needed to talk with my mother privately. I walked out of her office, but made sure not to close the door all the way behind me. I wanted to hear what the grown-ups were saying. I pressed my ear to the slit I'd left open, being very quiet.

"Dr. Tower, at this point I have no choice but to recommend we terminate the sessions. I've done everything I can for Matthew. He's sullen and withdrawn and nothing has changed in three months."

Love Wars

"All of these therapy bills, and you've made no progress with him?"

"Yes, I'm afraid so. He's quite stubborn and he's been silent whenever I bring up his relationship with his parents, especially his father. I wish I could do more."

I heard my mother sigh. "Thank you so much, Dr. McCrantock, I know you've done your best and I doubt anyone else could have done more. Nate has brainwashed him against me."

"Good luck, Dr. Tower."

I moved away from the door quickly. When they walked out of Dr. McCrackpot's office, I was sitting in the plush chair in the waiting room, minding my own business like a good boy. Thank God they didn't catch me spying or I'd be on the receiving end of a Mom screamfest.

* * *

Late that spring, Johnny showed up at my mother's house to play while she was out grocery shopping with Thomas. As usual, he'd brought over a backpack full of Atari video games, but this time he also had two boxes of cake mix and two tubs of frosting.

"Why'd you bring those over? Do you want my mom to bake them for us?"

"Nope, other way around."

"What do you mean?"

"It's Mother's Day on Sunday, so I'm gonna bake one for my mom. I thought I'd do it over here, 'cause I want it to be a surprise. Do you want to bake one too?"

"Sure, but I don't know how."

The Shrink

"My mom taught me; I can show you. Here, take your pick," he said, waving the two colorful boxes at me. I grabbed the chocolate one—of course. I loved chocolate.

Johnny clambered up onto the countertop and rummaged through the cabinets, making loud crashing sounds as he searched. Then he set to work, dumping his cake mix into a big silver bowl and adding water, and I did the same. Standing on chairs so we could reach, we whisked away, beating the lumpy mixtures smooth, then pouring them into cake tins.

While the cakes baked, we played *Frogger*, *Yars' Revenge*, and *Pitfall*. Finally, the cakes were done.

"Now for the best part—the frosting." Johnny opened the two containers, grinning. "It's okay to lick your fingers."

We spread the frosting over our cakes—strawberry for Johnny's and chocolate for mine—but the frosting wouldn't stay put, and the cakes started to rip apart.

"Oops. I think we're supposed to wait for the cakes to cool," he said. Just then I heard my mom open the front door.

"Quick, hide the cakes," I cried. We ran down to the basement and stuck them in the extra fridge.

"Something smells delicious in here. What is it?" My mother plopped down on the couch and turned on a soap opera. "Did someone bring you a treat from Ms. Callaghan's kitchen?"

"Wouldn't you like to know," I replied, grinning.

Johnny and I finished icing the cakes Sunday morning while Mom was at her aerobics class, and we used tubes of yellow frosting to write "Happy Mother's Day" in barely legible chicken scratch. I drew a heart on mine. I hoped no one would notice the cakes' odd shapes. They'd both acquired a bizarre deformity while cooling in the fridge.

The Shrink

Johnny's family came over for a combined Mother's Day celebration that afternoon. My mother danced around like a giddy schoolgirl, kissing Thomas and me on the head. I let Thomas pretend he helped bake the cake so he'd get some of the credit. Neither mother breathed a word about the cakes' lopsided presentation.

"You two are the best sons in the whole wide world," my mom said.

"I don't know about that—my sons are pretty excellent too," Ms. Callaghan bragged.

It was such a relief to be around a happy mother. I wished it could always be like this.

* * *

The Mother's Day sugar high didn't last long. Mom seemed to only become more upset about my father as time went on. She often took me into my room, shut the door, sat me down, and started talking and crying, rambling on for an hour, two hours, or more, about what a horrible human being my father was.

The sessions became a routine. My brain went numb. I tried to pretend it wasn't happening. I stared at my clock, stared at it as hard as two eyes can stare, willing the hands to move. I played clock games in my mind. I visualized the second hand moving faster than it really was. Then I closed my eyes, waited for long moments, and opened them to see that the second hand had, in fact, advanced quite a ways; sometimes it even advanced all the way to the point I had imagined it would. I must have had superpowers to make the clock move faster.

Love Wars

I prayed for an excuse, any excuse, not to have to listen to her. I prayed for the phone to ring so she'd have to answer it. I prayed for Thomas to come into the room, or for him to trip on the stairs and hurt himself and cry so she'd go running. I would have prayed for my father to come over and rescue me if I didn't know that was impossible.

Sometimes I asked Mom if I could go outside and play, but when she got into a rant, there was no stopping her. A few times she let me go, but usually she told me I needed to hear her and I could play outside some other time. The moment a session ended, I ran outside as fast as my legs could carry me to go play with Johnny Callaghan. Or I found Thomas and teased him, spit on him, or hit him in the face.

My mother started getting wise to me. She must have known that I didn't want to listen to her, so she picked times when I had no escape. One of her favorite tactics was to launch into a rant in the car. I dreaded long drives with her, like trips to Washington, DC, or to New York to see our grandparents. She did it on short drives, too, like from my father's house to her house. I hated being alone with her anywhere.

My mother never seemed to have any concern for how her angry speeches were affecting me. Sometimes I told her that I didn't want to hear her talking about my father. She argued and said, "Don't you want to know what kind of person your father really is? Don't you want to know what he did to your mommy? Don't you want to know what he did to you and your brother?"

I tried sticking my fingers in my ears, but when she caught me, she pulled my hands away and told me I had to listen.

One of my mother's favorite topics was the custody and separation agreement, which she only ever referred to as

Love Wars

The Contract. The Contract was an eternal wellspring of pain, and she forced me to listen to all her resentment about my father's violations of The Contract.

The Contract was like the Ten Commandments, only more important. As The War dragged on, the number of references to The Contract and Dad's violations of it increased to such a degree that I often heard about it several times a day. The Contract seemed like the single most important thing in the entire world to my mother—even more important than Thomas or me.

During a particularly unbearable monologue, my mother decided I needed to see The Contract. "Matthew, you're a big kid, you should read The Contract. Then you'll understand why I'm so angry at your father." She took me into her room, and fished a stack of papers out of a messy filing folder. She flipped to a page and pointed to a line.

"See right here. Look what it says. Your father broke The Contract."

I tried to make sense of the adult words, but the small type swam as tears clouded my vision. Even though I'd never signed my name to it, I wished I could get out of this Contract.

* * *

After a year of tension-filled, back-and-forth visits, Dad showed up on a Wednesday afternoon and announced that he had something special to show Thomas and me.

"I'm taking you to my lab for a surprise," he said.

"What is it, Daddy?" I asked.

"You'll see."

We climbed into the green jalopy and he drove us to his creepy,

The Shrink

mysterious lab, which was housed in a huge brick building close to the university campus. Bright yellow lights lit the hallways, and medical posters covered the walls. Everything smelled terrible. In the basement, where they kept the monkeys and rats, it smelled like pee and poo, and the upper floors stank of ammonia. A plaque on the door to his lab announced, 'Nathaniel Perry Tower, Dept. of Genetic Engineering.' Inside, bottles cluttered the shelves with skull-and-crossbones stickers saying loud and clear: DON'T DRINK THIS OR YOU'LL DIE!

It was almost five o'clock, and Dad's lab assistants were getting ready to leave for the day. We'd have the place to ourselves. He made us wear goggles to protect our eyes, then he set up a cart in the middle of the lab with lots of chemicals in vials and test tubes. He dimmed the lights and started mixing and pouring the chemicals.

"Gentlemen, welcome to the first-ever Tower Labs magic show." Suddenly—*voila!*—a miniature volcano exploded, sending purple and red clouds into the air. As we clapped and cheered, nondescript clear chemicals turned into every color in the rainbow.

When he turned the lights on, my father said he had something else to show me, something even more special. He said it was only for me, because Thomas was too young to understand. Tacked to his bulletin board was a letter from his dad, Grampa Stanley. Dad asked me to read the last line.

"What does it say?"

I read the words aloud: "Free at last, free at last, thank God almighty, free at last." I looked up at my father, but he just gazed at me expectantly. "Daddy, why did Grampa write those words to you?" I asked.

Love Wars

"Because I'm free! The divorce is finalized. After months of court battle and thousands of dollars wasted on attorney fees, finally I'm no longer married to your mother." He beamed. "My father is quoting a wise man named Dr. Martin Luther King, Jr. who said those words many years ago. I've had them on my mind for a long time. Sometimes remembering Dr. King's marches was the only thing that kept me going. And now I'm free."

I was jealous of my father's freedom. Didn't he care about my freedom? When would I be free?

"Daddy, if you are free at last, why are you and Mommy still fighting?"

Dad's face darkened. "Damn, kiddo, I don't know. Your mother started a war against me. I don't want to fight with her, but she gives me no choice. I wish it would end, too, but I don't know how to make it end. Maybe now that the divorce is finalized, things will calm down."

I didn't share his optimism.

"By the way," he said, "all your visits to that shrink didn't make a difference. Your mother accused me of every conceivable crime, but the custody arrangement stayed exactly the same."

Chapter Five
WHO'S THE REAL PARENT?
Age 7 • 1982 • Second Grade

Despite the divorce being finalized, neither parent seemed ready for a ceasefire. Mom and Dad kept telling stories about each other, and whether I liked it or not, I had to listen.

"King Solomon was the wisest ruler of the Israelites, because he knew how to tell a real parent from a fake," Mom said while driving Thomas and me to her house one day. "Matthew, are you listening?"

"Yes, Mommy, of course." I stared out the window at cows grazing in the green fields outside Chapel Hill, trying not to look at her. I knew she was talking badly about my father as usual, and I didn't want to encourage her by asking questions.

Love Wars

My mother loved this fable, and she told it often.

"There's a point to this story, and it would do you good if you learned it."

"I know the story," I said, but she either didn't hear me or ignored me, and she plunged ahead.

"One day, two women came to wise King Solomon, carrying a small boy with them. Each woman claimed to be the true mother, and they asked King Solomon to issue a custody ruling. Unable to decide who was the real mother and who was the impostor, King Solomon said, 'Let the boy be split so that each parent shall have half. Come, servants, bring me my sword.'"

I imagined a powerful man looming over me. I was strapped down. I struggled and cried at the top of my lungs. I wanted to scream "NO! DON'T CUT ME!" but no words came out.

My mother continued the story: "One woman immediately agreed to the plan. The other begged, 'Give my son to her, just don't harm him!' Recognizing that only a real mother would care so much for her son's well-being, King Solomon awarded the boy to her and dismissed the claims of the impostor."

She paused, sucked in her breath, and then turned toward me.

"Matthew, do you understand the moral of this story?"

"Yes, I understand." My eyes clouded with tears.

"Do you remember how your father used to hit you and Thomas? A real parent would never hurt his children!"

"Mommy, why do you and Daddy still fight so much?"

"I've told you before and I'll tell you again: I didn't want The War. *He started it!*"

* * *

Who's the Real Parent?

My parents kept finding new things to drag into their war, even clothing. I had different sets of clothes at each house, and I wasn't allowed to take my clothes from my father's house to my mother's house, or vice versa. When one parent purchased new shoelaces for me, the other parent removed them and strung in their own pair of shoelaces.

One cold winter day, when Mom picked me up from Dad's house, the clothing squabbles got ugly. Mom carried my overnight bag and helped Thomas get strapped into the kiddie seat in the back of the Volvo. Just as I was settling into the front, Dad came running after us, yelling, "Wait! Wait! *Vanessa!*"

Mom paused, the door halfway open. "What is it?"

Out of breath, Dad said, "Holly knit some gloves and a hat for Matthew, and I accidentally left them in his bag. I want to keep them here because I don't want them to get lost and not come back."

"NATE, I'M NOT GOING TO LOSE MATTHEW'S CLOTHING! AND IT'S *HIS* CLOTHING, NOT YOURS!"

I looked at the floor of the car. Dad had told me the last time they argued about clothing, Mom drove her car over his foot as she sped away. I didn't want to watch them fight.

Sure enough, I soon heard the sounds of a scuffle, shoes furiously scraping gravel. I looked up and saw my father holding onto my mother, leaning over her. He was screaming about the effort Holly had put into making the gloves and the hat and trying to tear my overnight bag from her hands.

I looked away again, out the opposite car window, staring off into space, wondering when it would end. Over the sounds of their fighting, I heard the relentless clock go "*Click. Click. Click.*"

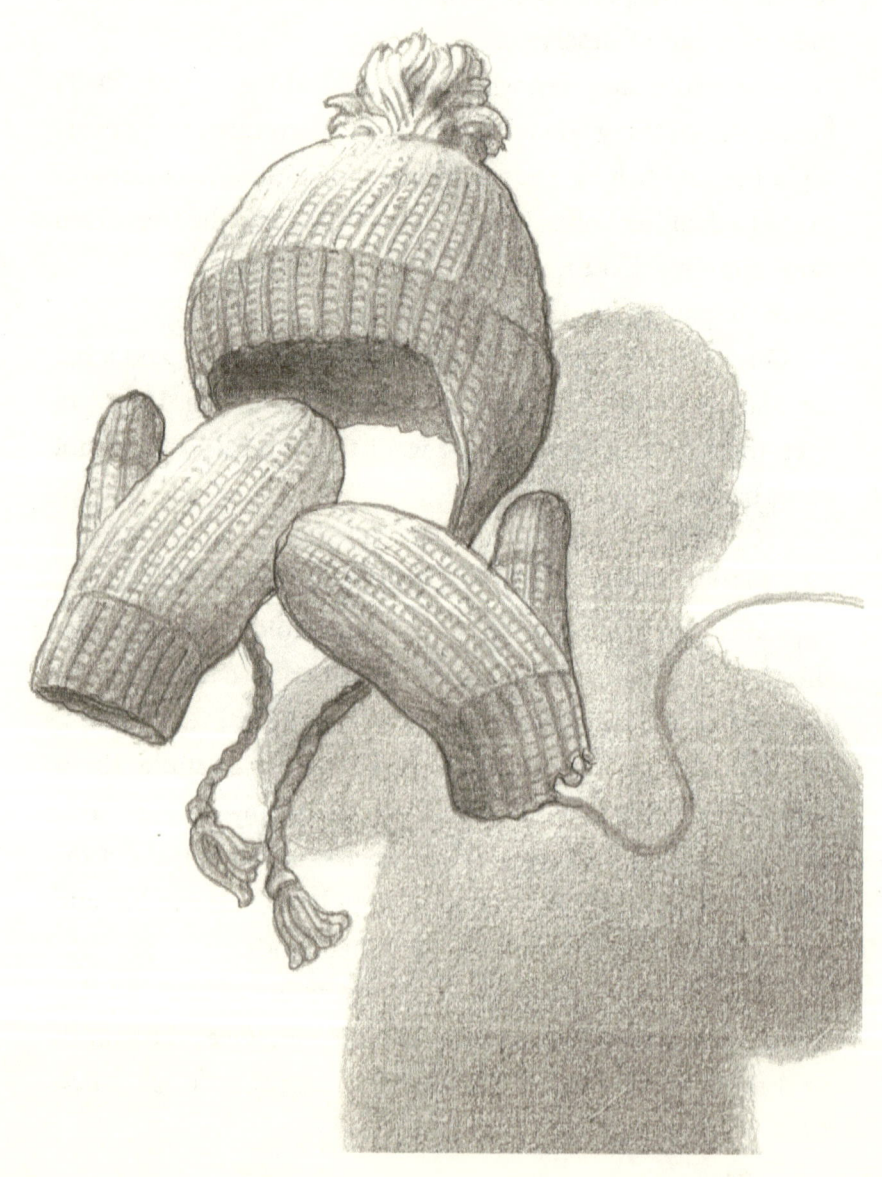

Who's the Real Parent?

A minute later, I looked up again and saw Dad walking back up the driveway, holding onto my gloves and hat. Mom got back in the car looking flustered, her hair disheveled and her face red.

We drove away in silence. The anger and fear and tension in the car felt so thick I could drown. Yet as painful as that wretched silence was, it was bliss compared to what was coming next.

"Matthew, *did you see that?* YOUR FATHER BEAT ME UP! That Neanderthal hit me! He used to hit you and Thomas, and now he's done it to me."

I looked up at her but said nothing. I tried not to respond when she got into one of her rants.

"Did you see what he did? You saw it. You saw him punch me in the arm."

I looked straight ahead at the road. I hadn't seen, didn't want to see . . .

"MATTHEW! Did you see what your father did to me?"

I knew I had to answer. "Sort of," I said, finally making eye contact.

"Sort of? *Sort of?* Matthew, grow up! Be a man for once in your life. Are you going to just pretend you didn't see what happened? Are you going to be a coward like your father? What kind of role model is he, beating up a woman? MATTHEW, YOUR DADDY BEAT UP YOUR MOMMY!"

I didn't want to get involved. It was like she was asking me to be the ref in a soccer game I'd never agreed to judge. Foul? Yellow card? Red card? I hadn't even watched the play.

"He's going to pay for this, *he's going to pay!*" she said. "Finally, I'm going to get justice! I'll have him arrested. He'll lose his job. He'll be out on the street, and you'll never have to see that child-abusing Neanderthal ever again. If there's a King Solomon who works for Chapel Hill Superior Court, your father will rue the day he laid a hand on me."

My head hurt, like my mother was moving a wrench inside my mind again.

When we got home, she showed me her arm, which she said was red and bruised and proved that Dad had beaten her up. It didn't look so bad to me. I got hurt on the playground all the time, coming home with a bloody cut, a nasty scab, or a fat black-and-blue mark. Mom's arm looked a little red, like a mild sunburn. I wasn't sure if it was really red or just her arm's natural color. She asked me to take some pictures of her arm to use as evidence in the police report and the lawsuit.

The incident was all Mom talked about for days on end. After she got the pictures developed, she showed them to me again and again. In the photos, she had the most sorrowful face I'd ever seen. I thought it would blow over, but she kept telling me how my father had hit her and beaten her up.

She repeated the story until I started to believe her. *She had to be telling the truth.* No one would make up such a terrible accusation. Dad had to be guilty. Why else would she be saying it? I couldn't let him get away with beating up my mom.

The next time my father came to pick us up, I screamed at him from the top of the stairs, "I DON'T WANT TO SEE YOU EVER AGAIN BECAUSE YOU BEAT UP MY MOMMY!"

My mother clutched my shoulder so tightly I thought I would be the one with red marks.

Dad left without picking us up. I hated him for what he'd done to my mother. In my nightmares, he beat me up, beat up Thomas, and broke into Mom's house and murdered her.

Who's the Real Parent?

* * *

A few weeks later, Mom told me the judge had ordered that Thomas and I had to visit Dad again. "Matthew, I did my best to protect you, but the judge says you have to go see that Neanderthal," she said.

When Dad came to pick us up, I hid behind the doorway, not wanting to go with him. Finally, Mom said I had to or she'd get in trouble with the judge.

For the first two hours, I gave my father the silent treatment. *He was a mean Neanderthal.* He tried to talk to me about school and soccer, but after a while he gave up and sighed.

"Matthew, what did you see that day?"

At first I bit my lip, but then I decided to hear his side of the story.

"I don't know," I confessed. "It was hard to tell what was happening, and I didn't really want to watch."

"Did you see me hold your mother down and take back Holly's hat and gloves?"

"I saw you holding her for a second." I thought about reminding him that they were *my* hat and gloves, but decided against it.

"Did you see me hit her?" my father asked.

"Mommy says you hit her," I said.

"So how do you know I hit her?"

"Mommy showed me photos."

"What did it look like in the photos?"

"I don't know, her arm might have been a little red. It was hard to tell."

"Do you have any evidence that I actually hit your mother?"

Love Wars

I looked out the window and felt sick. I was already a soldier in Mom and Dad's war, fighting for both sides. Now I had to be the judge too?

"Mommy said you beat her up. I guess I don't know what happened. But why would she accuse you of something you didn't do?" I asked.

"I don't know, kiddo, that's a great question. Why do you think she'd do that?"

I didn't answer and kept staring out the window. *Why?* The word throbbed in my head like a mallet pounding inside my skull.

Why why why why why?

My *whys* were a lot more about *me* than about my parents. Why does God hate me so much that I got stuck in this nightmare? Why do I have to choose between two parents who hate each other? Why can't I just play with my friends?

"Matthew, I did what I had to do to retrieve the gloves and hat, but I didn't beat up your mother. If I hadn't taken the gloves and hat away from her, they never would have come back, just like that fuzzy blue sweater of yours that disappeared."

I didn't say anything. Part of me was still angry at my father and wanted him to know. Part of me felt confused and didn't want to think about it anymore.

But Dad kept on talking.

"Your mother had me arrested. The police showed up at my laboratory in the middle of the workday with handcuffs. It was humiliating. I was in jail for a few hours before Holly bailed me out. Your mother tried to sue me, but the judge laughed it out of court due to a lack of evidence." He snickered contemptuously. "Your mother's getting crazier all the time."

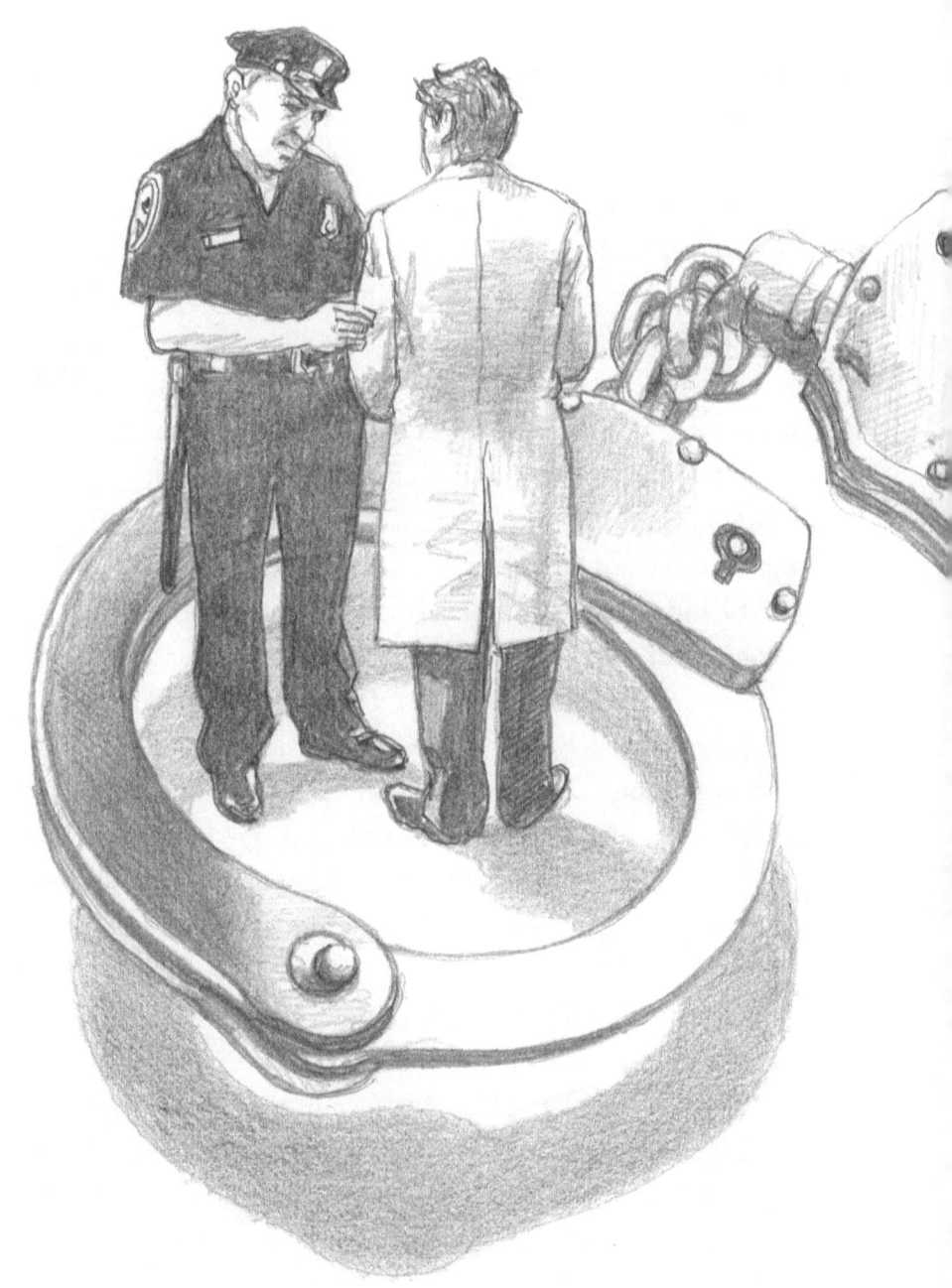

Love Wars

* * *

I was still angry with Dad the next few times I saw him, but he kept repeating his story, too, until I started thinking that maybe he was right. I stopped being angry at Dad and started feeling angry at Mom. The hat and gloves were Holly's, not Mom's.

Now each of them had new favorite stories: The Time Nate Beat Me Up and The Time Vanessa Had Me Arrested On False Charges. What the stories lacked in charm, my parents strived to make up for in repetition.

Before the hat-and-gloves battle, I thought I could take both sides. But now, I felt I had to choose. One of them must be lying. If my father was lying, and I didn't punish him for it, I'd be letting him off the hook—which meant I wasn't being a man, and I was taking a risk that he'd beat me up some day. On the other hand, if my mother was lying, that meant I couldn't trust anything she said. I decided to become like my hero Encyclopedia Brown and solve the mystery of "Who's the bad parent?"

Encyclopedia Brown was a schoolyard Sherlock Holmes who could unravel any small-time mystery. Encyclopedia looked for clues, talked to witnesses, and questioned his suspects. Under the harsh glare of Encyclopedia's sophisticated logic and carefully laid verbal traps, the criminal kid would always confess.

According to Mom and Dad, one of them was the worst human being who had ever lived, and one of them was the greatest parent who had ever walked the face of the earth. One must be guilty, the other innocent. I clung to this idea like a piece of logical driftwood amidst a raging divorce river to keep myself from drowning in the other possibilities: that they were both horrible

Who's the Real Parent?

parents, or that they were both wonderful parents telling lies about each other for no reason.

Every time I tried to investigate my parents' accusations, I failed to reach a satisfying verdict. Remembering that Dad had spanked me when I was little, I asked him, "Did you ever beat me and Thomas?"

"What? Never! Did your mother tell you that?"

"She says you used to hit us."

"Maybe a light spanking now and then when you did something bad. All parents do that."

The next time I saw my mother, I said, "Dad said it was just a spanking and all parents do it."

"*All* parents do it? Do I do it? Would I ever hurt you? It's not okay to spank kids, ever! And it was more than a spanking, Matthew. It was a beating!"

Whom to believe? My Encyclopedia Brown investigations always turned up empty. I just couldn't pin them down.

While I was trying to figure out who was the good parent and who was the villain, my parents used me as their little messenger boy.

Dad would order me: "Ask your mother to trade weekends with me next month."

I'd relay the message, and Mom would say, "Tell your father there's just no way."

I'd inform him, and he'd proclaim, "Your mother has absolutely no reason why she can't trade. She's being unfair and unreasonable."

The next time I saw my mother, I'd badger her, "Why don't you just trade weekends with Daddy? If he really wants to trade, you should be fair and reasonable." Then she'd yell at me, "*I don't need a reason!* I'm the parent and you're the child!"

Love Wars

I hated being in the middle of their negotiations. One night, Mom called when I was at Dad's house. As I was telling her about my day at school, Dad interrupted. "Matthew, tell your mother I'm taking you and Thomas out of town this weekend to visit your grandparents."

"Just tell her yourself," I said, and handed him the phone. He said a few words and within moments, he was holding the phone away from his ear. My mother's screaming was audible even from halfway across the room. While he helped Holly cook dinner with one hand, he held the phone at arm's length, and every so often he mumbled "Uh huh" into the receiver.

After at least fifteen minutes of my mother screaming into empty space, Dad pulled the phone back to his ear and barked, "Frankly, my dear, I don't give a damn!" before hanging up with a flourish.

"You know, Matthew, that's the greatest line in movie history," Dad said. Before I could even ask, he beat me to it and said, "Yup, even greater than 'I'd just as soon kiss a Wookiee!'"

We both cracked up.

That was how Dad taught me to fool Mom into thinking I was listening to her. All I had to do was say "Uh huh"; I didn't actually have to pay attention.

* * *

When Dad talked about Mom, he seemed less agitated than he had been in the early days after their separation. But when Mom talked about Dad, her face turned into a raging storm. She could be perfectly calm and quiet, but if Dad's name came up, a light switch in her heart would flip and she'd change from a normal person to an emotional wreck.

Who's the Real Parent?

With Dad, the feelings were there, but he usually didn't force them on me. I was certainly invited, though. When we talked about Mom, we fed off of each other. He said what he didn't like about her, I said what I didn't like about her, and it went around in a circle. It felt good, because I knew there was someone else who had problems with her.

I told Dad about how my mother forced me to listen to her rant about her problems for hours on end. He put a label on the anguish I was going through and called it "dumping." This word brought a little logic to the chaos at my mother's house. We also talked about "guilt tripping," which is what she did to me whenever I said anything nice about Dad or asked her to do something for me; and "lecturing," which was when she told me what I needed to do or how I needed to behave. Dad lectured me frequently, too—especially about my schoolwork—and occasionally he gave me a guilt trip. But with Dad there was very little dumping. Dad was logical. Dad made sense.

Unlike Mom, Dad said he knew the fighting was having a terrible effect on me and Thomas and he wished it would end. He said it, but I wondered if he really meant it, because whenever he was in Mom's presence, the hatred would overtake him.

Even though my mother made my life a lot harder than my father did, I couldn't choose between my parents. I wished King Solomon, Encyclopedia Brown, or any of my favorite superheroes would magically appear and tell me which parent was the real one and which was the impostor.

Did I even have a real parent? What about Holly? What would King Solomon say about her? She knit gloves and hats

Love Wars

and scarves for Thomas and me, cooked delicious food, and never pestered me about my weight, unlike my father, who was constantly reminding me to "suck in my gut." We talked a lot, she asked me about my friends, and she never dumped her problems on me like Mom did. Holly was the only grown-up in my life who seemed to care more about me than winning a pointless war.

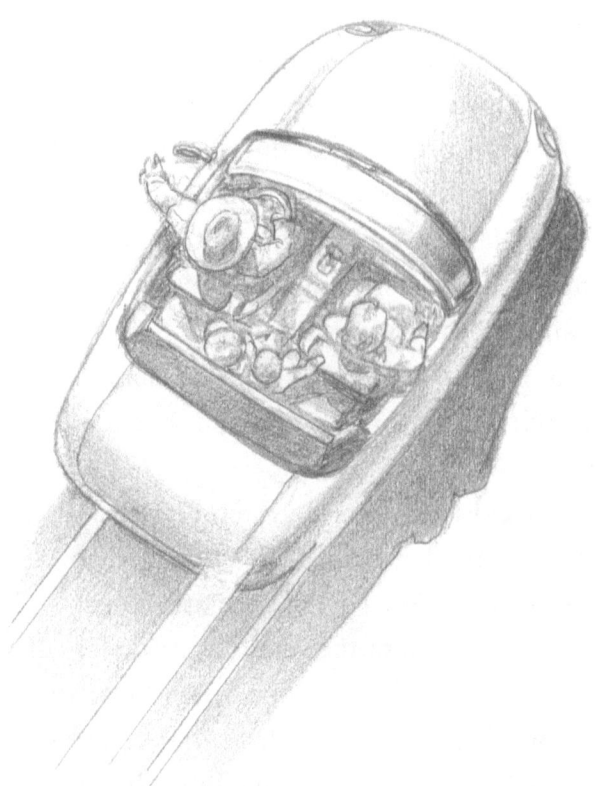

Chapter Six
MY NEW DADDY
Age 7 • 1982 • Second Grade

"Matthew, the world doesn't revolve around you," my mother reminded me as she fussed with my little red bowtie.

"But I want to stay home and watch TV." I twisted my head to catch a glimpse of *Family Feud* over her shoulder. I stretched my arms out to the side and shook them furiously, feeling hot and stuffy inside the navy blue blazer.

"Stop squirming so I can get your tie right. Mommy needs to have some fun, too, you know. My whole life can't be just working and raising you kids."

Love Wars

The doorbell rang, and Mom rushed off to greet the babysitter who'd come to look after Thomas.

As I settled down into the fluffy blue armchair, TV host Richard Dawson turned up the heat on the Coopers and the Andersons. "Name a kind of product on which the lid gets stuck," he challenged. I imagined Mom and Dad standing on opposing sides of the game board, their hands poised to ring the buzzer. Then they jumped across the podium, grabbed each other's throats, and simultaneously screamed, "Honey!"

Mom walked back into the room and slapped the power button, ending any chance I had of learning who won the feud.

"Time to go! It's Date Night!" she announced.

I dug my fingers into the cracks and crevices of the armchair. If I reached deeply enough, maybe I'd discover a magical spring that would launch me up through the chimney and onto the set of *Family Feud*, so I could finally just be a member of the audience.

My mother hooked my elbow and pulled me onto my feet. I went limp and allowed her to escort me to the garage.

"Now hold the car door for me like I taught you. You need to learn to be a gentleman."

I sighed and opened the door to her station wagon limousine. It was Thursday night, my mother's weekly night to go out on a date, and since things weren't going well in that area of her life, she'd decided that I was going to fill in—again.

"Who needs men, anyway? They just break your heart. Matthew, I'm so glad I have you in my life," Mom purred on the way to the evil dance hall.

Dancing. If there was one thing I hated, it was dancing.

My New Daddy

Given the choice, I'd rather be forced to play with My Little Ponies or dropped off at Sunday school for a week of *blah blah blah* religious education.

Without having to be asked, I held the dance-hall door open like a genuine Southern gentleman. As I caught sight of the middle-aged men and women kicking up their heels in a square dance, my teeth clenched so tightly that one of my loose ones almost popped out. My mother led me onto the dance floor, where I floundered my way through several hoedowns as her pint-sized partner. *Ick.* My face burning with shame, I focused on projecting an invisibility force-field around us, but the older couples spinning past kept grinning and calling me "adorable." One woman pinched my bright-red cheek, and I almost swallowed my tooth.

That night, before I went to sleep with the tooth under my pillow, I decided I was done praying for Mom and Dad to get back together. Since Holly was a positive addition to my life, my new prayer was for my mother to start dating someone, *anyone*, other than me.

* * *

"Do you, Nathaniel Perry Tower, take Holly Eileen Spires to be your lawfully wedded wife, for better or for worse, in sickness and in health, 'til death do you part?" Judge Handelman asked.

"I do," my father said, looking sharp in his tuxedo, like James Bond out for a night at the casino. His brown eyes sparkled in a way I hadn't seen since before The War, when he and my mother sang show tunes to me in the bathtub.

Love Wars

"And do you, Holly Eileen Spires, take Nathaniel Perry Tower to be your lawfully wedded husband, for better or for worse, in sickness and in health, 'til death do you part?"

"I do," my new stepmother said, smiling broadly in her fancy powder-blue dress, almost as tall as my father in her high heels. Holly's father stood behind her and beamed. He was hosting the wedding in his enormous living room in a stately manor outside Chapel Hill.

Dad motioned to Thomas, who walked over bearing a small purple cushion. Thomas fidgeted and rocked back and forth as my father leaned forward to grab the rings. I could tell Thomas had to pee, badly. *Hold it just a little longer, Thomas.*

"With this ring, I thee wed." Dad placed the ring on Holly's finger. Holly did the same.

Was that it? Nothing else? Weren't they going to kiss?

"The groom may now kiss the bride," I called out to the newlyweds.

Everyone laughed and turned to look at me. I felt my face on fire.

But Dad and Holly took the cue and smooched. The laughter turned into applause, and the old gray-haired judge winked at me.

Please God, let this work. Let Holly and my father love each other. Let them never fight, never get divorced.

* * *

My mother was incensed when I told her about the wedding. It was like my parents were in a race to see who could get remarried first, and she had lost.

Love Wars

"Do you know the *real reason* your father married that harlot?" Mom asked me when she'd absorbed the news.

I thought about repeating to her my father's favorite quip, "I married Holly for her furniture," but caught my tongue just in time. Somehow, I knew that wouldn't have gone over well. No matter, Mom barreled ahead like an out-of-control train about to jump the tracks.

"He just wants to increase his chances of stealing you kids away from me in court!" Mom practically spat the words in my face. "And I did some research on that Holly woman. It turns out her biological clock is ticking, and she's using your father because she's desperate to get pregnant. She doesn't really love him . . . or you, or Thomas. I'd watch out if I were you!"

My mother seemed to be unhappy with her dating life. Other than her sporadic dates with me, Thomas and I were always home with a babysitter when she went out, so I never met any of her dates. But shortly after she learned about my father's wedding, Mom settled on a boyfriend.

"Matthew, Thomas, tomorrow you're coming with me to meet my man, Bob Trapp," my beaming mother announced over dinner one night. "He lives on a farm with cows and dogs. You two like dogs, right? You'll love his farm."

My prayers were answered—I was finally off the square-dancing hook.

It was a hot May afternoon when we drove out to Bob Trapp's farm. Suddenly, I felt nervous. What would he be like? Was he a good guy or a bad guy?

"Does Bob Trapp like kids?" I asked Mom.

"Of course, he does! He has three kids of his own. But they're all a lot older than you. They're teenagers, and they probably

My New Daddy

won't be around to play with you."

After thirty minutes in the car, we pulled up a dirt road leading to an enormous farm. I could see dozens of fat black-and-white spotted cows behind a fence chewing grass.

Bob Trapp came out to greet us smoking a disgusting, smelly cigarette. Lanky and strong, he was as tall as a basketball player and towered over my mom. He had graying hair, salt-and-pepper stubble, and wore a big-brimmed cowboy hat. He looked way older than my mother. He took the cigarette out of his mouth, reached over, and with one hand grabbed her and gave her a big sloppy kiss, while with the other hand, he tapped cigarette ash onto the ground.

They turned toward Bob Trapp's small wooden cabin and were about to start walking when he looked over his shoulder at Thomas and me like we were a pack of Marlboros he'd left behind at a bar.

"You two must be the pint-sized products of your mother's first marriage, huh? Come along, follow me."

Mom wrapped herself around Bob Trapp and we walked toward the house. When Bob Trapp opened the door, the first thing I saw was . . . *parrots*. They were everywhere! Dozens, perhaps hundreds of ceramic green and red parrot statues lined the walls, the window ledges, and the top of the refrigerator.

"You like parrots?" I asked.

"Yeah, kid, how'd you figure it out?" Bob Trapp said. My mother pulled bottles out from behind the bar and set about pouring adult drinks, while Bob Trapp gave us instructions.

"Okay, boys, here's the deal: go have fun. You're welcome to play *Pong* or watch TV or listen to my tapes. There's a badminton court outside, and you can play to your heart's content. Just

My New Daddy

don't let the cows out, and above all, *do not touch my car!* That's the biggest rule, and you can *never* break it or there'll be hell to pay. Your mother and I need some . . . alone time, so don't interrupt us. What's your name again?" he asked me.

"Matthew." I felt excited about the *Pong* and the badminton.

"Matt, you're in charge of your munchkin brother. Keep him happy, play with him, but whatever you do, don't let him open the door to my bedroom. There are no locks on these doors, and I wouldn't want him to be unnecessarily traumatized. Got it, boy?"

I wanted to say, *Matt is not my name. It's something you step on*, but I thought better of it. This guy was huge.

"Okay, Matt, have fun, and keep your nose clean."

Done with me, he dashed over to my mother and scooped her up in his muscular arms. She laughed as she desperately held onto the two drinks, their contents clinking and sloshing onto her shirt and all over Bob Trapp's chest. He didn't seem to mind.

"One other thing, boy—*no alcohol!* I'll be smelling your breath later." Bob Trapp carried my mother into his bedroom. The door slammed, and I heard muffled giggling.

* * *

Outside, Thomas and I found Bob Trapp's bright red convertible parked in an open wooden garage. The sports car was polished and spotless, and I thought about jumping inside, grabbing the steering wheel, and going *vroom vroom!* But I recalled Bob Trapp's warning and decided instead to go play fetch with the dogs. Then we played badminton and got hot and sticky in the sweltering midday heat. It was fun for a little while but got boring fast. Three years younger and a lot smaller than me, Thomas could

Love Wars

barely hit the birdie. I wished Johnny Callaghan would teleport through the sky and land in Bob Trapp's farm so I could play with someone my own age.

We went back into the cool, air-conditioned cabin to play *Pong* on the TV. I beat Thomas every time, and again felt bored. I looked through Bob Trapp's cassettes and found a colorful tape called "Jingle Dogs." A cute little tail-wagging bulldog wearing a red Santa hat slobbered and grinned at me on the cover of the tape. What the heck? I put the tape in the player and was instantly captivated.

Usually, I *hated* Christmas carols. The only ones I liked were the twisted parodies I learned at school. My favorite went, "Jingle bells, Batman smells, Robin laid an egg. The Batmobile lost a wheel and the Joker got away—hey!" But this was *far* better: A chorus of dogs barked to the tune of "Jingle Bells." Thomas loved it too, and we both laughed hysterically. We kept rewinding and listening to the tape, for more than an hour. I turned up the volume to its max, wishing the barking dogs would block out the moans coming from Bob Trapp's bedroom.

After a long time, Mom and Bob Trapp walked out in their underwear. It was getting late, and they started cooking dinner together.

"Mommy, Mommy, I want you to hear something." I tugged on her slip.

"Matthew, children should be seen but not heard. I'm busy. Go watch TV and when dinner's ready, you can tell me about it," she said.

I went back to sit next to Thomas and we watched *The Dukes of Hazzard*. Finally, dinner was ready, and we sat down to eat. Bob Trapp and my mother sat next to each other as he gazed into her eyes and stroked her hand.

My New Daddy

"Let's go on vacation, Bob," Mom said. "We should travel together."

"Where do you want to go, doll?"

"How about Florida? We can take the boys to Disney World, then we can go out on the town and have some fun together." She batted her eyelashes.

"Perfect. I've got some real estate deals to do down that way."

"Mommy, do you want to hear the tape?" I asked.

She didn't look away from her boyfriend. "My parents have a condo in Miami where we can stay." Her fingernails grazed over his thick, sun-spotted arm.

I pressed her again. "Mommy, the tape, the tape."

"What is it, Matthew? You've found a tape you like? Okay, go ahead, play it for us."

I played "Jingle Dogs" and fell on the ground, laughing. Thomas laughed too.

"You like that tape, boy? You can keep it," Bob Trapp said.

"Really, Mr. Trapp? Thank you!" Maybe he was a good guy after all. He seemed a little gruff, but maybe deep down he really liked kids.

After dinner, my mother said, "Time for us to go home. You boys need your sleep so you can be alert for Sunday school tomorrow. But we'll come back in the afternoon, and you and Thomas can listen to more of Bob's tapes."

Great. Just what I wanted to do: waste another day with no one to play with other than Thomas. But I said nothing. Maybe Bob Trapp had more hilarious tapes.

On the way home, I insisted we play "Jingle Dogs" over and over. Thomas and I couldn't stop laughing.

Love Wars

* * *

The next day, Mom picked us up from Sunday school and drove us back out to Bob Trapp's farm.

"You boys need some exercise; you play too many video games. We're going for a walk," she said. Bob grabbed his big walking stick, opened the gate to the cow pasture, and we started through the grass and brush.

The two of them walked slowly, arm-in-arm like high school sweethearts, with Thomas and me plodding along beside them. Once again they talked to each other and didn't look at me.

"We'd make a great team, doll," Bob Trapp said, squeezing my mother.

"Yeah Bob, we'd be unstoppable! With my medical practice and your real estate holdings, we'd be set. We'd never have to worry about money," Mom told him.

I didn't want to listen to all their adult talk, so I wandered ahead.

"Come back here, Matthew. You're going too far. We can't keep up," my mother called out.

I sighed and stopped in my tracks, waiting for the three of them to catch up. We resumed walking, and again I grew impatient and walked faster. My mother called me back again.

I hated this walk. It was even hotter and stickier than the day before, and there were smelly piles of cow dung everywhere. I avoided the patties. Thick black clouds of buzzing flies swirled around the crap. I walked faster. I wanted to go back inside the cool cabin and play video games, watch TV, or do anything else but this.

My New Daddy

Suddenly, something slimy struck me in the back of my head. I turned around to see what had happened, and more of it hit me in my face, eyes, and mouth. *What?* I reached up to wipe off the nasty substance and realized what it was as the stench overpowered me: *cow crap.*

When I could see clearly, I saw the cowboy holding his walking stick aloft in one hand. Smirking, he could barely suppress his amusement.

"You should listen to your mother, you little runt. It's a dangerous world. Something bad could happen to you if you don't respect your elders," he said, biting his lip and stifling a big grin.

I stared down at the ground and my tears mixed with the cow dung. The bitter, salty, disgusting sandwich assaulted my senses. I would *not* let him see me cry. *No!* My mother walked over to me, bent down, pulled a handkerchief out of her purse, and cleaned up my face as best she could.

"Don't cry, Matthew. Boys don't cry. Bob's right, you know. You should listen to your mother," she said.

I looked up at Mom and something snapped inside my chest. I felt an anger like I'd never known rise in my body. *Your boyfriend just flicked crap on me, and you're not going to do anything about it?* My lungs filled with rage, but I couldn't touch it, couldn't feel it, couldn't release it. Instead, I bottled it up tight. I knew that if I gave my mother any hint of what I felt, things would get worse. Much worse. As angry as I was with my mother, I was even more terrified of Bob Trapp and what he might do to me if I challenged him—or her.

But I had my pride. As soon as she was done wiping, I decided: *I'll walk with you, I'll do what you say, but I won't say a word to either one of you. Both of you are getting the*

My New Daddy

silent treatment. My mother had taught me all about the silent treatment; she'd given it to me the day I tried to escape from the shrink's office and several times since. For the rest of the afternoon, I refused to say anything to either one of them. I didn't even look at them, and turned my head ninety degrees to the left while we walked. When they spoke to me—infrequently—I didn't reply. Seething, I just did what they told me to do.

They didn't seem to care. To my surprise and annoyance, they seemed to like it. Now I was exactly the son my mother wanted: seen, but not heard.

When we got back to the cabin, they disappeared into the bedroom. Once again I heard giggles, moans, and loud bangs as if they had picked up a bed and were slamming it into a wall. I couldn't believe my mother was making those adult sounds with a crap-flicking jerk.

While Thomas watched *Tom and Jerry* cartoons, I wandered outside, leaving him alone in the cabin. I picked up a big rock and walked toward the garage. I stood a few inches from the spotless bright red Corvette and tossed the rock up and down, up and down in my hand. I envisioned throwing the rock right through the windshield, glass shattering everywhere.

"Take *that*, craphead!" I said, louder than I'd intended. I looked around. No one was watching. No one was listening.

I reared back with the rock in my hand, like Sandy Koufax about to hurl the final pitch in a no-hitter. I froze and held the position for long minutes, staring at the windshield like it was the biggest catcher's glove I'd ever seen. I wanted to do it *so bad*.

Finally, something gave way and I lost my nerve. Not getting beaten was more important than revenge. Fear won. Seething with tears, feeling pitiful and weak, I walked back inside,

Love Wars

knowing I'd get in trouble if they noticed I'd left Thomas alone. We watched cartoons, and every now and then, Mom or Bob Trapp would come out in their underwear to get a glass of water or wine or beer. I felt nauseous every time I saw them.

* * *

Bob Trapp liked to take Mom driving in his Corvette. Before he'd flicked crap on me, I thought the red sports car was so cool, a real-life Hot Wheel. Now, I hated it. The car didn't have a proper back seat. What kind of person would own a car without a back seat? The kind who didn't want kids around.

Sometimes Bob Trapp would stuff Thomas and me in there anyway. The back had no seatbelts, and I felt cramped and scared. Bob Trapp would drive really fast and I'd just stare out the side window, feeling sick to my stomach, letting my eyes glaze over and hoping and praying the car would stop.

When school let out, Mom told us we were going to Florida with Bob Trapp. We drove all the way there in Mom's brand-new white Toyota Camry. It was an endlessly long, hot, sweaty, horrible drive. Bob Trapp insisted on driving the whole way.

About two-thirds of the way there, I got sick and threw up all over the back seat, spraying vomit on the precious parrot statues Bob Trapp had purchased at South of the Border, a scummy South Carolina rest stop.

"You stupid idiot, you got vomit on my parrots," he yelled. "Why didn't you warn us to stop the car?"

I felt miserable. I wanted to say, *I tried*, but didn't bother.

At another rest stop, Bob Trapp dropped one of his stinky cigarettes on the ground right outside the car door. I didn't see it,

My New Daddy

and I stepped on it with bare feet. I screamed and cried, and Bob Trapp pointed at me and laughed.

When we finally arrived in Miami, we stayed in our grandparents' winter vacation apartment. We ended up going to Disney World without Bob Trapp because he had to work on a real estate deal in Fort Lauderdale. What a relief. Mom took us on all the best rides: Big Thunder Mountain, the Jungle Cruise, Space Mountain, and Mr. Toad's Wild Ride, which was like the kiddie version of getting stuffed in the back of Bob Trapp's Corvette.

When it started to get dark, Mom told us it was time to leave. On the way out, we passed the Haunted Mansion, a huge gray building with tombstones in front, steam blowing out of vents, and flashing lights that illuminated bats, witches, and skeletons. Moans, groans, and cackles played on a speaker, and a deep, creaking voice said, "Beware . . . Beware . . . Abandon all hope, ye who enter . . . *Ha ha ha!*"

We couldn't skip this one—my friends had told me it was the *best* ride in the whole park.

"Mommy, please let's go. I want to see the ghosts," I begged.

She frowned. "Matthew, your brother's only five years old. It might be too frightening for him. I don't think so."

My brother clutched Mom's dress, his face white as a sheet.

I wanted nothing more in the whole wide world than to step into the Haunted Mansion. *Lie. Fast.*

"Mommy, this is the kiddie Haunted Mansion. I've heard from friends that the ghosts are friendly, not scary. It's a calm, fun ride," I told her.

"I don't know. I don't want to upset your brother. It's been a long day and I think we should go home."

Love Wars

My brother still looked scared out of his mind.

Wrong approach. There was only one thing I could do: convince Thomas.

I went over to Thomas, put my arm around his shoulder, and told him what he needed to hear.

"Thomas, look, I'm your big brother, and I promise you're going to have fun. The Haunted Mansion is full of happy, friendly ghosts, and if you wave at them, they'll smile at you. Johnny Callaghan came here with his family and he told me the secret is to wave. So just remember, wave at all the ghosts, and they'll smile."

"Are you sure? The ghosts are friendly? They're not mean?" He stared off at the mansion and wrung the edge of his bright blue Mickey Mouse T-shirt.

"No, I told you, they're friendly. For real. Look, if you don't like it, tomorrow I'll take you to the candy store and buy you anything you want with my allowance. What do you say?"

At age seven, I was old enough for an allowance. I got three dollars per week, whereas Thomas got nothing. Thus, I had direct control over my candy supply, and Thomas was utterly dependent on my rare generosity. That did the trick. He nodded, saying nothing.

"Mommy, Thomas and I want to go into the Haunted Mansion," I said.

My mother looked down at Thomas.

"Only if you're sure you want to go, Thomas." She looked at him with one eyebrow raised.

I'd been hitting Thomas a lot recently, beating him up, ordering him around, making his life miserable—always when Mom wasn't watching. I gazed at him with a look that was half an offer to give him candy, half a threat to punch him in the face.

Love Wars

Thomas looked up at Mom.

"Matthew says the ghosts are friendly," he said.

The next twenty minutes were the most enjoyable of my post-divorce childhood to date. The ghosts were scary and evil, and I loved every minute of it. I was the star of the best *Scooby-Doo* episode ever, on the case with Scoobs and the gang, out to clean up the mansion and reveal the truth about all the ghosts.

"You're fake! You're fake! Oh yes, you too, you're *fake!*" I cried out gleefully as I pointed at each ghost in turn. Every time I said it, I felt braver. I reveled in being one of the meddling kids who exposed all the fraudulent grown-ups.

Meanwhile, my brother wailed and buried his head in Mom's lap. It was hilarious. I kept saying to him, "Remember, Thomas, wave at the ghosts and they'll smile at you," as I nearly bit my tongue in two, stifling laughter. He tried it a few times, but gave up and sobbed. What a scaredy-cat. Wasn't it obvious that the ghosts were *all fake*?

When we exited the ride, no one said anything. Thomas stared at the ground, refused to look at me, and cried silently, tears streaming down his face. I looked straight ahead, but suddenly felt all mixed up and weird. Maybe I'd been unfair to Thomas. Meanwhile, my mother said nothing other than a stiff and frustrated, "Time to go home." She was annoyed that I'd fooled her so easily.

When we finally got into the car, my mother exploded.

"Matthew, you shouldn't be mean to your brother! You lied to him and made him really scared. That's the *last* time I'm taking you to Disney World, young man! I may take Thomas back, but I'll *never* take you again—that is, unless you learn how to be decent to your brother!"

My New Daddy

"I'm sorry, Mommy," I said.

"Don't tell me, tell your brother!"

"I'm sorry, Thomas," I said. I felt both sorry and not sorry. I realized I'd been cruel to him, and I felt bad about making him cry. But I couldn't imagine *not* having gone inside the Haunted Mansion. Returning home and hearing Johnny rub in my face that he'd been brave enough to confront the ghosts and I hadn't would have been unbearable. And I would never have forgiven Thomas if his pathetic fears had stopped me.

The next day, my brother and I walked through the sweaty, humid streets of Miami to a convenience store near the apartment and I bought him Gobstoppers and Willy Wonka Worms. It was the least I could do. My brother offered me half the candy, which I gladly accepted. Thomas was so sweet. He always seemed ready to forgive and be nice to me, no matter what I did.

* * *

The day before we left Miami was my eighth birthday. Bob Trapp was back in Fort Lauderdale closing his real estate deal, and Mom had calmed down enough to do something special for me. She took us to see *E.T. The Extra-Terrestrial*, which opened on my birthday. We all loved the cute little gray alien, who was cuddly enough not to scare Thomas.

After the movie, over cake and ice cream at Baskin-Robbins, my mother's face lit up like a jack o' lantern. "Kids, Mommy has some *great news* for you! You're going to be so excited!"

I'd already opened all my presents—including three new Atari video games and Luke's lightsaber—so I wondered if she had a secret, special treat for me.

Love Wars

"What is it? Are you taking us to a sneak preview screening of *Return of the Jedi*?"

She laughed.

"No, I don't have any special connections to George Lucas. You'll just have to wait for the movie to come out next year like all the other kids. But it's even better than a movie."

What could be better than the new *Star Wars* movie? I was stumped. This was going to be awesome.

"What is it?"

She looked so excited, I thought her face would burst.

"Boys, you're going to have *a new daddy!*"

She said it like Bob Barker would say "*A new car!*" on *The Price is Right*. I felt like Santa Claus had slid down the chimney and kicked me in the gut. I stared out the window at the palm trees. I couldn't allow myself to make eye contact with her. I'd rather the big news had been that she was forcing me to go back to the shrink. Ten shrinks, even twenty would have been a mild discomfort compared to the burning rage I felt about the idea of Bob Trapp being my new daddy.

"Matthew, look at me when I'm talking to you!" I'd been lost in a fantasy about E.T. wandering the universe, searching for home. She'd been prattling on about Bob Trapp for ten minutes and finally noticed I wasn't paying attention. I sighed and turned to meet my mother's bright, happy eyes.

"Bob's a great man and he's accomplished fifty times more just in the last year than your father ever will in a lifetime. He's strong, he's tough, he's a *real man*, and he's one of the richest men in Chapel Hill. Look!" She flashed a huge, glittery diamond ring at me.

"Do you remember I told you the story about the wealthy

My New Daddy

investment banker who wanted to marry me when I was in college, and I turned him down for your father? I've regretted that decision every day for more years than I can count. Now I'm finally going to make up for it," she said with pride.

"Mommy, when are we going home?" As much as I dreaded the sweltering, long trip in the back seat of her Toyota, *anything* was preferable to listening to her talk about Bob Trapp.

"Look, I know you're still in your father's thrall, but at least give Bob a chance. Some day you'll see he's the best daddy a little boy could ever wish for, and you'll forget all about Nate. Everything's going to be great from now on. Matthew, we're rich! We're millionaires! Don't you see? We're going to live like royalty, in a huge house in the countryside, and we'll all have our own private horses. We'll have money forever."

I thought of *Richie Rich*, the Saturday morning cartoon about the wealthy eight-year-old who had every toy in the world and a piggy bank filled with gold. *Maybe this won't be so bad after all*, I thought. I would make Mom buy me every toy I'd ever wanted, including a go-kart. It was the least she could do to make up for turning a blind eye to Bob Trapp flicking crap on me. I wasn't going to forget about my real dad, but I also wanted toys and money and my own private horse and a go-kart, *bad*.

* * *

A few days after we returned to Chapel Hill, Mom and Bob Trapp took us on a drive into the countryside.

"Matthew, we're going shopping for a mansion," my mother announced.

"A mansion? You mean like the Haunted Mansion?"

Love Wars

"No, a real-life mansion. We're looking for a place to live."

They drove us through the wealthiest areas just outside Chapel Hill while Bob Trapp gave me a history lesson.

"You see over there, boy? That mansion, and that one, and that one, too. Slaves built them before the Civil War. Most of them were passed down from one generation to the next. But times are tough for some of these farmers, and a few of the mansions are getting sold off or foreclosed. Bad news for them, good news for us."

Finally, we pulled into a long, circular driveway, and Mom and Bob Trapp took us inside the most enormous house I'd ever seen. I couldn't believe it. It was easily five times bigger than our small house on Lark Lane. And it had a swimming pool. *And a tennis court!*

"This is going to be our new home," Mom cried gleefully.

"*If* we win the auction," Bob Trapp reminded her.

A few days later, my mother took us down to the auction, where we met up with Bob Trapp. We had to dress in our best clothes and sit quietly.

"Matthew, silence is golden," my mother scolded me every time I fidgeted or tugged on her sleeve or asked her what was happening or asked her when it would be over. She and Bob Trapp held hands, her head resting on his shoulder. Watching them together, I wanted to barf.

The auction went on for hours. Lots of sharply dressed old people with cups of tea and little plates of cookies on their laps sat quietly, whispered in each other's ears, and occasionally raised their hands and called out numbers. Bob Trapp raised his hand and called out a number. What was happening? Mom and Bob Trapp looked at each other and smiled.

Love Wars

Finally, it was over and we walked outside. Mom practically skipped, she was so giddy.

When we were away from the crowd, Mom and Bob Trapp screamed and laughed, and then they started singing, "We're in the money, we're in the money, we've got a lot of what it takes to get along."

"Matthew, Thomas, sing with us," my mother commanded.

We all sang together. Visions of go-karts vroomed through my head.

On our way back to our small, simple home on Lark Lane, Mom told us that one day, when she died, the mansion would belong to Thomas and me, and all the money would be ours. Somewhere in my heart, I drooled.

* * *

Over the next several weeks, I kept asking my mother when we were moving into the mansion, and when she and Bob Trapp were getting married. Her answers were confusing and ever-changing. One day, they were getting married in winter. Then it was spring. Then it was winter. We were moving next month, then next year, then in three months.

I told Dad about Bob Trapp and the engagement and the mansion. He laughed and laughed, and laughed some more.

"So your crazy mother wants to marry Bob Trapp, huh? Word on the street is Bob Trapp's a jerk of epic proportions. He's known around town for suing everyone and always being in court. Your mother took me to the cleaners, but I bet she's no match for Trapp and his army of lawyers. She better watch out; if she tangles with that guy, she might end up on the short end of the stick."

My New Daddy

I told Dad how Bob Trapp had flicked crap on me and laughed at me when I stepped on his cigarette butt. He winced. I told him that my mother said Bob Trapp was going to be my new daddy. He just groaned, but didn't look concerned.

"Do you want him to be to your new daddy?" he asked.

"Of course not, you're my daddy. But I wouldn't mind having lots of money. Then I can buy all the toys you won't let me have, like a go-kart."

He snorted. "If you get a go-kart out of it, more power to you. Just be careful driving it and don't go fast. Those things can be dangerous. Have an adult watch over you while you drive, and I *don't* mean your mother—or Bob Trapp! But if I were you, I wouldn't hold your breath on getting anything. If half the things I've heard about this Bob Trapp character are true, your mother's in for a rough ride."

* * *

The next time I saw Mom, she told me she wasn't going to marry Bob Trapp after all. Then, a month later, the engagement was back on. Then it was back off. She was engaged to Bob Trapp no less than three times before finally, after several months of on-again, off-again wedding plans, she said she was done with Bob Trapp forever. She took me into my room, closed the door, sat down, and launched into a dumping session.

"Matthew, Bob Trapp is a horrible human being," she said. "He smokes, he drinks too much, and he's disgusting. His breath is wretched and he smells even worse than your father. He's a money-grubbing, sexist bastard, and he just wanted to use me in the bedroom. He never loved me. I don't know why I put up with his crap for so long. Some things just aren't worth it."

Mom prattled on for almost an hour, listing a string of angry accusations about Bob Trapp. She even said Bob Trapp had been mean to Thomas and me. Of course, she never mentioned the crap-flicking episode.

At first, I was shocked to hear how she'd turned against Bob Trapp. How could she hate him so much now and have loved him so much a few months ago? How come she didn't like the way he'd treated Thomas and me now, but she'd been just fine with it then? Could she really hate someone as much as she hated my father?

"Matthew, my father gave me crap when I was growing up, your father gave me crap when we were married, and Bob Trapp gave me crap the last couple of months while we were negotiating finances before the wedding. Men have been giving me crap all my life. It just isn't fair!"

Fair? *Fair?* Inside my chest, I felt a mountain of rage I wanted to throw at her with all my eight-year-old might, but I was too scared to let it out. I just stared out the window. Then a thought crossed my mind that almost made me laugh out loud: *For once, you and Dad agree on something. Both of you think Bob Trapp is a jerk.* Then I had another thought, and it made me queasy: *Once Mom's done hating on Bob Trapp, who's next?*

I remembered Bob Trapp smirking as he held his walking stick aloft. I had to know why she didn't stick up for me.

"Mommy?"

She kept right on rambling.

"Why are men always making me the target? What did I ever do to deserve this? I'm not a terrible person. It's their fault! It's not my fault. They're the ones who have the problem if you ask me, they're the ones who have the problem, and I just have to put up with it. I mean, this is my burden in life. I just don't understand why I always get these awful, awful men."

"Mommy!" I said more firmly.

"Matthew! You shouldn't interrupt your mother. *Show some respect!* I'm trying to explain to you how evil men are ruining my life. Pay attention. You might learn something important. You can *never* trust a man."

"I have a question about Bob Trapp."

That got her attention.

"What is it? I'll tell you anything you want to know about what a jerk he was to me."

Summoning up all my courage, I asked her the question that had been on my mind for months. "Why didn't you stop Bob Trapp from flicking crap on me?"

"What are you talking about?"

"You were standing right there. You saw the whole thing."

"Saw what?"

"Mommy, you wiped the crap off my face!"

"When?"

"At Bob Trapp's farm. When we went for the long walk through his cow pasture and he flicked crap on me with his walking stick."

She looked at me with wide eyes, then her eyes glazed over for a moment as she remembered.

"Oh, that time you got dirty. I thought you slipped and fell. I didn't see what happened. And I didn't know it was poop."

I stared back at her, the anger building in my chest, bigger, tighter, more powerful than I'd ever felt. *You didn't see? You didn't know? Are you blind?*

LOVE WARS

The rage swelled inside me and I thought I'd explode. But as I looked into her face, something popped and all the air went rushing out. She was telling the truth. She believed that I'd fallen. She believed that I'd just gotten dirty. She'd seen, but at the same time, she hadn't seen *me*.

She was totally incapable of seeing me!

I bottled up my anger and walked out of my room. *You're getting the silent treatment.* I didn't speak to her for days.

In the end, Dad was right: Mom's relationship with Bob Trapp did not get me a go-kart, money, or my own private horse. The only thing I got was more and longer dumping sessions, because now, on top of all her complaints about my father, I had to listen to her talk about how much she hated "that sexist pig" Bob Trapp.

After the Bob Trapp meltdown, my mother seemed to give up on romance altogether. Even though she was single again, she never took me out on another date.

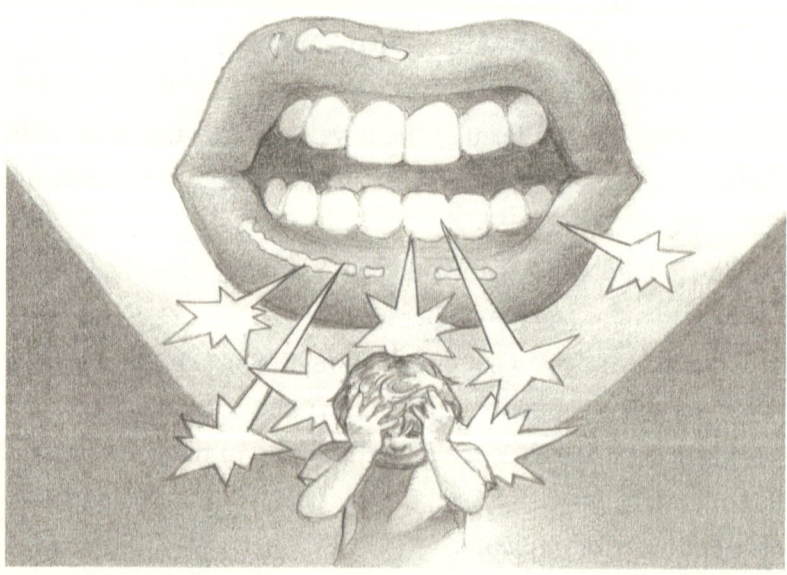

Chapter Seven
ESCAPE FROM THE PARKING LOT
Age 8 • 1982 • Third Grade

"NATE! WHEN ARE YOU GOING TO PAY YOUR HALF OF THE KIDS' SUNDAY SCHOOL BILLS?"

"GIVE IT A REST, VANESSA! CALL MY LAWYER IF YOU HAVE A PROBLEM!"

The three of us—my mother, my father, and I—stood in the darkening, dreary parking lot in front of Dad's laboratory. The sun had set, and we cast long shadows against the building's red brick wall. Mom stood on one side of me, Dad on the other side. They screamed like they always did whenever they got within twenty feet of each other. I was in the middle. Always, I was in the middle. Little Thomas sat by himself in Mom's car, playing with his stuffed rabbits. As usual, he didn't have to be in the middle like I did.

Escape from the Parking Lot

"NATE, YOU'RE A MISERABLE FATHER AND YOU'RE RUINING MY LIFE!"

"GO TO HELL, VANESSA!"

As different as my parents were, in this moment, they looked like twin Dark Lords of the Sith. Their eyes shot icy daggers at each other. They screamed so loud and with such force, I thought whoever yelled loudest would win the hate competition and cause the other to drop dead.

They weren't Mom and Dad anymore, but hateful monsters. As I gazed up at their twisted faces, my tears erupted. I cried for them, but most of all, I cried for me. I felt so sorry for myself.

Before my parents got divorced, I'd thought they were basically gods. They could do no wrong. They always had an answer when I asked a question. They always knew how to take care of me, how to punish me, and what I deserved. If I challenged them, usually their answer was: "Because I'm the adult and you're the child." Or, "That's just the way it is." Or, "Someday you'll look back on this and thank me." Sometimes I didn't like what they did. But I'd wanted so much to believe they were perfect.

After the divorce, I still wanted to believe they were supermom and superdad, just like always—that their rules were fair and just, that I was just like all the other kids, and that we had a perfectly normal family. How could anyone else be different? What happened in my family was all I knew.

But as I stood in the dark parking lot, with their hateful words pouring down on me like acid rain, something in my brain clicked. *This is not normal. This is not right. This is not fair. This is not the way it's supposed to be.*

They weren't looking at me. Their eyes locked onto each

Love Wars

other's like rams locking horns. The yelling only got louder. They moved closer together so that they were only inches apart as they screamed into each other's faces. I couldn't believe that two people could possibly hate each other that much and not fight with their fists.

Their words were full of blame, guilt, and accusation.

"You're the one who—! No, you're the one who—! You did this! You did that! Shut up and let me speak! Stop interrupting me! You're a bad father! You're a bad mother! You can't even take care of the kids! You don't know what's best for the kids! I know what's best for the kids! I take care of the kids better than you! You're not paying enough money for this! You owe me money for that! I want my records back! I want my furniture back! I want my photo albums back! I want my books back! Your parents are responsible for this! Your parents are responsible for that! You never loved me! You never listened to me! I'm a better parent than you! I'm going to sue you for this! I'm going to sue you for that! You'll hear from my attorney! I will never let you have custody of the kids! I will get custody of the kids! Drop dead! I HATE YOU!"

As I listened, a black hole threatened to suck me in and make me disappear forever. My parents weren't paying attention to me. I wasn't there. They were yelling about the house, the furniture, the books, the cars, the money, and the kids. I was just another possession.

What happens to the things they fight over, split in two by their tug-of-war? What happens to me?

Sobbing, on the verge of collapse, I struggled to disentangle myself from my mother's grasp. She had a tight death-claw grip on my shoulder, which only intensified as the yelling grew worse.

Escape from the Parking Lot

It was as if by tightening her hand, she could vampirically suck the energy she needed to fuel her hatred out of my little body. Using all my strength, I wrenched open her fingers and stumbled away in a daze, a flow of tears streaming down my face.

I crumbled against a wall at the end of the parking lot, far enough away from my parents so that if I stuck my fingers in my ears I could block out their fighting. I let my mind wander and left that miserable godforsaken parking lot with the angry monsters who were trying to suck me down into their ocean of hate.

I went somewhere else—to a different time, a different place, a different life. I had different parents, who never ever fought and always listened to me. I had a brother I never picked on, a sister I could laugh with, and lots of friends. I still played soccer, but on a different team. I wasn't fat. Everyone loved me, and I loved everyone.

I was happy. I wasn't totally sure what that was anymore. But somehow, somewhere, in another life, I was happy—like all the normal kids.

A hand on my shoulder snapped me back to reality. It was my father. It had been many long minutes before either of them had realized I had left. What if I hadn't stopped at the wall and just kept going? I could have run away, I could have boarded a train, a car could have hit me, but they never would have noticed because they were too busy yelling.

"What's wrong, Matthew? Why are you crying?" he asked.

During my fantasy of a different life, I had almost stopped crying. But when Dad touched my shoulder, and I saw him standing there with Mom yelling in the background, I started crying again even harder than before. I couldn't speak. The tears were so intense that my whole body shook.

Love Wars

I didn't want to answer him. I turned away and shook my head violently back and forth—*no!* I wanted them to leave me alone. My throat was sore. Snot dribbled out of my nose, but I didn't bother wiping it away. It mixed with the tears and went into my mouth. The bitter mixture of snot and tears made me cry even harder.

Mom came storming up, shoved Dad to the side, and grabbed me. For a moment, I thought there would be another tug-of-war. But my father let go of me, and my mother resumed her iron death-claw grip. It was like, "You've had your time-out, Matthew, but the time-out's over, and you're back in our world of hate."

My leaving hadn't accomplished anything. I wasn't in a different life where people loved each other. I was back in my life, where everyone hated each other, and there was no escape. My parents wanted to hate each other more than they wanted to take care of me. And both of them wanted me on their team, both wanted me to join in their hate.

From deep inside, something rumbled, bubbled, and burst. I screamed like I'd never screamed before.

"STOP FIGHTING! STOP YELLING! CAN'T YOU SEE WHAT THIS IS DOING TO ME? CAN'T YOU SEE WHAT THIS IS DOING TO ME? *CAN'T YOU SEE WHAT THIS IS DOING TO ME?*"

I repeated it, over and over again, yelling it as loud as I could, crying up to the Mommy I once knew, the Daddy I once knew, God, someone, anyone. I wanted to be heard. I wanted someone to answer my prayer and make my parents stop fighting with each other. Or, for someone to take me away to some other life so my parents could fight their stupid war forever and I wouldn't have to listen or be part of it ever again.

Escape from the Parking Lot

I put every bit of energy I had into my scream, every ounce of courage, every piece of me that wanted my childhood back.

I wasn't sure about much of anything anymore. I didn't know what was true and what was false, what was real and what wasn't. Encyclopedia Brown had failed me. I couldn't figure it all out. It was too big of a mess, and there never seemed to be any answers.

I wasn't sure if I loved my parents, or if I loved my brother, or if I loved myself. I wasn't sure if I hated my parents, or if I hated my brother, or if I hated myself. I wasn't sure if I knew what love was. I was absolutely sure what hate was, though. I didn't know if I wanted my parents to live. I didn't know if I wanted my parents to die. I didn't know if I wanted to live. I didn't know if I wanted to die.

Through all my confusion, only one thing felt absolutely clear and real and true: *Can't you see what this is doing to me?* I held onto this question like a life preserver.

I had said a lot of things to my parents, and nothing had made a difference. Repeating what one parent said about the other hadn't helped. Taking sides hadn't helped. Accusing them of things hadn't helped. Trying to use verbal games to trap them hadn't helped. They hated each other more than ever.

As I screamed my truth, I realized something so important I knew I'd never forget it for the rest of my life: If they listened, if they really listened to this one question, it would make a difference. It would matter.

Suddenly, the monsters of hate were speechless. Somehow, I had done it. Through my crying, my screaming, and my praying, I had gotten through to the gods who ruled my life. An eight-year-old had made the grown-ups change. I held my breath.

Love Wars

Time slowed to a crawl. The whole world moved in slow motion, then came to a halt. The birds stopped singing, the cars stopped motoring, the engines stopped humming, and the generator shut off. A happy couple walking down the street, so in love that their eyes glistened with contentment, turned away from their love for a moment to observe the spectacle. Children playing with each other, brothers and sisters who loved each other and loved their parents, turned away from each other to look at us. The entire world looked at my parents with expectant, sorrowful, hopeful eyes, not wanting to make a single sound, not daring to break the silence, waiting, waiting, waiting for an answer to a very simple question... *Which was more important: Matthew or Hate?*

And then, the world knew the answer. The cars started motoring again, the birds and squirrels chattered, the engines hummed, the couple returned to their love, the children played and laughed, and the generator turned back on. The world turned away, with a slight tear in the corner of its eye.

My parents were arguing again. I couldn't believe it. God couldn't abandon me like this! The flame of hatred was being fed. Soon they were screaming just as loudly as before.

"Vanessa, why the hell did you steal all the furniture out of the house?"

"Nate, you know damn well it was *my* furniture. And when are you going to replace my orchids? You smashed them!"

"Oh *please*, enough about your orchids. You owe me for the boys' health insurance. Do I have to go to court to make you pay?"

"Nate, you owe me thousands of dollars. You're a deadbeat! You've been trying to steal the boys away from me for years!"

"GET A GRIP ON REALITY, *YOU LUNATIC!*"

"GO TO HELL, *YOU GODLESS BARBARIAN!*"

Love Wars

It was more important to yell than to listen to me. It was more important to fight than to be my parents.

Hate was more important than Matthew. 'Til death do they fight.

I turned my back on my parents, and even as my mother gripped my shoulder, I gazed off into the distance at the train tracks that I could barely glimpse in the hazy dusk and fantasized about running away for real. I'd hop onto the next train to anywhere and disappear from The War forever. My picture would appear on the back of a milk carton, and maybe then my mother and father would stop fighting long enough to go looking for me.

Finally, the screaming ended. My mother spun on her heel, yanked Thomas out of her car and deposited him on the ground, then jumped in the driver's seat and peeled out of the parking lot. Her last words were, "NATE, YOU'LL BE HEARING FROM MY LAWYER!"

Dad drove us to Mud Flats in total silence. I wondered if his lack of words meant that somewhere deep inside, he was ashamed that he couldn't control his rage but didn't want to admit it.

After long minutes hearing only the car's engine, he clicked on the tape deck and The Police came on playing "Every Breath You Take." I looked up at my father's tight face, his gritted teeth, his eyes staring off at a dark road only he could see. I reached over and hit the fast-forward button until the song I wanted him to hear came on. I silently mouthed the words:

> Love can mend your life
> But love can break your heart

Escape from the Parking Lot

> I'll send an S.O.S. to the world
> I hope that someone gets my
> Message in a bottle.

Back at home, Dad disappeared into the basement with Thomas to develop a shoebox full of film canisters. Other than his precious garden, snapping candid close-ups of everyone in the family was my father's favorite hobby. Usually I tagged along and sat quietly with him in the darkroom waiting for the images to appear, but I was in no mood to look at pictures. Instead, I slunk into the kitchen and plopped myself onto a stool while my stepmother cooked my favorite dinner, Holly's Casserole.

Holly and I had been getting along quite well. I liked hanging out with her in the kitchen and watching her bake bread. Tonight, although I usually loved the fragrance of bubbling noodles and ground beef, I had no appetite. The kitchen became a blur, and I couldn't fight back the lone tear that rolled down my face. Holly heard me snuffle and somehow read my mind.

"Matthew, what's it like being in the middle of your parents' fighting?"

I stared at her, open-mouthed. *No one had ever asked me that question.* Not my mother, not my father, not the shrink, not my grandparents, not my teachers, not my friends—no one.

I burst out crying. I knew it was okay to sob in front of Holly, that she wouldn't insult me for it like everyone else did.

"*I hate it I hate it I hate it I hate it!*"

Holly enveloped me in a huge hug and stroked my hair. "Shhh, shhh, it's okay. I understand. I hear you. I'm here."

She held me for a long time, and I felt like *finally someone saw me, heard me, and believed me.*

Love Wars

"I'm going to talk to your father about it, okay? You didn't start The Craziness. You don't deserve to be in the middle of it."

"The Craziness?" I asked, wide-eyed.

"Yeah, The Craziness. I know your parents call it The War, but I think it's just a bunch of crazy, juvenile fighting. Your father's a good man, but I've seen him lose it when he's around your mother. Lord, does she know how to push his buttons. Both of them are acting like out-of-control kids. They're driving each other crazy, but the one who's suffering most is *you*, because they always put you in the middle. Thomas is lucky. But if this keeps going, he's going to end up in the middle, too."

I couldn't believe what I was hearing. I couldn't believe any adult could be so smart.

"Make it stop, Holly! Please make it stop!"

Holly pulled away from me so she could look into my eyes.

"I'll do my best. I can only do so much, but I promise I'll talk with your father. I don't know if he has enough self-control to not fight with your mother, but the least he can do is keep you out of it."

Maybe someone had heard my prayers after all.

I was grateful to Holly for offering to talk to Dad. But I didn't just want my parents to stop putting me in the middle. I wanted them to stop their whole stupid war.

As I imagined The Craziness coming to an end, something shifted, as though a rusty can of radioactive worms had evaporated from my belly. Suddenly, the angry monsters of hate seemed less tyrannical. I imagined them as misbehaving kids flinging mud at each other in the schoolyard.

"Holly, do you remember the last scene in *Star Wars*?" I asked, one eyebrow raised.

Escape from the Parking Lot

"How could I possibly forget? Didn't we bake Death Star cookies together last Christmas?"

"If we could somehow get our hands on a copy of the secret plans, there's got to be a way we can blow up the Divorce War Death Star!"

Holly laughed. "Yeah. *Right*, kid. You, me . . . and an army of lawyers. May the Force be with us!"

PART II:

THE REBELLION

Chapter Eight
TUNING THE VIOLIN
Age 8 • 1982 • Third Grade

I moved the bow back and forth, and the violin made noises. I wasn't sure how or why. But somehow, it worked—sort of. My little brother did the same.

"You kids are so talented!" My mother giggled. "Let's dance the hoedown. Play it again, Sam!"

We took it from the top, and Mom cavorted around her friend Caroline's cluttered living room, being careful not to trip over the myriad dog toys strewn over the plush blue carpet. Caroline, a tall doctor with long auburn hair, jumped up to dance with Mom. The two women held hands and kicked their legs in all directions like Broadway show girls.

"You two are destined for the London Philharmonic," Mom said. "Caroline, aren't they superstars?"

"I've never seen such talented young violinists," Caroline lied enthusiastically.

Mom beamed. "Can you believe my Mozarts are only eight and five years old?"

Love Wars

Violin lessons were finally starting to pay off—for my mother. Now, instead of two sons who didn't know a violin bow from a bow and arrow, she had two sons capable of creating a glorious, infernal cacophony, a tribute in her mind to her exceptional mothering skills.

When my mother had announced that she'd signed Thomas and me up for violin lessons, I asked why.

"Nate is corrupting you and Thomas. You need to learn more civilized activities, or one day you'll end up uncouth, smelly athletes, just like your father."

"You don't want me to play soccer anymore?" I asked.

"No, you can still play soccer, but next week you're going to learn to play the violin."

Six months later, the point of our lessons was clear: Mom wanted a private traveling orchestra to entertain her friends. We worked for no pay, we played on command, and we didn't get weekends off. But, on the bright side, at least we sucked.

Every weekend, she took us on the road to a new friend's house and made us dress up in our finest suits. Some applauded politely. Others squeezed our cheeks and asked, "What do you want to be when you grow up? A musician?" *No, I want to be a writer, a soccer player, or Luke Skywalker.* I'd force a smile and say nothing.

After completing the grand tour of her entire social network, Mom took Thomas and me to a huge convention hall to play a concert with other beginner violinists. This seemed like a very bad idea. When dozens of klutzy kids clanged spoons together, what would happen? Would the vile noise shatter the windows and shower our parents with glass? Would it blow a hole in the space-time continuum and destroy the universe?

Love Wars

Before the concert started, we were all supposed to tune our violins. I had absolutely *no idea* how to do such a thing. All I knew was how to move my elbow back and forth in a memorized pattern, creating what my instructor proudly called a "song" and which I secretly called "making a racket." My instructor had tried to teach me how to tune the instrument by turning the black knobs in certain directions, but I didn't understand how this made my violin sound any better or worse.

While my fellow violinists fiddled with their black knobs, I haphazardly did the same and hoped no one would notice my cluelessness and accuse me of ruining the concert. I was afraid I'd stand out like a broken string. Luckily, it turned out no one could hear me above the obnoxious din.

Back on Mom's musical tour, we returned to Caroline's house for an encore performance. Like the last time, my mother sat with Caroline to talk about adult stuff and sent Thomas and me out to the backyard.

"Remember, children should be seen but not heard. Go outside and play," she told us. "I'll let you know when it's time for the hoedown."

"Yes, ma'am." I was happy for any excuse to play outside. Caroline had the best dog ever: Black Orpheus, a Labrador whose tail always thumped the grass whenever I got near. The old boy didn't run much, but he loved to stretch and roll around in the sunshine. I lay down on my back, put my head on the furry pillow, and stared up at the clouds that passed overhead. Orpheus's regular, predictable breathing comforted me.

I squinted and turned the clouds into my favorite shapes.

"That one's a soccer ball. That one's Scooby-Doo's tail. That one's an X-wing fighter . . ."

TUNING THE VIOLIN

I turned over to pet Orpheus, and he nuzzled my face. Thomas liked Orpheus too, and the big dog licked my kid brother's hand.

"Boys, come inside! Showtime!"

For long moments, I lay still with my head buried in Orpheus's sleek, warm coat and wondered about the future. When I grew up, would I have a happy family and kids? Would I get my kids a dog? Would I make my kids play the violin?

When Mom called a second time, I obeyed.

* * *

"Mom, does Caroline want to keep her dog?" I asked on the drive home.

"Young man, of course she wants to keep her dog! Why would you ask such a silly question?"

"I dunno, just wondering," I said.

For long minutes, we drove in silence.

"What does the name Black Orpheus mean?" I asked.

"It's the name of an adult movie. You're too young to understand," she said.

Again, silence. Then I sucked up my courage.

"Mom, can I have a black Lab just like Black Orpheus?"

I cringed in anticipation. I was sure she'd say no and harangue me about what she wanted and needed from me. After what seemed like forever, my mother said, "Let me think about it. I'm not saying yes and I'm not saying no. Keep practicing the violin and we'll see."

I could barely contain my joy. Although she hadn't said it directly, I knew what her response meant: *Keep playing for my friends and I'll get you a dog.*

LOVE WARS

When we got home, Mom rubbed my head. *Oh, no.* I knew what was coming.

"Matthew, it's time for me to get the crud out of you," she announced. "Come on, let's go."

She marched me upstairs, took up her usual perch on the big wicker chair she'd set up in my room for her dumping sessions and plopped me into her lap. Her perfume and body odor washed over me like an enormous Mom tidal wave I couldn't stop or control. All I could do was wait for the wave to pass and hope I'd wake up breathing on the beach.

She pulled out her black rubber comb and *scraped*.

"Ow. Ow. Ow. Ow," I said. As usual.

Streams of white flakes fell like snow onto my Superman T-shirt, my shorts, and Mom's flowery dress. The more the flakes fell, the more my scalp burned.

"Matthew, you know I do this because I love you. I could be a bad mother and just let you go to school with all this dandruff, but then what would the kids say? Someday you're going to look back on this and thank me."

I wasn't listening. Or at least, I tried not to listen. Projected onto my bedroom's closed white door, Pac-Man darted around in his eternal quest to eat the ghosts. I felt like Pac-Man, one moment chasing the flashing blue ghosts, the next trying to escape before they caught me and . . .

"Young man, I bet no other mother in the world would do this for her son. I bet you all the bad mothers just let their kids walk around with crud in their scalps. I must really love you if I'm willing to spend an hour every week digging your crud out." She rammed the sharp edge of the comb deep into my head and *scraped*.

Tuning the Violin

"OW!"

"Sorry. Dr. Mom is doing her best," she said.

After an hour, we both looked like a snowplow had driven by and doused us with fresh powder. Touching my raw scalp was like brushing up against a knee skinned to the bone.

"It's time for your shower, young man," she said, handing me a bottle of Denorex.

The foul-smelling green liquid stank like a cesspool, made my eyes red, and made my scalp convulse in pain. I bit my lip to stop myself from yelping.

When I got into bed, I couldn't lie on my back because my head hurt so much. I lay on my stomach and read Hardy Boys books until weariness finally overtook me. I tossed and turned all night, and my head felt like a thousand needle pricks.

* * *

A few weeks later, Mom took Thomas and me to the animal shelter.

"I'm so proud of you boys and how well you're doing at violin that I've decided you can have a dog."

I was in luck. They had a friendly, young black Lab who needed a home. I told Mom, "That one, that one." Thomas didn't object.

We took him home, and I named him Black Orpheus, just like Caroline's dog. Once I had my dog, I lost all motivation to play the violin.

The next time I saw my father, I told him about the violin lessons.

"Mom forces me to play the violin. I don't like it."

"Well, have you told her?"

Love Wars

"No, I'm scared to. I don't like it when she gets mad."

"Matthew, you know I can't help you. I would never force you to play the violin, but it's her house and her rules. Holly talked to me about not putting you in the middle of my arguments with your mother, and I think that's a good idea. All I can tell you is my opinion, which is that a third grader doesn't need to learn the violin to get into a good college."

I thought about saying, *Dad, you force me to work in your stupid garden. What does that have to do with getting into a good college?* But I thought better of it.

"Speaking of which, I know you can do better on your next report card. My brother and I got straight As throughout our entire school careers. Are you going to do your *best* next time?"

"Yes, Dad," I muttered. I hated it when he guilt-tripped me about grades.

The next time I saw my mother, I steeled myself for the confrontation.

"Mom, I want to tell you something." I was like Luke Skywalker going into the cave to confront Darth Vader.

"What is it, Matthew?"

I paused a long time, looking at my shoes. *Luke wouldn't have just sat here like a dummy, doing nothing.* Finally, I made eye contact with my mother.

"I was talking with Dad, and he said I don't need to learn the violin to get into a good college."

Mom's face darkened into a scowl.

"Young man, it's not up to him! It's *my* house and *my* rules. And you like playing the violin, right? You're so good at it."

Oops. I knew I shouldn't have quoted my father, but somehow his words had flown out of my mouth. I hesitated to respond.

Tuning the Violin

Oh well, here goes nothing.

"Honestly, Mom, I don't really like playing the violin. I know you and your friends love it, but I don't. Can I please stop?"

"Young man, I *just* got you a dog. I didn't want the stupid dog, but I got it for you as a reward because you've been practicing your violin. Now you want to quit? What kind of scam is this? *Did you trick me?*"

"No, Mom! I didn't trick you! I never promised anything. We never made a deal."

"Oh yes we did! You're just like your father, breaking The Contract. Enough of your antics! Go to your room and practice your violin. *NOW, young man!*"

Crying and scared, I trundled myself upstairs, shut the door to my room, took out my violin, and . . . just held it for long moments. I pulled out the bow, waxed it with resin, and started playing halfheartedly. I couldn't focus. All I could think about was poor Black Orpheus. Surely my mother would return him to the pound—or worse.

After an hour of distracted violin playing, I walked downstairs. Mom was lying on the couch, watching TV.

"Mom, are you going to let me keep Orpheus?"

Her lips were firmly zipped while she watched her soap opera, her face a mask of annoyance. I waited with butterflies in my stomach.

Finally, she responded. "Are you going to keep playing your violin?"

I was about to answer yes but stopped myself short. *Don't promise anything—she'll use it against me later.*

I sat down on the floor and forced myself to watch *One Life to Live*. Neither of us said a word. I *hated* soap operas with a

Love Wars

passion, and didn't understand why she liked them so much. But I felt compelled to sit there. Why, I wasn't sure, but a little voice inside my head said: *Wait. Say nothing.*

Finally, when the episode ended, my mother turned toward me.

"Matthew, we adopted the dog, and I'm not going to get rid of it as long as you keep your end of the deal. Okay? Are you happy now? But you have to keep playing the violin. Furthermore, it's *your dog*, and you better take care of it. *Don't let your dog become a nuisance!*"

I took Black Orpheus for walks every day. I loved him so much. He was so friendly and never looked sad. Oblivious to the Hoedown Showdown, all he wanted to do was fetch balls and chase squirrels. He had no idea that his place at my side depended on my willingness to continue making ear-shattering noises with a small wooden instrument.

* * *

The next Friday, Mom picked us up from school. But instead of taking us home to meet Dad, she took an unexpected turn into an all-too-familiar gated community.

"Mom, where are we going?" I dreaded the answer.

"You'll find out when you get there," she said.

My innards tightened like violin strings about to snap.

We pulled up to the violin teacher's house, a stately brick manor with a perfectly manicured lawn and a black sedan parked out front.

"Matthew, the teacher says you're not making any progress, so I've added an extra day of practice."

"*On Fridays?* But Dad's supposed to pick us up at four!"

Tuning the Violin

"He can wait 'til five-thirty. Civilized kids are worth the wait." She retrieved the accursed instruments from the trunk.

Thomas didn't say a peep and clambered out of the car. I would have complained more, but I remembered my pooch and kept my mouth shut.

I was annoyed, but my father was outraged.

"What the hell is your lunatic mother up to now?" my father asked when he arrived at the violin instructor's residence. Apparently, Mom's lawyer had provided his lawyer with instructions on when and where to find us.

"I don't know, Dad. She thinks I need to practice more."

"*Not on my time!* My attorney's going to file a complaint with the judge. She owes me several thousand dollars for your medical insurance and back property taxes anyway."

* * *

Scared about my dog being taken away, I halfheartedly practiced violin for another couple of weeks. But boredom and loathing overtook me once again. I had to do something. What? It dawned on me that my mother didn't have to know whether or not I was practicing.

You can force me into my bedroom all by myself for an hour every day, but you can't make me play.

Instead of playing the violin, I pulled it out of its case and placed it on the floor next to me so I could grab it at a moment's notice. Then I cracked open one of my favorite books, *Call It Courage,* and escaped from my bedroom prison to the Pacific Islands. I was the teenage Polynesian hero Mafatu on a voyage across the treacherous sea to conquer my fears and test my will

Love Wars

to survive. Mafatu's only companions on his long, lonely journey were his yellow dog, Uri, and the albatross, Kivi.

After about half an hour, I heard the door handle turn. Fast as lightning, I threw the book under my bunk bed and it landed with an all-too-loud *thud*. Just as my mother walked in the door, I pulled the violin to my shoulder and moved the bow. But I didn't fool her.

"Why aren't you practicing, young man? *Play!* I spent a lot of money on your violin."

I banged out one of her favorites. She waited for five minutes, listening with the faintest hint of a smile. Finally, she walked downstairs, satisfied. I played for a couple more minutes, then put the hated instrument down and retrieved my book. I searched through the rumpled, creased pages to find my place in the story with Mafatu and Uri:

> It was the sea that Mafatu feared. He had been surrounded by it ever since he was born. The thunder of it filled his ears; the crash of it up on the reef, the mutter of it at sunset, the threat and fury of its storms—on every hand, wherever he turned—the sea.

After the hour was over, I ran downstairs, brushed past my mother, who was calling me to dinner, and cuddled with Orpheus, my very own Uri.

* * *

Tuning the Violin

We fought The Violin War for several months. Mom routinely caught me not playing, and rushed home from work every day to monitor my practice sessions. She punished me for disobedience and told me I was not allowed to watch TV, eat dessert, play video games, or see my friends if I didn't practice. Sometimes the punishments worked and I found myself playing for a full hour against my will, crying and feeling weak and helpless. Sometimes her punishments only made me more determined to resist, and I devised new ways to outsmart her. I stood perfectly still with my ear pressed against the door, listening for any hint of an approaching mother. The moment I heard footsteps on the stairwell, I rushed over to the violin and played, so when she threw open the door, all she saw and heard was a son who followed orders. This way, I sometimes managed to play the violin for only five minutes out of the hour.

Like everything else in my life, The Violin War became yet another topic of parental interrogation. Mom frequently asked me what Dad said about it, and Dad asked me whether I'd figured out how to get out of it, reminding me that my crazy mother had no right to steal ninety minutes of his visitation time. I agreed, especially since I hated the violin. (I might not have taken his side had it been go-kart lessons.)

I had nightmares. In one, my mother and I each had ahold of the violin and we were pulling with all our might. I wanted to take it away from her so I could throw it in the trash. I didn't know what she wanted to do with it, but I was afraid she'd shove it down my throat. Suddenly, I turned into my father, and the violin turned into me, and they were pulling me apart again. I screamed and woke up. Mom appeared at my door and asked, "Matthew, what is it? What's wrong?" I looked away and mumbled, "Nothing."

Love Wars

In another nightmare, Mom towered over me. She was the raging giant from the movie *Attack of the 50 Foot Woman*.

"MATTHEW!" her voice thundered from far above. She was so tall I could barely see her angry face.

"GIVE ME YOUR DOG."

"No no no," Orpheus whimpered. *Wow! My doggie could talk!*

But before he could say another word, Mom ripped him out of my arms and held him aloft by his tail. Orpheus dangled above her enormous mouth, crying and barking.

"I'M HUNGRY," my mother announced to no one in particular, licking her lips. "AND WE'RE OUT OF DONUTS!"

"NOOOOOOOOOOO!" I screamed, waking up drenched in sweat.

Again, my mother came into my room to see what was wrong.

"Are you okay, Matthew? I heard you scream again."

"It's nothing, Mom."

* * *

One day, I came home from school and walked down into the basement to grab Orpheus so I could take him for a walk. He wasn't there. The side door swung in the breeze. *What? Someone let my dog out?* I went out into the neighborhood and walked from house to house, calling him.

"Orpheus! Orpheus! Where are you?"

At first I wasn't overly concerned. Orpheus had gotten out before, and it had been pretty easy to find him. Usually he hung out in a neighbor's backyard.

Tuning the Violin

But this time, none of the neighbors had seen him.

By the time dusk descended, I felt frantic. I looked everywhere. Where was my Uri? I asked Johnny Callaghan to help me find him, and we kept circling the block for hours. Johnny went home for dinner, and I felt so alone.

I trudged home, waiting for my mother to return from work so she could drive me around the block looking for my dog. I went down into the basement and picked up Orpheus's red leash, holding it, wishing with all my heart for my pooch to magically appear on the end of it. As I fingered the taut fibers, in my mind's eye I saw my first dog—Carrie—and fear gripped my heart. Suddenly I realized that I had forced myself to forget about her. For the first time in years, I remembered the day she'd disappeared...

I was five years old and had arrived home from kindergarten, but couldn't hear the sounds of scratching and pawing, sniffing and yelping, the fast familiar beat of my doggie's wagging tail. Carrie wasn't running up to greet me like she usually did. Where was she?

I walked all around the house, looking everywhere, inside our indoor jungle gym, behind the couch, under the coffee table, in the basement. Where was my dog? I asked the maid, but she didn't know anything.

I had a horrid feeling in the pit of my stomach. Something wasn't right. I locked myself in my bedroom, fearing the worst. What if Mom gave Carrie away to some other family? I stroked Winnie-the-Pooh for comfort, but for the first time I saw that Pooh Bear was just a lifeless object.

After what seemed like hours, my father got home. The moment I heard the key turn in the door, I raced downstairs,

Love Wars

and before the door even fully opened, I cried, "Daddy, where's Carrie? What happened to her?"

He only glanced in my direction, unable to look me in the eye. He looked deflated. It was the first time I'd ever seen him like this. Usually he was so tall, proud, and strong. I'd never seen him back down in any confrontation. Now he looked like a cartoon chipmunk whose nuts had been stolen, and he was too embarrassed to tell his baby chipmunks he'd lost their dinner.

"Matthew, come with me for a moment. We need to sit down and talk," he mumbled.

We sat in the living room. I looked up into his lined face, scared of what I was about to hear.

"Matthew, I don't know how to tell you this . . ." He didn't look at me, just stared off into the distance. "This morning, Carrie pooped on the carpet again and your mother decided she'd had enough. She took your dog to the animal shelter and had her put to sleep."

"NOOOOOOOOOOOOOOOOOO!" I screamed and hit him furiously. "Why didn't you stop her? *Why didn't you stop her?*" Somehow, I was angrier at him than I was at her. She'd always hated my dog. But Daddy, who was always talking about his beloved childhood dog, Skinny—how could he stand by and watch while Mommy had my dog murdered?

"Matthew, I . . . I . . . don't know what to say. I couldn't stop her. It was her decision. Things have been hard between us, and I just . . . well, I . . ." He finally looked into my eyes. "Kiddo, I know this is hard, but it's not the end of the world. You still have lots of friends at school. Maybe someday you'll be able to get another dog. You had some good times with Carrie and now it's time to move on. Your mother was upset about the dog and we need her to be happy too."

Tuning the Violin

I felt a tightening in my chest. I felt something shrivel, gasp, die. My whole body shimmered into invisibility. My tears suddenly stopped. They were worthless. My father tried to hug me, but I pulled away. My feet pounded up the stairs and I flung myself onto the floor of my room, my mouth and teeth pressed against the cold wood. I slammed the floor with my fists, my whole body shaking with huge gasps that took my breath away.

That night I dreamed I was running away from a big evil man with a gun but I couldn't run fast enough. I fell off a bridge while trying to dodge his bullets, landed on railroad tracks, and then a train ran over me. As I died, my last vision was the face on the locomotive: my mother's . . .

* * *

As Carrie's fate came flooding back to me, I felt my stomach turn to ice. I heard Mom's car roll up. I froze, but then for Orpheus's sake forced myself up the stairs. I dreaded having to ask her the question.

"Mom, what happened to Orpheus?" I choked out as she got out of the car and made her way up the driveway. There was a lump in my throat like a sharp, pointy rock. "Where is he? What did you do with him?"

"What do you mean, Matthew? I didn't do anything with him. Isn't he in the basement where he usually is?"

"No, Mom, he's gone, and someone left the side door open."

"Really, he got out? Did you leave the door open?"

I paused. *I didn't know.* I couldn't remember what had happened that morning.

Love Wars

"I don't know, Mom. I don't think so. Are you sure you didn't leave the door open?"

"I would never do such a thing. I don't want your stupid dog running from here to kingdom come and bothering the neighbors. Show some respect for your mother."

I didn't trust her, but there was no way to figure out whose fault it was.

"Mom, can you please drive me around and help me look for Orpheus?"

We were about to walk back to the car, Thomas in tow, when we heard the phone ring. My mother went inside to answer, and I followed her.

"Hello? Yes, this is Dr. Tower. What is it? Uh huh . . . Yes, yes. That sounds exactly like our dog, yes. Are you sure? Thank you for the call."

She hung up and turned to me. Her voice on the phone had been cold and expressionless.

"Matthew, that was Kevin, Johnny's older brother. Apparently he was riding home on his motorcycle about a mile from here and came across your dog in the middle of the road. I'm sorry to tell you your dog is dead."

I'd been preparing myself for this moment. When I hadn't found Orpheus after school, a voice in my head, cold, flat, and final, had said, *Matthew, your dog is dead and there's nothing you can do.*

I turned away from my mother and ran outside, sprinted over to Johnny's house and told him what happened. He took me up to his room, shut the door, and let me cry without saying a word. He didn't insult me like he usually did when I cried. Johnny loved his dog, Tessie, and we both knew he would have cried just like me if Tessie was dead.

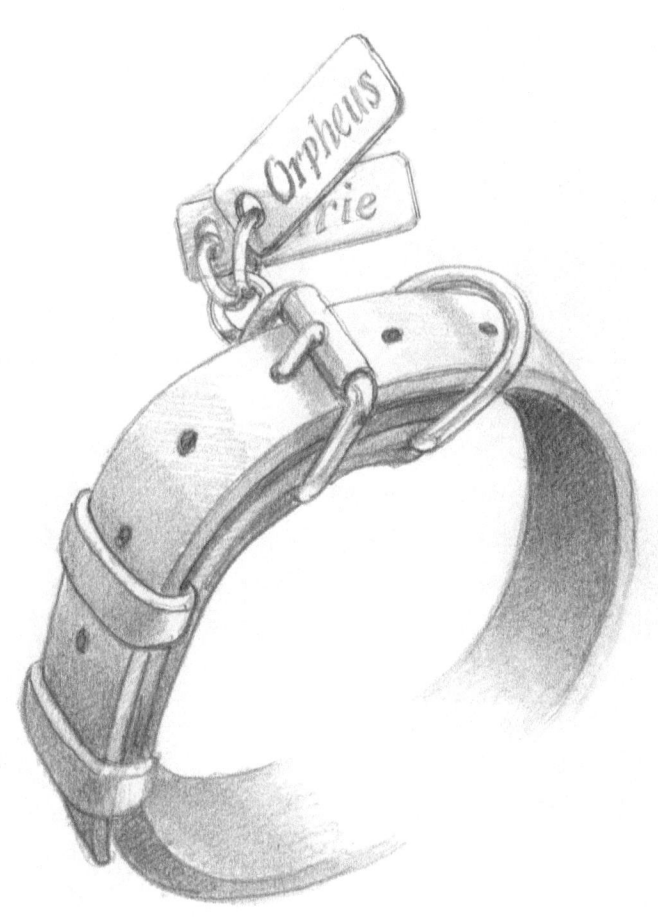

Tuning the Violin

Returning home long after sunset, I didn't say a word to my mother and went straight to bed without supper. There was nothing to do but read about Billy and his faithful hounds in my tattered copy of *Where the Red Fern Grows*. As my empty belly heaved with cold sobs, I suddenly realized why I'd always cried at the end: my previously forgotten love Carrie had been my Little Ann, and now Orpheus was my Old Dan. I imagined their bodies side by side, with a red fern growing in the soft earth of fresh graves.

* * *

After Orpheus died, I had little enthusiasm for anything. I stopped playing violin, stopped playing video games, stopped doing my chores, stopped doing my homework. My English teacher sent a note to my mother telling her that I wasn't performing up to my usual high standards. I brought home a book report with a D grade. I hadn't bothered to read the book, and just wrote a quick note based on the description on the back cover.

Mom came into my room to have a talk with me.

"Young man, whatever's troubling you, you need to pay attention in school. If the teacher tells you to read a book, you have to read it. And you can't neglect your violin. Life goes on, and you can't just mope around forever. Don't you remember the story of *Alexander and the Terrible, Horrible, No Good, Very Bad Day?*"

I silently nodded my head.

"Everyone has bad days. Even I do! Maybe it'll make you feel better if you can think about Alexander's life instead of your own, and you'll see how good you really have it. Do you want to hear the story?"

Love Wars

I liked it when she read to me, even if the story was far below my reading level. She sat in the chair and plopped me into her lap.

> I went to sleep with gum in my mouth and now there's gum in my hair and when I got out of bed this morning I tripped on the skateboard and by mistake I dropped my sweater in the sink while the water was running and I could tell it was going to be a terrible, horrible, no good, very bad day.

My mother read the story of Alexander's unfortunate misadventures as he faced his definition of a bad day. He got smushed in the middle seat of a car, opened his lunch sack to find no dessert, got treated for a cavity at the dentist's office, and was forced to sleep in the stupidest-looking pajamas any kid had ever worn. Things were so rotten that he threatened to run away to Australia.

I wanted to feel better after hearing poor Alexander's tale of woe. But somehow, I didn't. I wondered if Alexander's mother had done even half the things to him that my mother had done to me. At least it helped me to stop thinking about Orpheus and Carrie for a moment.

Then the distraction ended. "Matthew, I've let you go too long without digging the crud out of your head." Mom reached for her comb-shaped scalpel.

Ow. Ow. Ow. *Ow!*

That night, I slept a deep, dreamless sleep, exhausted from crying and feeling wretched.

Tuning the Violin

* * *

The next day, my tears were gone. Maybe it was because I'd decided to try to forget all about my canine companions. Mafatu would have carried on even if Uri had drowned, and I had to be brave.

At school, I told some of my friends about how I was sick and tired of my mother's lame violin lessons.

"So what, Matthew? I have to take piano lessons, and most of the kids I know have to take music lessons too," Daniel Griswell said. "We don't like it either, but it's just what you gotta do."

"Danny's right. Life gets easier when you stop complaining and do what your parents say. Plus, they'll buy you more toys," Johnny Callaghan said.

"But I *hate* the violin," I said.

"Doesn't matter. Eventually, they'll notice that you suck and they'll stop forcing you to play. That's how it always ends—my older brother told me so," Johnny said.

"But my mother's so mean to me!"

"What are you talking about? Your mother's *so nice*. I overheard her telling my mom that you have an attitude problem," Johnny said.

Danny piled on. "I know what your real problem is: You want to be more popular. You could be one of the cool kids, but you're so fat."

Before I even had a chance to react, Danny added, "Try losing some weight, then maybe everyone will stop calling you Goodyear."

Suddenly, my soccer-ball-shaped tummy felt as heavy as a bowling ball. I gritted my teeth. I wanted to punch them both, but said nothing. I made a decision: *Today, when I get home, I'm NOT playing the violin.*

After school, I walked into my room, my sadness replaced by hot anger. I paced around the room, thinking about how much I hated the violin—hated it like I'd never hated *anything* in my life. I walked around in circles, trying to figure out what to do. Finally, it came to me: nothing. *No matter what Mom says, I'm not going to play.* I sat down at my desk to work on school assignments. My anger helped me to focus.

I decided to finally read the book that had caused me to get the D grade. It was about a pack of talking mice who ran a cheese-stealing crime syndicate in the tunnels of New York City. It was a fun read and not at all challenging.

By the time Mom burst into my room, I'd completely forgotten about the violin.

"I don't hear anything, young man."

I didn't look up. I tried to keep reading, but my attention wavered.

"I said, 'I don't hear anything, young man!'"

I refused to look at her.

"Matthew, it's 4:15 and you were supposed to start practicing fifteen minutes ago. If you're well enough to read, you're well enough to play your violin!"

Silence.

"MATTHEW, WHEN YOUR MOTHER TALKS TO YOU, YOU LOOK AT HER!"

I kept my eyes on the book.

She grabbed the book out of my hands and threw it across the room. I looked at the wall.

"YOUNG MAN, YOU GET ONE MORE CHANCE!

Tuning the Violin

I'm leaving and I'm going to count to sixty. When I come back, either I'm going to find you playing the violin, OR ELSE! *Do you hear me? OR ELSE!*"

"ONE. TWO. THREE. FOUR—" she yelled as she stomped out of my room, slamming the door shut.

I stared at the door and heard a buzzing in my ears. The buzzing got louder and louder.

What will she do to me? What's the "Or Else"? I imagined never seeing Johnny Callaghan again, *ever*. I imagined her taking away my precious Atari, or even worse, only letting Thomas play. I imagined her telling me I could never eat another dessert for the rest of my life.

I pushed my chair back. Shaking, my fists clenching and unclenching, I walked over to the violin and picked it up. I gripped the violin's neck so tight, the metal strings bit into my hands, cutting my fingers. Butterflies swirled in my stomach. *She's going to kill me.*

For long moments I held the violin out in front of me like a baseball bat. I turned sideways, facing the wall. I hesitated. The butterflies turned into vicious child-eating moths, devouring my stomach.

Then I remembered how all the kids teased Mafatu in *Call It Courage*:

> "Mafatu is afraid of the sea. *He* will never be a warrior." Kana laughed, and the scorn in his voice was like a spear thrust through Mafatu's heart. . . . Mafatu—Stout Heart—was a coward. He was the Boy Who Was Afraid.

Love Wars

NOOOOOO! NO NO NO NO NO!!

I smashed the violin against the wall, again and again. Each time I swung it, the violin made a *twang* like the whimpering cry of a defeated enemy. After so many fruitless attempts to tune the violin, finally I made a beautiful song. I smashed and smashed until I was left holding a few inches of violin neck and snapped strings. My hands were bloody. I didn't care.

I dropped the neck onto the shattered pile of wood, retrieved my book, and returned to my chair, smearing blood on the pages.

The door opened. I didn't turn around, so I could only hear my mother's gasp. After almost a minute of silence, she laid down her verdict.

"I'm *not* buying you another one, young man."

"Good," I said, not looking up from the book.

She said nothing for long minutes, then . . .

"Fine. *Fine.* You're excused from violin lessons. Thomas likes the violin. He's going to be a great musician. He's destined to make lots of money in the London Philharmonic. *Someday you'll regret this! Someday you'll look back and wish you'd been more like your brother!*"

She stormed out, leaving me alone with the talking mice and my bloody hands.

After a few minutes, I went to the bathroom, washed up, and found some Band-Aids. I looked into the mirror, and I saw a proud boy with strong blue eyes whom I'd never seen before. The boy's determination and courage reminded me of Mafatu in his moment of triumph:

Love Wars

> "Moana, you Sea God! Fear of you has haunted my sleep. But now I no longer fear you, Sea!" He sprang to his feet, flung back his head, spread wide his arms in defiance. "Do you hear me, Moana? I am not afraid of you! Destroy me—but I laugh at you. Do you hear? *I laugh!*"

Head held high, I walked out of the bathroom and down the stairwell, taking every step deliberately. I looked straight ahead, and never faltered in my stride. As I reached the bottom, I overheard my mother talking with my little brother in the living room.

"Matthew's a terrible son, but you're such a good boy, Thomas. You're making your mother proud. I love you so much. You play beautiful music..."

I reached for the front door, and just as I pulled it open, Mom stomped toward me.

"*Just where do you think you're going, young man?*" she asked.

"To play with my friends."

Before she could say another word, I walked out into the crisp North Carolina afternoon.

Chapter Nine
THE TEN PLAGUES
Age 8 • 1983 • Third Grade

"What is the name of the Jewish homeland?" the test paper asked.

Hmmmm . . . What to write? Feeling clever, I scribbled "Mississippi."

"Who enslaved the Jews?"

Who indeed? A real stumper.

"Hey Micha, what'd you put for question number three?" I called out. Unlike real school tests, the teachers at Sunday school had left the room, leaving no one to monitor the inmates.

Love Wars

"The Duke Blue Devils," Micha answered. My eight-year-old co-conspirator looked at me with a sly, knowing grin.

Nice. I copied his answer. I briefly wondered if there was a penalty for deliberately copying wrong answers. If there was, I welcomed it. I was hoping to sink my Sunday school grade into negative territory.

"On what Jewish holiday do we light the menorah?"

That one was so easy, and so obvious: "Halloween." Duh!

The following week, the test came back with precisely the grade I expected: F. And not just an F, an *F-*. I had gotten zero answers correct, and I was proud of it. If Mom insisted on forcing me to go to Sunday school, at least I would make it fun.

When my mother picked us up after Sunday school, she drove us to the Tar Heel Café on the downtown mall, where we had burgers, fries, and milkshakes for lunch. I ordered an adult-sized burger, whereas my brother got the kiddie meal.

"Matthew, I'm going to give you the opportunities I never had," Mom said while noshing her burger.

"What do you mean?" I asked.

I immediately regretted the question. Asking my mother *anything* about her life was an invitation for her to launch into a big speech about how her life was a disaster and it was all her father's fault, my father's fault, and/or Bob Trapp's fault.

"You just cannot imagine what it was like for me as a child, the hell I endured. You are so lucky to have a mother like me. My father was a tyrant, and my mother wasn't much better. I desperately wanted to get a *bat mitzvah*, and my father wouldn't allow it, that sexist jerk."

She rambled on about her horrific childhood, which, based on her level of resentment, sounded like it was only one step

The Ten Plagues

removed from growing up in a concentration camp. I tuned her out as there was nothing new to learn about my mother.

". . . and I've signed you up for Hebrew lessons," she concluded.

"*Huh?*" That snapped me back to reality.

"I told you, you're getting the opportunities I never had. You're getting a *bar mitzvah*, and the first step is to learn Hebrew. You're going to see a tutor on Tuesday."

"I don't know if I want to learn Hebrew," I whined.

"That's right, you don't know, because you haven't tried it. Try it, Green Eggs and Ham, you might like it."

Sigh. After The Violin War, I didn't have the energy to start another battle with Mom about something she wanted me to do. I decided to go along and give it a try. Besides, she wasn't asking me. She was telling me.

* * *

My first Hebrew lesson was okay, neither particularly fun nor utterly revolting. I liked that the tutor worked with me one-on-one, and there wasn't a whole classroom of kids competing for his attention. I learned the Hebrew alphabet, and I somewhat enjoyed the challenge of it. But I didn't feel much motivation—what was the point?

After a few Hebrew lessons, I asked my mother, "Why am I doing this? I know you want me to learn Hebrew, but I just don't get it. What's the big deal about the *bar mitzvah*?"

In response, later that month she drove Thomas and me to our cousin Josh's *bar mitzvah* in New York City, which coincided with the annual Passover holiday family gathering.

Love Wars

"Matthew, you're going to see one of the most beautiful sights you've ever seen. Your cousin is going to become a man. *That's* what a *bar mitzvah* is all about."

At the service, Josh delivered a long-winded Hebrew monologue. What did this have to do with becoming a man? Josh looked like a big kid to me; he was only a few years older. I couldn't understand a word and was so bored I had to pinch myself to stay awake.

At the hot, stuffy, nauseating reception, lots of aging relatives whom I barely knew squeezed my cheeks and asked me what I wanted to be when I grew up. Then Mom took me into a small room to witness Josh's spoils: stacks of presents.

"Look at all the presents Josh got! And he'll get *lots of money* from all our relatives. Young man, if you get *bar mitzvahed*, you'll get lots of presents and money too. Don't you want presents and money?"

I couldn't help thinking: *Can I have lots of money and presents, and skip the bar mitzvah?*

But instead, I said, "Uhhh, I guess so."

* * *

The next day, Mom took us to meet up with her parents and her two sisters, Kendra and Ellen, to go shopping at fancy women's clothing stores in Manhattan, while I fantasized about digging a hole to China. After shopping, I endured a cramped car ride back to my grandparents' walk-up flat in Queens. Sitting in the back seat of my grandfather's Lincoln Town Car, I listened to them argue about the usual subject: The Will.

"Mom, you need to revise The Will. You promised you'd

The Ten Plagues

leave one-third of the antique statues to each of us, but I read the fine print. You're still favoring Ellen," my mother said. That started the brawl, like dropping a bloody chicken's head in a shark tank.

"Vanessa, *give it a freaking rest already*," Ellen shot back. "Mom and Dad have changed The Will at least three times in the last year, and what's done is done."

Mom returned fire at her sister, who was a trial lawyer just like her father. "What's done is done? Easy for you to say. The current draft gives you an unfair portion of the inheritance. I bet you wrote the text!"

"Children, children, calm down," Grandma Libby said.

"Calm down? *Calm down?* Dammit, Mom, I put up with you and Dad playing favorites with Ellen my entire childhood, and I'll be damned if you're going to do it to me again," Mom retorted.

"*Vanessa!* Listen to yourself!" Ellen practically spat back. "You sound like a spoiled brat, making demands of our parents. It's *their* choice, not yours."

"*Both of you, shut the hell up!* Your father deserves some peace and quiet while he drives," Grandpa Avi commanded.

The car was quiet for about twenty seconds.

"*Fine*, Dad. If that's the way you want to be, go right ahead. You always made it abundantly clear who you really love," my mother said, breaking the silence with another bucket of chum.

Mom's twin sister Kendra chimed in, "Mom, Dad, I can't stand listening to these two going at each other's throats. But Vanessa has a point. You need to make The Will fair to all of us."

"Fair? *Fair?* Who are you to be judge and jury of what's fair, Ms. Self-Righteous?" Ellen said.

Love Wars

"ALL RIGHT! *THAT'S ENOUGH!*" Grandpa Avi pulled the car to the side of the road and looked over his shoulder at the three sisters crammed in the back seat like rabid monkeys in a cage. I sat on my mother's lap and Thomas sat on Kendra's, neither of us daring to make a sound. Grandpa Avi's face had turned bright red, like a mobster about to put a hit on his worst enemy.

"THE NEXT ONE OF YOU TO MAKE A GODDAMNED PEEP ABOUT THE WILL GETS *DISINHERITED*. YOU GOT THAT? HAVE I MADE MYSELF CLEAR, YOU LITTLE BRATS?"

None of them said anything. The brawl had concluded, as always, with a threat of disinheritance. Disinheritance was like the death penalty, the ultimate red card, and neither my mother nor her sisters was willing to risk it. I knew that was the last I'd hear about The Will . . . at least, until our next visit to New York.

* * *

That night, my ten relatives and I celebrated Passover. We had to squeeze tight to fit everyone at the Seder table: my mother and brother; Aunt Kendra, her husband Rod, and their two children, Josh and Rachel; Aunt Ellen, who was divorced—just like my mother—and her daughter Wendy; and, of course, our grandparents. Plus we saved an empty chair for the prophet Elijah, a wise adult who never seemed to show up at family gatherings.

The usual buffet of non-delicacies covered the table: horseradish, parsley, lamb bones, disgusting gefilte fish balls in jelly, and sweet wine that tasted like cough syrup. The only Passover food I really liked was matzoh ball soup, but we couldn't eat that until the end.

Love Wars

In somber yet celebratory tones, Grandpa called out the names of the Ten Plagues that cursed the Egyptians before Moses led the Jews out of slavery.

"Blood, frogs, lice, wild beasts, pestilence...," he proclaimed as he spilled a drop of wine for each one on his plate.

I silently finished the list for him. *Screaming matches, crud-removal sessions, fights about The Will, custody battles, and death to the first-born son's childhood.*

"Grandpa," I interrupted, "I know it's a good thing Moses and the Israelites escaped, but why are we supposed to be happy about all the Egyptians drowning?"

"Because the Egyptians are all evil bastards who tried to ruin the lives of our people," he said. "And the Arabs are *still* doing it to us today! We should never have given up even a single inch of the Sinai."

I knew from Sunday school, where we sang songs of allegiance to the blue-and-white flag, that the Israelis were still fighting the Egyptians. No one could explain why. One day our teacher said, "Today is a special day, the Israeli army is withdrawing from Egypt. We all have to pray for the safety of our soldiers." I asked, "Why are we still there? I thought we left Egypt thousands of years ago." The teacher sighed and told me, "It's complicated."

The Seder was long and *boring*. Finally Grandpa gave us permission to eat, and the dinner conversation turned to my grandparents' favorite subject: religion. As much as Mom loved to harangue her parents about their will, they loved to browbeat her about Judaism.

"So, Vanessa, you're dating a new man?" Grandpa Avi asked.

"Yes, I told you about Gordon," Mom replied, her mouth full of matzoh ball soup.

The Ten Plagues

Surprisingly, I liked Gordon, a welcome change from Bob Trapp. A math professor and Navy reservist, Gordon didn't smoke, didn't drink, and perhaps most importantly, had not flicked crap on me. Gordon was kind to his two daughters and didn't dump his problems on them like Mom did to me, or berate them if they didn't get perfect grades like Dad did to me. Occasionally he raised his voice, but there was far less yelling in Gordon's household than in Mom's or Dad's.

I had a big crush on his tall, attractive, blonde, eldest daughter, Cindy, but kept my affections carefully hidden. Anyway, I saw her infrequently as she was usually out with her high school friends. Gordon's other daughter, Lisa, was a year younger than me, and my brother and I enjoyed her company quite a bit. She spent the night frequently, and we made fortresses out of pillows and blankets and chairs. Lisa was the one kid who I could talk to about *anything*. I got along perfectly with her and never teased her or bullied her the way I did Thomas. We'd sit together for hours and just talk about stuff.

"So Gordon's a Catholic?" Grandpa Avi asked.

"Yes, I already told you that," my mother said.

"What are you doing dating a Catholic? You know the church has a long history of anti-Semitism. Pope Pius said *nothing* against the Holocaust, may that evil bastard rot in hell. As far as I'm concerned, Pius and company were Hitler's cheerleading squad. How could you betray our family, our people?" Grandpa Avi scolded.

"Dad, we've already had this conversation, and I have nothing more to say to you," my mother shot back. "Why are you bringing it up over dinner? Clearly you just want to embarrass me in front of everyone!"

Love Wars

"Look, Vanessa, all I'm saying is tradition matters. That's it. You can do whatever you want with your life; I certainly can't stop you. Just think of the example you're setting for my grandsons, and ask yourself if you want them to marry *shiksas* someday, God forbid."

I pushed my food around on my plate without looking up. I hated listening to them fight, but at least Grandpa Avi was focusing his intimidating energy on Mom and not me.

"Matthew. I hear you're taking Hebrew lessons," Grandpa Avi said.

Yikes! I'd jinxed myself.

"Uh huh," I mumbled, intentionally answering with my mouth full in an effort to cut the conversation short. Making the mistake of looking up, I noticed his bald, liver-spotted head perfectly reflected the chandelier's light like the polished surface of Darth Vader's helmet.

"That's my grandson. Don't listen to anything your atheist bastard of a father says; he'll corrupt you. Study your Hebrew lessons and you'll be a good Jew."

I nodded, hoping he'd shift his focus to Thomas Rabbit.

"You saw your cousin Josh yesterday. You heard his mastery of the Torah. You saw how many presents he got. I promise you'll get at least three hundred dollars from me at your *bar mitzvah*, which is fifty more than I gave Josh." Grandpa Avi winked at me.

"What the hey?" Josh complained, but Grandpa ignored him.

Three hundred dollars? That's a lot of video games, I thought.

"Thank you, Grandpa Avi," I said.

My mother glared at her father.

Love Wars

"Don't try to bribe my son! Matthew is enjoying his Hebrew lessons and he doesn't need your money. You two are going to spoil him rotten."

Grandma Libby cackled, her throaty laugh made scratchy from half a century of smoking. She ignored my mother and turned to me, grabbed my cheek, and said, "Tomorrow, we're going to FAO Schwarz and you can have any toy in the store. The rest of you kids, too."

That was the best part about visiting my grandparents: toys. Lots of toys.

After dinner, my cousins and I took center stage for the traditional game: find the *afikomen*, the hidden piece of matzoh flatbread. The grown-ups had stashed it somewhere in the house and the Seder couldn't conclude without it.

The moment Grandpa Avi said, "All right, kids—go!" we all pushed our chairs back and scampered around the small apartment, searching behind stiff, uncomfortable furniture, underneath the small beds (Avi and Libby had separate beds), inside closets overflowing with old vinyl records, behind the washing machine . . .

"FOUND IT!" Wendy cried. Even though she was three years younger than the eldest cousin, she was the biggest, toughest, strongest, and cleverest of the five of us. She'd physically overpowered me plenty of times in the past. She was like Boba Fett the bounty hunter, stalking her prey, and she wouldn't be denied.

We all sat down, wondering what she was going to get out of Grandpa Avi. Traditionally, the victorious kid could ask for just about anything: a new board game, candy, tickets to a movie, even money.

Love Wars

"So, my gorgeous granddaughter," Grandpa Avi said, pinching her cheek. "What will I need to do in order to retrieve the *afikomen* from you so we may conclude the Seder?"

"Give me a BMW convertible," Wendy responded.

The entire room fell silent. I almost laughed, but bit my tongue just in time. If I'd found the *afikomen*, I'd planned to ask for a go-kart.

"Excuse me, young lady? *What did you just ask for?*" Grandpa Avi sputtered, showering half the table with little droplets of saliva.

"I'm not asking you, Grandpa, I'm telling you. A BMW convertible. Or, we could just never finish this Seder, if you prefer," Wendy replied.

"Ohh, *I know!*" Grandma said, laughing. "She wants a toy car, like those Hot Wheels that Matthew loves so much."

"Grandma, excuse me, I'm *not* a little kid like Pipsqueak." Wendy glared at me. "I mean it. A BMW convertible. I realize I'm not old enough to drive—*yet*—but soon enough I'll be taking driving lessons, and I don't want to get stuck with a piece-of-crap, hand-me-down car from my mom."

Aunt Ellen rolled her eyes. "*Whose* car is a piece of crap, young lady?" Then she laughed. "Dad, I gotta admit, she's my kid, through and through. She may be stubborn, but at least she has taste."

Grandpa Avi finally managed to spit out whatever bone he'd been choking on. "A BMW? You should be ashamed of yourself! Don't you know what BMW stands for? *Bavarian Motor Works.* What the hell do you think they made during the Third Reich? Sports cars for Jews to escape the country? You want your grandfather to buy you a Holocaust joyride?"

The Ten Plagues

Wendy stuck out her tongue at the family patriarch and made a loud, pronounced *pffft* sound.

"Holocaust, shmolocaust!" she said. "That was ages ago. Grandpa, American cars *suck*. Good cars come from Germany and Japan."

A thirty-minute verbal sparring match ensued, in which Grandpa Avi matched wits and wills with his ten-year-old granddaughter. At one point, the two of them had to leave the table to talk privately.

When they returned, Avi held the piece of matzoh aloft in his wrinkled old hand like it was the Holy Grail.

"Everyone, I have good news. We're ready to conclude the Seder!" he proclaimed as his cane thudded into the floor.

"So what happened?" I asked.

Grandpa Avi avoided the question. He didn't want to talk about it, and no one else seemed willing to push the issue except me.

I kept pestering him, and he finally whispered to me between macaroon bites and sips of cappuccino, "I promised to give your cousin a nice car when she turns sixteen. She's absolutely right, she needs some class if she's going to find a good Jewish boy. But don't you go getting any smart ideas."

Years later, I finally figured out what Grandpa Avi had been up to with his high-stakes matzoh negotiations. He was training litigators.

* * *

The next day, Grandma Libby bought me four Hardy Boys books to complete my collection, and Thomas got three new

Love Wars

stuffed rabbits to join his ever-growing rabbit warren. My three cousins picked out toys, too. Then Grandma told us we were in for a special treat.

"Kids, we're going to Broadway! Have you ever seen a Broadway show?"

I shook my head. "What's a Broadway show?"

"You're going to love it."

She took us to see the stage production of *Annie*, the story of a little orphan who desperately wants to find her real parents. Somehow, Annie's spunky, hopeful attitude keeps her going through thick and thin, until a billionaire named Daddy Warbucks rescues and adopts her. The cloying musical numbers were as barftastic as my grandmother's perfume:

> The sun will come out tomorrow,
> bet your bottom dollar that tomorrow,
> there'll be sun. . . .

After the final curtain call, Grandma Libby gushed, "Kids, wasn't that the most amazing story ever? And it felt *so real!*"

While Grandma tried to hail a cab outside the theater, I stared down at the dirty sidewalk with the gum and cigarette butts stuck between the cracks. *No, Grandma, look down there for one minute—that's real*, I thought.

On our way back to my grandparents' apartment, my mind wandered: *When will my tomorrow come? Will someone rescue me? Does the forecast call for a sunny mother? Or more Mom thunderstorms?*

Chapter Ten
Hebrew Lessons ... *Or Else!*
Age 9 • 1983 • Fourth Grade

After we returned home from New York, my mother told me I was ready to upgrade from Hebrew tutoring to classes at the temple.

"But I like the tutor," I whined. "Do I have to go?"

"Yes, Matthew. The classes are on Wednesday evenings," she announced.

What? Wednesday was one of our nights with Dad!

Love Wars

When Mom dropped me off at the Hebrew class, I didn't pay attention to a single word the teacher said. He criticized me twice for zoning out. All I could think about was Dad.

When it was finally over, my father came to pick me up. It was eight o'clock, and he was not pleased.

"Hi Dad. It's so good to see you," I said.

"So your mother decided to schedule your Hebrew classes during my time?"

"Yeah, and I'm not happy about it either."

"Do you want to take Hebrew lessons? Or would you rather spend time with me?"

"I'd rather be with you, Dad."

The whole way back to my father's house, I weighed my options. I realized I was about to get into a battle with my mother that would be ten times worse than the violin showdown. But I had no choice. I wasn't willing to give up Wednesday evenings with Dad so Mom could live out her unfulfilled dreams through me. By the time we got home, dinner was over and Holly was reading Thomas a bedtime story. Dad heated up some leftovers in the microwave and I realized how much I'd missed being part of the family dinner.

* * *

The next day after my mother got home from work, I told her right away. "Mom, I don't want to go to Hebrew classes at the temple if it means I can't see Dad on Wednesdays at four o'clock."

"Matthew, you don't have a choice. The classes are only offered on Wednesdays, and this is my decision, not yours. *This is for your own good.*"

Hebrew Lessons... Or Else!

I was about to shoot back at her when an idea suddenly occurred to me.

"Why don't you trade visitation days with Dad? Maybe Thomas and me could start seeing him on Tuesdays or Thursdays."

"No way, young man. We're going to follow The Contract *to the letter*."

"But Mom, you're the one who wants me to go to Hebrew lessons. It's only fair for it to come out of your time."

"Matthew, *stop being so insolent!* I'm the parent, you're the child. The Contract says that I have the right and responsibility to provide for your religious education, and that's exactly what I'm doing."

"But I want to see my dad on Wednesdays!"

"You can see him *after Hebrew lessons*, young man. *This is what's best for you!*"

"*NO!*" I screamed. "NO NO NO NO NO!"

"MATTHEW, SHUT UP! SHUT UP, SHUT UP, AND *SHUT UP!* GO TO YOUR ROOM! THIS DISCUSSION IS OVER. CASE CLOSED. *THE END!*"

I glared at her. My mother was at maximum rage, the anger rising to her cheeks like steam erupting from a geyser. I wasn't going to get anywhere in this debate, so I spun on my heel, furious, and went up to my room.

I tried to read one of my Hardy Boys books, but I couldn't concentrate on the adventures of Frank and Joe. All I could think about was: *How can I outsmart her? What can I do to get out of Hebrew class?*

That weekend, when I saw my father, I told him I had a plan.

Love Wars

"Dad, on Wednesday after school, I'm not going home to Mom's house. I'll take the bus and stay at Johnny Callaghan's house next door. When you pick up Thomas at four o'clock, come get me from the Callaghans'. Mom will never be able to take me to Hebrew class if I don't come home."

My father grinned.

"How'd you get to be so smart?" he said.

When I saw my mother after school on Thursday, she looked like she wanted to rip my head off.

"I was worried sick about you when you didn't come home. I waited for *hours*. You missed your Hebrew class!"

I stared back at her, thinking carefully about what to say.

"Where do you think I was?"

"Oh, you think you're so clever, but I found out where you were—at the Callaghans' house. You're grounded! You're not allowed to play with Johnny for a week. And Ms. Callaghan won't let you come over. She knows you're being punished for your disobedience."

Damn. I tried to think what I could do next week. *Think, Matthew, think.*

Suddenly, it occurred to me: the schoolyard. I could wait at the schoolyard while my mother was still at work, and there was nothing she could do to stop me. No one at school would throw me off the grounds if I told them my father was picking me up at four o'clock.

I smiled.

"Fine, I won't play with Johnny Callaghan or go over to his house for a week," I said. Already I knew a way around that problem: I'd go to Daniel Griswell's, then Johnny would come over. Mom would never know.

Hebrew Lessons ... Or Else!

"Matthew, *so help me God*, you are going to Hebrew class next week ... *OR ELSE!*"

Or Else? Where had I heard *that* one before? *Go ahead, Mom, hit me with your best shot.* I said nothing and walked out.

The next day, when I got home from school, my Atari was gone. When my mother arrived home from work, I asked her about it, even though I already knew the answer.

"It's simple. You want your Atari back? Go to Hebrew class. Thomas can play Atari all he wants," she said.

All my friends have Atari. I can play at their houses, I thought. *You are not going to use Hebrew lessons to keep me from my father. No way in hell. No threats, no punishments, nothing you do will make me give up and submit.* I said nothing more to her.

I called my father later that evening while my mom was in the shower. I told him to pick me up from the schoolyard on Wednesday. Again, it worked like a charm.

That night at Dad's house, the phone rang, and within seconds, my father was holding it at arm's length. The faint sound of screaming could be heard. I noticed how much less unpleasant my mother's rants were with the volume turned down.

After a good twenty minutes, my father put the phone back to his ear. "You don't want me to see my son, you lunatic? Fine. SUE ME!" He slammed the phone down.

"NATE! Watch your mouth," Holly called from the living room.

We looked at each other and cracked up.

The next day when Mom got home from work, she looked like she'd acquired a case of late-stage rabies.

"Matthew, *your name is Mud!* You're an awful son. You're just like your father! You're just like my father! Men have been

Hebrew Lessons... Or Else!

giving me crap all my life, and now you're giving me crap too. What did I do to deserve this? Why am I always the target? Why are you making me the target?"

I said nothing. There was nothing to say. It was pointless. She rambled on and on. It became an hour-long dumping session focused primarily, for the first time ever, on me. After she'd decided that Bob Trapp was a jerk, I knew someone was going to be next on her crap list—it turned out to be me.

I stared out our front window, but it was hard to ignore her words. Her venom leached into my heart. *My mother hates me.*

I refused to let her see me cry. I just kept thinking, *I'll be at Dad's house tomorrow.*

For the rest of the night, Mom barely spoke to me, and when she did, it was with a sharp, angry voice. She doted over Thomas, and she went out of her way to show me how much she loved him.

"Thomas, you are *such* a good son. I *adore you*, Thomas," she cooed at my younger brother. "Can I get you anything, Thomas? Do you want dessert? I have Drumsticks in the freezer." She knew full well that was my favorite dessert. Then she turned to me and said loudly, "Good boys who love and respect their mothers get dessert. Matthew, you're excused. Go to your room and do your homework."

As I walked away, she yelled after me, "MATTHEW, I TOLD YOU NOT TO DISOBEY ME. YOU'RE GOING TO GET WHAT'S COMING TO YOU!"

* * *

Love Wars

Friday after school, I didn't want to go to Mom's house, so once again I asked Dad to pick me up from the schoolyard.

"Matthew, your mother is suing you," he said as I clambered into his red station wagon.

I looked up at him, half-expecting a big goofy grin. But his eyes were haunted.

"Dad, what did you just say?"

"Your mother has filed a lawsuit against you to force you to take Hebrew lessons. Her attorney served me with the papers at work today."

My father guided the car out of the elementary school parking lot and headed home. I stared up at him like he was a Wookiee who'd just told me I'd won the intergalactic space travel lottery and we were blasting off for Planet Alderaan.

"Dad, cut it out!"

"I wish it were a joke. I thought your mother was certifiably insane, but now I'm certain of it," he said. "Oops. I promised Holly I wouldn't say bad things about your mother to you, and I guess I just did. But this is a *special occasion*. It's not every day a mother sues her nine-year-old son, you know."

"Umm, Dad, aren't lawsuits for adult stuff, you know, like murder, bank robberies, and divorce? Right?"

"Well, kiddo, see, here's the thing. Technically, she's filing a complaint to enforce the terms of the custody agreement. She claims that you're in defiance of the agreement and I'm a party to your defiance. She's asking the judge to order you to take Hebrew lessons. So in a sense she's suing you. On the other hand, one could say she's suing me, because she's arguing that I'm in violation of the custody agreement by seeing you during the time of the Hebrew lessons. Of course, I'm only seeing you

Hebrew Lessons... Or *Else!*

during the time I'm allowed to, per the custody agreement! So I guess she's suing both of us." He let out a long sigh.

So, that's my mother's big, scary "Or Else!" A lawsuit? Am I about to get what's coming to me?

"There's going to be a court hearing next month to determine whether or not you have to take Hebrew lessons," my father continued. "I've never heard of anything so preposterous in my whole life, but that's the game your mother wants to play. And the good news for you is, you don't have to cough up any of your allowance to defend yourself, but I have to spend more of my retirement nest egg on lawyer's fees."

I couldn't believe it. After three years of Mom and Dad's War, and their endless court battles, my mother had declared war on me too!

I looked up at my father, my eyes as wide as if I'd just seen the Loch Ness Monster.

"So what's going to happen, Dad?"

"Beats the heck out of me. If you want me to, I can file a counter-complaint and have my lawyer argue that you shouldn't have to take Hebrew lessons."

"That sounds like a good idea. But what will the judge say?"

"I don't know, kiddo. If you want, my lawyer can subpoena you so you'll have the opportunity to testify."

"*Subpoena*? What does that mean?"

"It means the judge will talk to you and ask you for your views on the matter."

I thought about it for a minute. Going to court and talking to a judge sounded scary—the scariest thing I'd ever had to do in my entire life—but missing out on seeing my father was worse.

213

Love Wars

"Okay, Dad, I'll talk to the judge. This is so crazy. Do you ever think this whole thing could be a movie?" I asked.

He burst out laughing.

"Absolutely, tiger, I think about that all the time!"

"What would they call it?"

"I don't know, tiger. What would you call it?"

I thought about it for a moment, and then it hit me.

"I know—Love Wars!"

"That's a great name, kiddo."

"Who would play you, Dad?"

"I don't know. Someone really good-looking, I hope."

"How about Harrison Ford?"

Dad laughed.

"Thanks, kiddo, but I'm not *that* good-looking."

"By the way, Dad, there's something else you should know. But I want you to promise to keep it a secret and not tell my mother."

"What, are you kidding? We're not even on speaking terms. You know that. Your secrets are safe with me."

"Last night, at Mom's house..." I paused for dramatic effect.

"Go on, what is it?"

"I didn't finish my vegetables. They tasted like an old sock, so I threw them out when she wasn't looking," I said, proud of my sneakiness.

Dad's face fell as if he'd been expecting a big slice of juicy gossip and all I'd served up was a half-eaten saltine cracker.

"Why is that such a big secret?"

"I'm worried if she finds out, she might sue me for that, too."

Dad's eyes started watering, and he had to pull the car over to avoid driving and laughing like a madman.

Love Wars

* * *

On Saturday, when I saw Mom again, she had some unexpected news for me. I thought nothing could be more surprising than the impending lawsuit. Boy, was I wrong!

"Matthew, we're going to church tomorrow."

To church? *What?*

"What do you mean, Mom? Like . . . Christian church?"

"Gordon has invited us to explore his religion with him, and I'm bringing you boys along for the sake of the relationship."

"But Mom, you're suing me to force me to take Hebrew lessons!"

"*Don't get smart with me*, young man! We're going, and I don't want to hear another word about it."

"But I don't want to go to church," I said in my whiniest possible voice. Sometimes whining bugged her so much that she gave in.

Not this time.

"SILENCE! Not another word!"

Fine. She wanted me to go to church, I'd go to church. Besides, I was secretly curious about who the heck this Jesus Christ character was and why everybody was so obsessed with him.

At church the next day, I didn't get it. I found it just as boring as Shabbat services. Blah blah blah blah blah. At least the priest spoke English instead of Hebrew, but still . . . *boring*.

Afterwards, on the drive home, I asked her my burning question: "Mom, why is it you're suing me to force me to take Hebrew lessons while at the same time you're going to church with Gordon?"

Hebrew Lessons... Or Else!

My mother sighed the enormous sigh of a long-suffering parent who must endure her child's ceaseless insolence.

"Matthew, it's *really* simple. I'm the parent and you're the child. I'm old enough to make decisions about my religion. You're too young, so I make decisions for you. When you grow up, you'll make decisions for yourself and for your children. Until you're an adult, zip it."

"But it isn't fair, Mom! I don't want a *bar mitzvah*. And I don't want to go to church either."

"Tough. Life isn't fair. Now be quiet. I've had just about enough out of you!"

* * *

The next time I saw my father, he had an update on the legal situation.

"Matthew, your mother wants to quash your subpoena."

At first I thought he said, "Your mother wants to squash your penis," but then I realized he'd said that big adult word again: *subpoena*.

My father handed me a long piece of paper with small type and pointed to a few lines. I read them aloud, only stumbling over a few words:

> "Vanessa M. Tower, by counsel, asks this court to quash the subpoena issued to Matthew Alan Tower for appearance in a hearing on the seventh day of October, 1983. To have this nine-year-old child called to court for the purpose of being

Love Wars

asked about religious preference will turn his religious instruction into a dispute between his parents, and will preclude any positive feelings resulting from such religious education. Additionally, requiring the child to testify in a hearing like this may have a lasting negative impact on his own growth and development. Wherefore, Vanessa M. Tower respectfully requests that the hearing go forward without necessity of testimony of Matthew Alan Tower."

I paused. "Dad, what does preclude mean?"

"It means to eliminate, to rule out, to make impossible."

I read the whole thing again, slowly and carefully, and then I said, "Mom doesn't want me to talk to the judge, because then she might lose."

"Wow! You figured it out! How'd you get to be so smart?"

I smiled. I loved it when my father told me how smart I was.

"Sometimes I think you're an adult trapped in a child's body," he added.

I felt my whole body sag and the gleam left my eyes. I stared out the window. When, oh when, would I ever get to be just a kid?

* * *

And so it went on—me running away from Hebrew lessons to see my father; my mother going to church with her new boyfriend and occasionally dragging my brother and me with her to the house of Christ. Of course, it was only when she brought

Hebrew Lessons... Or Else!

us to church that she'd let us skip Jewish Sunday school, never because I wanted to go play with my friends.

As I anxiously ticked off the days until the court hearing that would determine whether I would get *bar mitzvahed*—and thus, in the eyes of my Jewish tradition, "become a man"—I couldn't have imagined any further plot twists. But as usual, I underestimated my family's capacity for craziness.

One day at Dad's house, the telephone rang.

"Hello," he answered, while a pregnant Holly cooked dinner and Thomas played with his toys. They had just announced the big news to the family, and I couldn't wait to find out if it was a boy or a girl.

"Yes... Yes... Uh huh... Uh huh..."

The strange tone in his voice made me stop watching the football game on TV. His face was pale, and his voice quivered. I'd never seen him so shaken.

When Dad got off the phone, he didn't say a word. He walked to the couch, collapsed in a slump, and clapped one of his big hands over his eyes.

At last, he collected himself, and delivered the news in a hollow, tinny voice.

"Matthew, that was Vanessa's father. He called to tell me if I don't make you take Hebrew lessons, he'll have my entire side of the family killed."

* * *

At school, I tried to explain The Craziness to my friends, but when I told Johnny about my mother suing me, he didn't believe me.

Love Wars

"Cut it out, Tower! I mean it. Your mom's awesome," Johnny said as we swung on the jungle gym bars. "Whenever I'm over at your house, she's always making us hot chocolate and giving us quarters for candy and letting us play video games."

"Johnny, it's for real. She filed a lawsuit! I have to go see the judge."

"You're *so* full of it. Tag, you're it!" Johnny slapped me on the back, jumped off the jungle gym, and ran away across the grassy schoolyard.

Part of me felt like crying. I looked down through the bars of the jungle gym at the ground, and I just wanted to drop. But I sucked it up, jumped off, and ran after Johnny. I hit him a little too hard when I caught up, and he tripped and fell to the ground.

My fourth-grade teacher, Mrs. Kaputnik, saw me hit my friend and called me over to take a time-out. If my best friend wouldn't believe me, I thought maybe my kindly teacher would. I walked over to accept my small punishment from the sweet old Polish lady with the wrinkled face, bright red lipstick, and flowing mane of crimson hair.

"Mrs. Kaputnik, can I ask you a stupid question?"

"Matthew, remember what I told you? There's no such thing as a stupid question. Go ahead, what is it?"

"Is it okay for a mother to sue her son?"

"Excuse me, I don't understand. Are you asking about a lawsuit?"

"I mean, do you think it's cool for a mother to go to court to make her son do something?"

"Matthew, what on earth are you talking about?"

"My mother is mad that I don't want to take Hebrew lessons, so I have to go talk to a judge."

Hebrew Lessons... *Or Else!*

Mrs. Kaputnik exhaled noisily, her brow furrowed, her eyes narrowed, and I could practically hear a *tsk-tsk* under her breath.

"I know your parents are divorced and I get the feeling it's messy, but that doesn't mean you can disobey them and get away with it. If you're asking for my advice, I suggest you just listen to your parents. They know best. Obey them both and you'll be fine."

I looked down at my shoes and sighed a big dramatic sigh.

Mrs. Kaputnik put her arm around my shoulders. "Someday, when you grow up, I promise you'll see that they did the best they could for you. Now recess is over, so why don't you go apologize to Johnny?"

I didn't say anything to her, and I didn't go seek out Johnny to offer him an apology. I just turned on my heel and walked toward the classroom. Once I got to my desk, I stuck my head between my hands just like I'd seen my father do after Grandpa Avi had called and threatened to kill his whole family.

When the bell rang and school ended for the day, Mrs. Kaputnik handed me a book, *It's Not the End of the World* by Judy Blume. "Matthew, I thought reading this novel about divorce would help you understand what your parents are going through."

That evening, I devoured the book in one sitting, and by the end I felt just as empty inside as I did at page one. I wanted to like twelve-year-old Karen, but mostly I envied her. Compared to my parents' smackdown, she was growing up in a divorce of hopscotch and tiddlywinks—no custody battles, no kidnappings, no lawsuits. Why weren't there any books for kids like me? Right then and there, I decided: *Someday, I'm going to write a*

Love Wars

book about all this, and maybe then my friends and teachers will finally believe my stories about my crazy life.

* * *

Finally the big day arrived, and for the first time ever, I got to skip out on school even though it wasn't snowing. My father drove me downtown to the Chapel Hill courthouse. Outside, stone warriors stood beside petrified cannons, with Confederate flags carved into the bases of the statues. The enormous brick building sported pristine white marble pillars, turning its entrance into the jaws of a dragon that threatened to devour all who entered.

Dad took my hand and led me into the courthouse, deep inside the dragon's belly, where a tall police officer with an enormous gun awaited us. I squeezed Dad's hand hard, digging my nails into his flesh.

"Don't worry, kiddo, the bailiff will take you to see the judge," Dad said. I relaxed just a bit.

The officer led me into a wood-paneled chamber, where a balding old man with flowing black robes sat behind a desk, absorbed in his papers.

"So, you're Matthew?" Judge Handelman asked kindly as he removed his reading spectacles.

"Yeah," I said and took a seat.

Wow, I couldn't believe it—*the same judge who had married my father and Holly*. Still, I fidgeted. The bailiff left, closing the door loudly behind him.

In the month leading up to the court hearing, I'd started getting nervous about what the judge might do to me. My mother's

Hebrew Lessons... Or Else!

punishments were annoying, but nothing compared to *jail*. Could the judge send me to jail if I refused to go to Hebrew class? I clenched my legs tight to stop my knees from knocking with fear.

"I remember you from your father's wedding," the judge said. "You're nine years old now, in the fourth grade?"

"Yeah."

"What are you learning about in school?"

"Public speaking."

"Really, at your age? You must be quite gifted." The old man smiled at me, and his eyes sparkled. "Come to think of it, you were quite outspoken about wanting your father and stepmother to smooch in public, much to their embarrassment as I recall."

"All the smart kids are learning public speaking," I told him.

I was in a program for gifted students, and our big assignment was to research a topic of our choice and give a speech about it. I'd plagiarized a *National Geographic* article about the history of chocolate for my speech. Mrs. Kaputnik, unaware of my sleight of hand, had told me I was one of the best speakers in my class. She said public speaking was my *forte*. After looking up the strange word in the dictionary, I'd decided that writing, soccer, and video games were my *fortes*, but I didn't mind adding a fourth talent to my repertoire.

The judge lobbed softball questions about school, my friends, and my favorite hobbies. And then: "Do you want to take Hebrew lessons?"

I paused for a moment. *What's the catch?*

"Uhhh... Not really?" I said, worried about what he might do to me.

"Not really?" he asked.

Love Wars

"No. Definitely no," I said, more certain.

"Thank you, Matthew. I have no further questions."

That's it? No way! Wasn't he supposed to grill me?

The judge excused me, and I went outside the courtroom to wait with Holly while my parents appeared before the judge. Waiting was pure agony, but during a break in the hearing, I found a way to entertain myself.

While Dad and Holly whispered to each other and my mother ran off to find a payphone to call her medical office, I looked out the window and noticed the two opposing lawyers chatting with each other under the courthouse's grand overhang. I slipped outside and crept slowly across the cobbled path until I was about twenty feet away—just close enough to make out their words, but too far away for my eavesdropping to be obvious.

"Bruce, I gotta tell ya," my mother's lawyer chortled as he slapped his colleague on the back. "I probably shouldn't say this, but off the record, this is the most looney-tunes case of my career!" With his other hand, he tipped his cigarette, spilling ashes onto the red brick courtyard, which the wind picked up and blew in my face. I stifled a cough as I didn't want to get busted.

"Tell me about it, Dick. Let's go down to the tavern for beers when this one's over—which I'm guessing will be very soon," my father's lawyer replied.

I fingered the pages of my weathered copy of *The Hobbit*, ready to open it in case they looked up. But they didn't even notice me and disappeared back into the courthouse to resume their arguments.

After another hour, my father emerged and said he had some big news for me.

Love Wars

"Matthew, your mother has been enjoined from taking you to Hebrew classes."

"Dad," I groaned, "I *know* Mom enjoys taking me to Hebrew classes. Duh! What did the judge say?"

He laughed. "No Matthew, *enjoined*, not enjoys. The judge issued an *injunction*. You have the right to make your own decisions about your religious education. You do not have to go to Hebrew lessons. You can see me on Wednesdays."

I'd won. My mother had lost. I'd never have to take another Hebrew lesson for the rest of my life, and, as a bonus, I could quit Sunday school, too. I'd miss making up random test answers with my mischief-making friend Micha, but playing outside was infinitely preferable.

I was quiet for a moment. Then I cackled like a hyena and started singing a ditty I made up on the spot to the tune of a *School House Rock* grammar jingle. Dad chuckled, and we sang the song together: "Injunction junction, what's your function? Saving my childhood from total destruction!"

We were singing and giggling when my mother stomped out of the courthouse. We both fell silent. For once, she said *nothing* to my father. She just grabbed my hand and pulled me to the car.

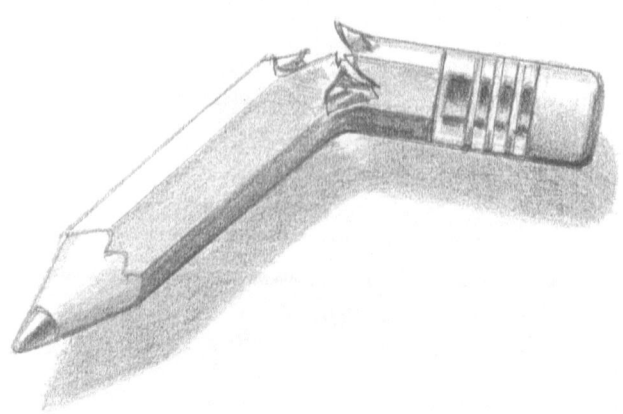

Chapter Eleven
MOTHER AND CHILD REUNION
Age 9 • 1984 • Fourth Grade

"What kind of good-for-nothing child humiliates his own mother in front of a judge?" my mother ripped into me as she drove us from the courthouse to pick up Thomas from school. "Matthew, you know that Grandpa Avi is a retired litigator. He's never going to let me hear the end of it that I lost to my nine-year-old son in court! *How could you do this to me?*"

But you started it. I thought about sticking my thumbs in my ears, waggling my fingers at her, and chanting *Nahnah nahnah naaaah naaaah, I kicked your butt in court*, but decided this wouldn't be wise. Instead, I said nothing. She ranted.

"You're *nothing* without an education, do you know that? You stupid little dropout, *you're illiterate!*"

That got to me; I hated it when anyone called me stupid. I felt compelled to respond.

"Frankly, my dear, I don't give a damn!" I cracked back.

Love Wars

"Well you should, Rhett Butler! I heard about your father's father being in the hospital with high blood pressure. Don't you realize God is punishing your grandfather for being an atheist? If you keep disobeying God, you'll be next! And *watch your mouth*—any more swearing and I'll wash it out with soap!"

I loved Grandpa Stanley, a smiling old baldie in excellent shape who had taught me to play tennis the previous summer. Physical fitness was the only religion on my father's side of the family. The thought of God striking him down filled me with a strange mixture of dread and disbelief. *If God really wanted me to take Hebrew lessons, why hadn't He made the judge rule against me?*

In any case, I was far more afraid of my mother's father than of God. After she'd talked herself blue, I asked, "Mom, is Grandpa Avi going to have my father's entire side of the family killed?"

My mother got a weird look on her face.

"*What* are you talking about?"

"Dad said Grandpa Avi threatened to kill his entire family."

"Matthew, you're so gullible. You shouldn't believe everything your father tells you. He's just brainwashing you. Your grandfather never said anything of the sort."

Who to believe? I decided to believe my father. Dad had told me it was an idle threat and that Grandpa Avi wasn't going to follow through on it. Still, the story cemented my image of Avi as The Godfather.

In the wake of her unexpected and devastating courtroom loss, my mother turned me into the primary source of all her woes. She made it clear to me that I was nothing but an obnoxious thorn in her side. When she dumped, she didn't just dump on me, she dumped *about* me. I caused her grief and sorrow, just like my

Mother and Child Reunion

father. I was an atheist, just like my father. I was out to get her, just like my father. She never failed to point out what a great son Thomas was and what a crummy son I was. Her life was a shambles and it was all the fault of men—including and especially me.

* * *

One cold winter night a few months later, I dreamt that I'd returned to swampy Dagobah to complete my training.

"No more training do you require. Already know you that which you need," Yoda told me.

"Then I am a Jedi," I marveled.

"Ohhh! Not yet. One thing remains. Vader. You must confront . . ."

My mother woke me, interrupting Yoda. Rubbing my eyes, I looked at Snoopy's hands on my wrist. It was two o'clock.

"Matthew, I just got a call. We have to go," she said.

"Huh? What?" I asked sleepily. It was a Monday night and I had school the next morning.

"I don't have time to explain. Just get in the car!"

I stared at her. *What was going on?*

"I don't want to go. I'll just stay here. You go ahead," I said groggily.

"Young man, *move your bottom. Get into the car*," she commanded.

She collected Thomas and packed us both into the car. As she peeled out of our driveway, the car almost skidded off the road. She drove through the snow and ice like a woman possessed.

"Mom, where are we going?" I asked as I saw us leave Chapel Hill city limits.

Love Wars

"You'll find out when you get there," she responded.

"If you need to go somewhere, why can't you just leave us with Dad?" I moaned.

"Silence, young man! You can see him on his visitation time."

She stuck a tape in the tape player—her favorite, Eurythmics. She loved "Sweet Dreams (Are Made of This)," and played it on repeat, like it was her theme song.

What was going on? Where was my mother driving us to in the middle of the night? When the hell would she turn off the stupid song about the woman traveling the seven seas looking for something she just can't seem to find, meeting men who want to use her or get used by her?

Fortunately, I had left my Walkman tape player in the car, so I was able to block out her music with my new favorite song, "Believe It or Not," the theme for *The Greatest American Hero*. Dad, Thomas, and I loved to watch the TV show about Ralph Hinkley, a mild-mannered special education teacher who gets visited by space aliens and receives a superhero suit with special powers but no instruction manual on how to operate it. Ralph flies through the air like a drunken pelican, routinely crashing into buildings. Still, he always manages to catch the crooks at the end of every episode.

As we drove through the quiet, snowy North Carolina roads on our way to who-knows-where, I thought about Ralph Hinkley and my father. Yeah, my father bumbled and stumbled, he didn't know what he was doing half the time, he got angry, he yelled at my mother, and he was strict about my grades. He wasn't perfect, but he was my dad; he was my Greatest American Hero, and I missed him. As I drifted off to sleep with the cheerful theme song in my ears, I imagined my father flying through the air on his way to rescue Thomas and me.

Love Wars

We pulled to a stop, and I was jolted awake. It was dawn, and I saw flashing red and yellow lights against the windshield. I struggled to sit up. I rubbed the window so I could see outside. *Ambulances.* We were in the parking lot of Bethesda General Hospital in Bethesda, Maryland. It was where Aunt Kendra, Uncle Rod, and my cousins Josh and Rachel lived.

"Mom, why are we at a hospital? Why are we in Bethesda? Is something wrong with Josh?"

My mother glared at me, frustrated that I was asking questions again.

"Stay here with your brother. I'll be back," she said.

She disappeared from the car. I fell asleep again.

By the time she came back, I was awake, drumming my hands on the door, sick of listening to the tape. No one had come to rescue us. Snoopy's hands said it was nine o'clock. I was supposed to be in math class. As she got into the car, Mom handed each of us a bag of McDonald's food, and we dug into our Egg McMuffin sandwiches, hash browns smeared with ketchup, and chocolate milk.

"She's going to be fine, Matthew, they've sedated her. We don't need to stay."

"What happened? What's wrong?"

"Kendra is sick in the head. Like you, Matthew. She's very ill. But there's nothing more we can do here, so we're going home." And just like that, she pulled out of the parking lot, turned the car around, and headed back to Chapel Hill.

I yawned and fell back asleep. But not for long—bright sunlight woke me up, and during the ride home, I started thinking about Mom, Dad, and what I wanted in my life.

Mom frequently told me she knew what was best for me, but

Mother and Child Reunion

I no longer believed her. Whatever she wanted for me, she really wanted because she hated Dad and wanted to get back at him. I no longer trusted her.

Encyclopedia Tower was back on the case. Older, wiser, and tougher, he'd reached some conclusions. One, despite his poor grades in Jewish Sunday school, he'd learned that his father was definitely *not* "worse than Adolf Hitler." Two, he'd decided that his mother was, in fact, "certifiably insane." Like his father had said all along, she was "sick and belonged in a mental institution."

After hours in the car of almost total silence, interrupted only by my mother's favorite pop music tapes, we pulled into the George Armstrong Custer Elementary School parking lot at two o'clock, in time for my final class of the day. Although I usually rejoiced when I got to miss school, I would rather have been there than stuck in Mom's car for the last twelve hours.

I'd had enough. I wanted *out* of my mother's crazy life, *out* of her dumping sessions, *out* of her constant reminders that I was a crummy son, *out* of her hatred and bitterness. I wanted *out* of my mother's house.

I imagined what life at Dad and Holly's house would be like, and in my visions it felt a lot calmer, happier, and more normal. I wanted to be just a normal kid, like the rest of my friends. Would my Greatest American Hero ever rescue me?

* * *

Following the Bethesda field trip, Mom seemed more distraught than ever, but to my great relief she started directing her dumping at someone other than me. She frequently scooped up the phone with its long, tangled cord and disappeared into her

Love Wars

bedroom for hours on end, whispering the ruination of her life (or so I imagined) into the ears of her friends. I wondered if they *liked* listening to her. What was she so upset about now? Was her relationship with Gordon on the rocks? I tried pressing my ear to the door, but I couldn't make out the words, so I gave up and played video games with Thomas.

Then one Thursday morning as she drove us to school, my mother said something so surprising, it made the Bethesda adventure seem like just another routine day in the life of the Average American Family; at least, the Average American Family that engages in custody battles, dog murders, kidnappings, threats to annihilate half the family, and lawsuits against fourth graders.

"Matthew, Thomas," my mother said in a soft, sickly voice that I almost had to strain to hear, "I'm going to Emerald Isle Beach, and I'm never coming back . . ." Her voice trailed off. I looked up at her, but couldn't read her face. Impenetrably dark sunglasses shielded her eyes, and her lips clenched together in a tight purse.

"Huh? What do you mean?" I asked. We'd *never* been to Emerald Isle Beach before! This made no sense whatsoever. Why was she going in the dead of winter? It wouldn't be any fun.

"Can we go too?" Thomas asked. I was sure he wanted to visit that beach as much as I did. And after all, it was Mom's weekend to be with us.

"No kids," she said, and looked away, staring out the window. Her voice was almost whisper soft, but choked and throttled, like a lost bird in a collapsing well. "You'll be fine with your father. You both seem to love him . . . He's the only one you love . . . Especially you, Matthew."

Mother and Child Reunion

My mother loved to provoke arguments about which parent which kid loved the most or least. I refused to take the bait.

"What do you *mean* you're never coming back?" I asked, suddenly suspicious. At first I thought it had been some sort of joke, the kind of thing people always say, like, "I'm going to Disneyland and I'm never coming back."

"Matthew, you heard me the first time. I'm never coming back. That's all. The end." She didn't even look at me.

I sat glued to my seat long moments while the car idled, not knowing what to say or do. *Is she serious? Is she really never coming back?* "Thomas and I love you," I tried to say, but the words just wouldn't come out. She stared out the window for a long time, then finally looked back at us.

"Go to school," she commanded softly but firmly, and we did, and then the wheels of her white Camry spun and kicked up gravel and she left the school parking lot—and, apparently, my life and my brother's life.

All day at school, I didn't hear a single word that any teacher said. It was as if the *Charlie Brown* cartoon creators had used their magical powers to hijack my teachers' vocal cords and replace all their typical droning with one sentence, on endless repeat: "Your mother went to the beach and she's never coming back." I saw these words scrawled in gigantic capital letters on every chalkboard of every classroom all day long: YOUR MOTHER WENT TO THE BEACH AND SHE'S NEVER COMING BACK!

What could it mean? At first, I'd been annoyed that she was going to the beach and she wasn't taking us. But as the day wore on, I became more and more certain of the truth behind her words: *She's not going on vacation. Mom's going to kill herself.*

Love Wars

And she didn't even really bother to say goodbye. I wasn't sure which of those two things I was angriest about.

What else could "I'm never coming back" mean? That she was running away with Gordon? I turned that over in my mind a few times, and it just didn't make any *sense*. Encyclopedia Tower was smart enough to know that Gordon had a great relationship with his daughters, he was usually in a good mood, and he had a stable job at the university. There was no chance—none—that he would sign up for a harebrained scheme with my mom like skipping town permanently on short notice.

Nope, "I'm never coming back" could only mean one thing: my mother was going to be dead by the end of the weekend, probably in some motel room overlooking a desolate beach I'd never seen and I probably never would see.

I didn't say a word about this to anyone. How could I explain this? Who would believe me? What could I say? I knew that my friends would just say dumb stuff like, "Don't worry, she didn't really mean *never*, she'll be back in a few days."

But . . . did I *want* her to come back?

* * *

When the bell rang to end the school day, the chimes sounded the sentence again in my head, like hammers chiseling important words into some sort of monument to The Madness of Vanessa.

Your mother . . . beach . . . never . . .

I walked to the pickup area, found Thomas, and suddenly froze. *Who will pick us up?* The obvious question only now occurred to me. It was a Thursday, and it was my mother's visitation day, and . . .

Mother and Child Reunion

Suddenly, a blue Honda Civic drove up, and my very pregnant stepmother rolled down her window.

"Holly? What are you doing here?" I asked as we got in the car. Previously, my mother had called the principal's office and convinced the administration to ban Holly from picking us up, even on my father's visitation days, because she wasn't our "legal guardian." But perhaps those rules were suspended for special occasions such as this one.

"Matthew, Thomas, I got a message on my answering machine from your mother. She said she's going away for the weekend, and the principal gave me permission to collect you. Your father's in London for a genetic engineering conference, so I'm going to look after you."

As we drove back to Dad's house, my brother was silent; I was anything but.

"Did she tell you why she left town?" I asked.

"No, and this is all *extremely strange*," she said, looking at me with an eyebrow raised to infinity. "Where did your mother go and why did she leave and why did she suddenly decide I have the right to pick you boys up? The last time I tried to come collect you two, she threatened to have me arrested!"

Finally, I had someone with whom to share the words that had been echoing in my skull all day. "She said she's going to Emerald Isle Beach and *she's never coming back!* And she didn't even really say goodbye!"

Holly looked at me, her face stiff for a moment as she absorbed this news. I was about to say more, but I noticed her looking over her shoulder at Thomas.

"Matthew, let's talk about this more later. This is all way too much adult stuff for your brother." I was about to blurt out more,

Love Wars

but I glanced at Thomas, and decided I agreed with her. The poor kid looked like he was ready to start bawling, but whatever he felt, he was holding it all in.

When we arrived home on Stonehouse Road, Holly did her best to set Thomas up with his toys, then took me outside. She towered over me in a long blue denim dress that stretched over her huge belly, the fabric stained with flour from baking bread. Big hoop earrings poked out from behind her flowing red hair. She bent down a bit to meet my eyes and hesitated for long moments, then sucked in her breath.

"Matthew, tell me again, what exactly did your mother say?"

"I told you, she went to the beach and she said she's never coming back!"

"And what do you think that means?"

"Isn't it obvious?" I said, even though I hadn't seen the truth of it when she first told me. "She's going to kill herself!"

Holly sighed, and her eyes looked away for a long moment.

"What do you think?" I asked. "What else could she be up to?"

"I don't know," she said at long last. "You might be right. I have no idea what your mother is doing or why she left town."

"What's going to happen to me if she commits suicide?" I asked.

"Well, I guess you'll come live with your father and me," Holly said.

And then, suddenly, without warning, I burst out laughing.

"Just like that, I can live here?"

Holly hesitated. "*Matthew.* You shouldn't wish bad things on other people . . ." Then Holly stopped, and her face puckered up. Her tone softened. "You don't like her very much, do you?"

"She hates me."

Mother and Child Reunion

"How do you know she hates you?"

"Her dumping sessions."

"Yes, I know about the dumping sessions," Holly said.

"She's added me to her hate list. She talks bad about me all the time, just like she talks bad about Dad."

Holly frowned.

"Holly, it's not that I want her to die," I lied. The truth was, *I did want her to die*. But I decided I'd better not say that out loud. "I just never want to see her again. She doesn't have to die, she can just never come back. That would solve everything."

"You may well get your wish," Holly said quietly.

"If she kills herself, it's not my fault."

"You're right, Matthew. She's an adult and she gets to make her own choices. It's not your fault. None of this is your fault," Holly said.

"I bet this is a little more than you bargained for when you married my father," I said.

Holly laughed for the first time since she picked us up from school. "You're a smart kid, Matthew. Let's go inside and see how Thomas is doing."

"You go ahead," I said. "I think I'm going to take a walk."

Holly disappeared into the house.

I walked through the grassy field in front of the house, then couldn't contain myself. I skipped, twirled, whooped, and hollered. I spun myself around in a circle, looking up at the clouds, until I collapsed on the ground. Dizzy with glee, only one joyous thought ran through my head: *No more Mom!*

Then, guilt struck. I knew it was bad to want someone else to die, to *really* want them to die. I'd thought about people dying before—Thomas, the shrink, myself—but a wish is just a wish.

LOVE WARS

You don't always act on wishes, and you don't always really mean them. I had said I wanted Thomas dead, but did I really mean it? I had wanted to stick a knife in my heart, but would I really have done it? No, I guess not.

But I hadn't wished for this, and it was happening anyway. I hadn't told her to go to Emerald Isle Beach to kill herself. She had figured out that plan all on her own. Maybe I was responsible. Was I? A little bit? Was she going to kill herself because of me? No. She had too many other problems. She hated Dad, she hated Bob Trapp, she hated her father, and who knew if she was still getting along with Gordon or not. Maybe she'd just had a big fight with him. Whatever the case, I felt guilty for wanting my mother to die, but it didn't stop me from allowing myself to imagine how amazing my life would be without her. I'd never have to see her horrible, ugly, hateful face again. *No more Mom!*

* * *

After school on Friday, Holly picked us up again. For an entire weekend, her caretaking was my oasis. She cooked for us, played games with us, and spoke to us nicely. I felt like a prince. Finally, someone wanted to mother me and didn't ask for anything in return—other than help carrying in the groceries.

While we played a game of Scrabble, I asked Holly, "When's the baby due?" for the millionth time.

"June eleventh," Holly said for the millionth time. "She'll be lucky if she gets to share a birthday with you."

I was so excited. I couldn't get over the fact that my little sister would be precisely ten years younger than me.

Love Wars

"Are they sure it's a girl?" I asked, knowing the answer full well. I'd always wanted a sister.

"Positive," Holly responded. If she was tired of this routine, she didn't let on.

"Holly, I have a question."

"What is it, Matthew?"

"Can I call you Mom from now on?"

She put down the Scrabble pieces she was holding for a moment, and a huge smile lit up her face.

"Of course you can!"

She gathered me in a hug, and I felt my sister kick. When I pulled away and looked up at Holly, tears were streaming down her face.

"I love you, Mom."

"Matthew, I love you too."

* * *

By the time I arrived back at school on Monday, my fantasy was becoming reality. From now on, I'd live with Dad and my new mom, and I'd never have to see my "biological mother" (that's what Holly called her) again. I couldn't wait to see my father that night. It would be the first Monday night my brother and I had spent with him since my parents split.

During class, I daydreamed about playing Scrabble with my new mom again, eating dinner together, and talking about my soccer games. The rest of my childhood stretched out before me, and I felt happy.

That afternoon, while I was waiting for my new mom to pick me up after school, a white Toyota Camry rolled up that looked suspiciously like my biological mother's car.

Mother and Child Reunion

No. No. Please God, NO!

The door opened, and my mother stepped out. She wore dark sunglasses and a black pantsuit, and the makeup smeared on her face looked like the scribblings a four-year-old might make with blue, purple, and black crayons.

"Let's go," she said curtly to Thomas and me.

I couldn't believe it. I hesitated for a moment, blinking my eyes, hoping I was seeing a ghost. When my mother didn't disappear, I got in the car, shattered.

We drove for a while, and I waited for her to say something about her trip to the beach. She said nothing. *She's pretending like she never left!* Finally, I couldn't contain myself.

"What happened at the beach?"

"Matthew, you couldn't possibly understand, you're just a kid. Everyone's out to get me! My life's a shambles, and I had to go to Emerald Isle to sort it all out. What did I do to deserve this crap?"

She rambled on, spewing her misery and suffering all over me. Finally, she paused, her face and eyes red; she blew snot into a tissue. I leapt at the chance to ask her the question that was burning a hole in my heart.

"Mom, why didn't you kill yourself?"

In a flash, her face changed from a black hole of despair into a cannon of rage.

"*What?* What did you just ask me?" Although I couldn't see through her sunglasses, I knew her pupils had turned the bright red color of molten lava.

Oops. How could I be so stupid? *Dammit!* I wanted the referee to call a do-over. If only I could take those words back—but it was too late.

Love Wars

"Did you want me to kill myself, you stupid brat?" She pulled the car over.

"No, Mom, of course not!" I lied. *Crap*. Now I was in *deep trouble*.

Desperate to prevent what I knew would be the worst verbal onslaught yet, I reached over to give her a hug, even though I felt icky whenever I touched her.

"I love you, Mom. You're a great mother, you try *so hard*, you do *so much* for Thomas and me. I'm so glad you're okay and nothing bad happened to you."

I stopped breathing. I prayed, *please please please please . . .*

It worked. *Somehow, it worked.* My mother was *so* gullible.

"Oh, Matthew, I knew you loved me. You've always loved me. You and Thomas are the only men in my life who I can count on. I love you so much! Thank God I have you two. I don't know what I'd do without you. I'd be lost without my sons—*lost!* Oh, Matthew, I knew you'd come back to me."

She babbled on about how wonderful Thomas and I were in contrast to the bastard men who were destroying her life and how we were both the perfect model children.

Whew. Somehow, I'd gotten myself off my mother's hate list. That was good. But I despised myself for hugging her, for lying to her, for giving her what she needed from a husband, when I was only nine years old. Images of the carefree weekend I'd spent with Holly blew away like dandelions in a hurricane.

As she drove us back to her house, she fished around in the messy glove compartment and found her prize: her favorite Paul Simon tape, its innards busting loose. "Fix this for me, will you?"

Mother and Child Reunion

Staring out the window, I wound the wayward tape backwards, secretly hoping it would snap. No such luck; it clicked into place. Sighing, I handed her the tape, and she inserted it into the deck. Soon she was gleefully crowing along to a song that made me feel like zombies were snacking on my flesh.

"No, I would not give you false hope, on this strange and mournful day," she screeched. "But the mother and child reunion is only a motion away!"

I wanted to ask her if there was still a chance, if she might consider going back to Emerald Isle Beach to kill herself. Instead, I sat and contemplated my miserable existence, stuck inside her sick little world.

* * *

At least I wasn't in my mother's doghouse anymore. She decided I was a good son after all—in fact, she said I was the best son *ever*. She stopped treating me differently from Thomas, and let me play video games and eat dessert again.

I still called her Mom, even though I didn't want to. It was confusing to call two different people Mom, and my mother didn't feel like a Mom. But I couldn't imagine how angry she'd get if she found out I called Holly Mom. So I pretended like nothing had changed. Being a good actor was one way to survive at her house.

One Friday afternoon in late May, my mother got home from work and told me something even more shocking than her lawsuit against me, our trips to Gordon's church, or her plan to kill herself.

"Matthew, your father will be picking you up late today."

Love Wars

What? My father was the most punctual human being who'd ever lived. He always arrived a few minutes early, and the idea of him showing up late was more incomprehensible to me than if he'd sent a pack of rabid wolves to collect us on his behalf, an apology note clutched in their salivating jaws.

"Mom, are you sure? Why?"

"It's a special occasion. Your father will explain when he gets here," she said. I noticed that for the first time in years, her voice was calm when she referred to "your father," containing none of her usual rage. I also detected a strange note in her voice when she mentioned the "special occasion"—was she *happy* for him? Jealous? Both? It was hard to tell.

Then she shifted into a more familiar tone. "If he's not here by five," she warned, "I'm taking you boys out of town with me for the weekend."

Great. Just what I needed: a weekend getaway with Dr. Mom and her thirty-one flavors of venomous ice cream.

I parked myself by the front door, my nose pressed against the peephole, tapping my foot, *praying* to a God I didn't believe in for Dad to show up on time. He arrived at 4:55, and I felt the breath whoosh out of my belly. Not asking for permission, I flung open the door and dashed out to his car.

"Matthew, Thomas, you have a little sister," he said.

I was shocked. It was only May 18th. My birthday was still three and a half weeks away.

"Is Mom okay?" I asked.

"Everyone's fine," he said. "Bethany arrived early and she's a little small, but she'll be all right. Your stepmother's doing great too."

He drove us to the hospital, where Holly was recovering. Then Dad took Thomas and me to see Bethany. She slept inside

Mother and Child Reunion

a plexiglass bassinet in a room with a dozen other newborns.

Dad, Thomas, and I made kissy faces at Bethany through the window and cooed at her. After a while, Dad said it was time to go back to see Holly.

"I want some alone time with my sister," I said. He smiled and nodded. After he and Thomas walked away, I looked through the window, pressing my face against the glass, and for the first time in my life felt a spiritual presence looking over my shoulder. I got down on one knee, put my hands together, and bowed my head.

"Please God, bless my little sister. May she have a long, happy life. Please spare her from nightmares, fighting, and craziness."

I thought about Thomas, and remembered how close we'd been before the divorce. And then I'd screwed it all up by bullying him. I was getting a gigantic do-over, another chance to be a good big brother.

On Sunday morning, the hospital released Holly and Bethany and we all drove to our new home in the city. Holly had insisted they move in order to have a fresh start and leave behind the Mud Flats home that my parents had custom-built before the divorce. Holly let me hold my sister for the first time, and I adored her.

This is my family.

And then, at precisely four o'clock, my mother's white Toyota Camry appeared in front of my father's house. *Why, God? Why must I go back to my mother's house?* I was more determined than ever to find a way to get out of her life. If she wasn't going to leave me, I would have to leave her.

* * *

Love Wars

On my tenth birthday, Dad and Holly brought out a triple-layer, mega-fudge, ultra-dark chocolate cake with chocolate ice cream. As I blew out the candles in one go, and everyone clapped, I made a special birthday wish.

"Now you can't tell us your birthday wish or it won't come true. Keep it to yourself," Holly said when the clapping ended.

I hesitated, then decided to throw caution to the wind.

"Mom, I'm not superstitious like that, and besides, I'm pretty sure if I *don't* say it, it'll never come true."

Then I turned to my father, because I knew only he had the power to make my wish come true.

"Dad, I want to live with you and Mom."

He seemed a bit taken aback.

"Are you sure?"

"Pretty sure," I said.

He was silent for long moments. Holly and Thomas didn't say anything either.

"I don't know, Matthew. I've spent so much money on lawyer's fees already. I've been before the judge so many times. When I go down to the courthouse, everybody knows my name, like I'm Norm on *Cheers*. Getting you out of Hebrew lessons cost me thousands of dollars. I don't know if I could handle another court battle with your mother."

"Please, Dad," I said. "I can't deal with her dumping and her craziness anymore."

"Let me think about it," he said.

The next evening before dinner, I crept down the hallway and stood a few feet away from Holly and Dad's bedroom door, where they were having a private talk. I was an expert spy by now.

Love Wars

"Honey, I know you hate going to court," Holly said. "But you have to do it."

"You think I wouldn't love to snap my fingers and get the boys over here? Of course I would. But the risks are enormous. I've asked the lawyer about this multiple times, and every time he tells me the same thing: The chances of getting sole custody are close to zero. The courts are biased against fathers."

"But this is a special case. Vanessa is not like most mothers. There's something very wrong with her."

"You think I don't know? But how do we prove that to the judge? Vanessa's court performances are Oscar-worthy. She's a successful doctor, she owns her own medical practice, and she makes nearly double my salary."

"Money doesn't mean she isn't nuts. She's driving Matthew crazy. He's very disturbed. Do you know that when I talk to him, half the time he doesn't know what's real and what's not? And his mother's lunacy is making him hate her. Do you know that he was actively rooting for her to commit suicide? I'm deeply worried about him."

"I'm worried too, but what can I do? If I go to court and lose, things could get worse."

"I don't see how."

"I could lose my son completely."

"NATE, YOU'RE HALFWAY THERE ALREADY!" I'd never heard Holly raise her voice before, *ever*. For the first time, I was glad to hear one of my parental figures yell. "You think it's hard now, picking him up from Vanessa's house after she's screamed at him and dumped on him? If this goes on for much longer, you're going to be visiting him at a mental hospital. What good's a psychotic son? *You have to rescue him! You have no choice!*"

Mother and Child Reunion

Silence. I waited, hoping, praying, then...

"I can't argue with your logic," he said. "All right, let's see what my attorney has to say. He's not going to like it, but we'll figure out a way to get it done—somehow. I hope. Actually, my attorney will love it. It'll be his biggest payday yet."

Yes!

"That's the spirit!" my stepmother said.

"Jesus H. Christ, *another court battle!*" My father sighed dramatically. "I gotta clear my head. I need to go for a run."

I took my cue, tiptoed away, and put on my tennis shoes. When the door opened, Dad came out in his gym shorts and I emerged from my bedroom pretending it was a coincidence that I was meeting him in the hallway. Normally I dreaded participating in my father's rigorous fitness routine; he frequently forced me to go running whether I wanted to or not. But this time I wanted to go with him.

"Dad, can I run with you?"

"Of course, tiger. Like father, like son!"

* * *

During our annual vacation to the Outer Banks beach the following week, Dad asked me, "How certain are you that you want to live with me and Holly?"

"Pretty sure," I said.

"How sure?" he asked.

"Pretty sure," I said again.

"What do you mean? What's 'pretty sure'?"

"Well, I definitely want to live with you and Mom, and I can't stand my biological mother's craziness, but I like Gordon. Now that he and Lisa and Cindy are planning to move in with my mom, it'll probably be a little better over there. And even though my biological mother's a pain in the butt, I know I should go see her sometimes, 'cause it's the right thing to do. I don't want to be a bad son. So I wouldn't want to see her *never*, just rarely."

"If you had to put a percentage on it, how much do you want to live with just me?"

"Ummm . . . 90 percent," I said.

"Not good enough, kiddo."

"What do you mean?"

"I spoke with my lawyer and he said the only way this is going to work is if you are 100 percent certain you want to live with just us, and that you never want to see your mother. Custody cases are very hard for a father to win, and the only way you're coming to live with me is if the judge is convinced your mother's unfit to be a parent."

"So I have to be 100 percent sure?"

"Yup," Dad said.

"Let me think about it," I replied.

Dad asked me the question again a week later, while we were hosing down the life preservers and the crab traps after returning from the beach.

"Ninety-five percent," I said.

"Still not good enough," he replied.

This went on for about a month. Dad kept asking the question, and each time I was a little more certain: 96 percent; 98 percent; 99 percent; 99 ½ percent—until finally, I gave him the answer he needed.

"One hundred percent, Dad."

"One hundred percent? You sure?"

Mother and Child Reunion

"Positive," I said. Given the two choices—keeping things the way they were or lying a little bit to give Dad the ammunition he needed in court to get custody of me—I chose the latter.

"Okay."

"You said after you get custody of me, I could always decide to visit her house if I want to."

"Right, kiddo, I wouldn't stop you. But you can't tell the judge you want to see her."

"I know. I'll tell the judge I'm 100 percent certain I want to live with you and Mom and I never want to see my biological mother ever again."

"All right. We're going to start preparing the custody case, and it will probably take at least six months."

"What about Thomas?" I asked.

"Well, your brother said he wants to live with both his parents. I think the worst-case scenario is things will stay exactly the same for Thomas. But judges almost always keep siblings together, so chances are if I win you, I'll get Thomas too."

"What are the chances we'll win?"

"I don't know, kiddo, hard to say."

"Can you give me a percentage?"

"I have no idea. Fifty percent," he said.

"*Fifty percent? That's it?*" My mind wandered into a nightmare. What if we lost the case? My mother would make my life hell. She'd *never* forgive me for trying to leave her.

"Matthew, the courts are impossible to predict, and they're biased against fathers. We'll do the best we can and hope for the best. I think the only thing we've got going for us with this judge is that he saw how your mother made a fool of herself over the Hebrew lesson issue. By the way, have you told your mother about this yet?"

Love Wars

I'd been *dreading* that question. I knew he was going to ask. "Uh, no."

"That's the next step. I'm not going to file the paperwork until you've told her. She needs to hear this from you first, or she'll claim I manipulated you. So let me know when you tell her, and then we'll move forward with the custody petition."

I'd never feared anything in my life so much as the prospect of telling my mother I wanted to live with my father. Given a choice between walking through the darkest alley in the worst part of town, getting drafted to fight in a real-life war, and telling my mother I wanted to live with my father, the alley and the war seemed like easy choices. It looked like Mom and Dad's War was about to go nuclear.

Chapter Twelve
HERE COMES THE BRIDE
Age 10 • 1984 • Fifth Grade

We'd stacked the pillows five high and ten deep, tied blankets to chairs to create a canopy over half of my new bedroom, and filled the plush tunnels with large piles of stuffed animals.

Thomas, Lisa, and I had created the coolest fort *ever*.

"Now what are we going to do?" Thomas asked.

"Dance party!" Lisa cried out, laughing. She plugged in her boom box and inserted one of our favorite tapes: Tears for Fears. The three of us danced and sang with wild abandon, a trio of preadolescent pop stars in pajamas.

> Welcome to your life
> There's no turning back
> Even while we sleep
> We will find you

Love Wars

> Acting on your best behavior
> Turn your back on mother nature
> Everybody wants to rule the world.

When Lisa's teenage sister Cindy heard us, she took a break from watching *The Cosby Show* and came galloping from the living room to join in the frolicking, her blonde hair in curlers and the cordless phone glued to her shoulder. With our bare feet against the carpet, we built up static charges, zapped each other, and giggled. I looked up at the overhead light, pretended it was a mirror ball bathing us in stardom, and imagined that if the four of us were in charge of the world, we wouldn't even need any grown-ups.

Then I realized: *Yup, pretty much everybody wants to rule my world!*

Exhausted, Lisa, Thomas, and I collapsed on the floor and crawled inside the fluffy fortress to play with Transformers. Cindy left to go call her latest high school crush. She was too busy being a sixteen-year-old flirt to play with us much.

After my mother came back from her brief safari to the beach, she had gotten her act together and decided she wanted to shack up with Gordon. Almost as big as the Brady Bunch, the six of us plus Lisa's friendly dog, Sandy, were all living together in a five-bedroom house in an exclusive gated community near Chapel Hill Country Club. We moved in just before the start of fifth grade, and Mom told me they were just living together for now to see if it would work, and they didn't have any plans to get married.

Gordon installed a basketball hoop in the driveway and let us mark our initials in the concrete. He played basketball with

us, told us silly jokes about his overseas adventures in the Navy, and gave me high fives every time he was impressed by something I did. I tried to hang out with Gordon and his daughters whenever I could.

But as much as I liked Gordon and my pseudo-sisters, I detested being anywhere near my mother. She still dumped her countless problems on me, and I'd had enough. I tried to avoid her, which was hard to do because she was quite skilled at getting me alone. As soon as she cornered me, she'd take me into my room, close the door, and force me to swallow one of her toxic tirades.

I had a hard time working up the courage to tell my mother that I wanted to live with my father. Ever since Dad told me I had to do it, I'd thought about nothing else for the rest of the summer before fifth grade. But every time I came close to saying it, I chickened out and hid in my shell.

Shortly after school started, Mom told Thomas and me she was taking us on a trip to Denver, Colorado, for a medical conference. She said we'd be staying at a fancy hotel, the Sheraton, and it would be lots of fun.

Spontaneously, I decided: *I'll tell her while we're on this trip.* It wasn't perfect, but would there ever be a perfect time?

During the flight, I read about the hobbit Bilbo Baggins for the eleventieth time. The hobbit snuck into the lair of a fire-breathing dragon, stole the treasure, and tried not to disturb the slumbering beast. How would Bilbo handle this? *Be brave, be brave, be brave.*

We arrived at the Sheraton. My mother was oblivious to what was about to happen. "Boys, we're going out to the movies tonight," she said. "Mommy has to get dressed up because I might run into some colleagues at the theater." While Thomas

Here Comes the Bride

and I waited for her, I rehearsed what I was going to say over and over in my mind.

I have to tell her, I have to tell her, I have to tell her.

My entire body turned to ice. My stomach wound up like a twisted rubber band. I felt goosebumps on my arms and chills down my spine. My mother did her makeup in the mirror.

I have to tell her.

"Mom . . . " I called out tentatively.

She didn't look up, just kept applying her lipstick.

"Mom, I need to tell you something."

"What it is it?"

"I want to live with my father."

Her hand stopped. She turned to look at me, still holding her lipstick against her lips.

"What did you just say?"

After one glimpse at her livid face, I looked down at the floor. I thought of the movie *Clash of the Titans* and remembered what happened to the men who looked into the eyes of the Medusa. I was afraid if I looked at her I'd lose my courage or turn to stone.

"I said I want to live with my father."

I kept my eyes on the floor.

I heard an enormous intake of breath, like she was sucking in all the air in the entire universe so she could exhale a fireball at my head. At first, nothing happened. Silence, a long silence—then the roar, the scream, the inferno of rage.

"MATTHEW, YOU'RE THE CRUMMIEST SON A MOTHER EVER HAD! WHO THE HELL DO YOU THINK YOU ARE, TRYING TO RUIN MY CONFERENCE? ARE YOU OUT TO GET ME? DO YOU WANT TO DESTROY MY CAREER?"

Here Comes the Bride

The carpet had such interesting patterns. Blue swirls, squiggles, lint... I imagined what it was like to be an ant, crawling among the enormous fibers of the carpet, completely unaware of the gigantic humans who trod on top and might randomly stomp on him and extinguish his life without warning or reason.

"YOUR FATHER PUT YOU UP TO THIS, DIDN'T HE? THAT MANIPULATIVE BASTARD! BOTH OF YOU CAN ROT IN HELL. FROM NOW ON, YOUR NAME IS MUD. DO YOU HEAR ME? MUD! *YOU NEVER LOVED ME! I WISH I'D NEVER GIVEN BIRTH TO YOU!*"

The sound waves echoed through me like an earthquake demolishing my heart. I kept my head down and stubbornly refused to look up at the Medusa.

But Mom wasn't done. She was just getting started. She cried, loudly blew her nose, and ranted on and on, reiterating for the millionth time—but with more conviction than ever—how all men are bastards and how I was in league with my father and I was out to get her and he had painted her to be the devil but it wasn't true and I was helping my father wreck her life and she wasn't a horrible mother and in fact she was a very good mother and my father had brainwashed me against her and I was a terrible son and he was worse than Adolf Hitler because he was trying to steal her son away from her and he had convinced her son not to love her anymore and she wished my father had never been born and she wished I'd never been born and she wished she'd never been born...

I tried to tune her out, but I couldn't. She was too emotional, too passionate, too insistent. She was determined to inject all her poison directly into my mind whether I liked it or not.

Love Wars

Thomas cried. I heard him scamper off into a corner of the room. Normally Thomas wasn't around for my mother's rants, but this time, his cry interrupted her. Otherwise, she could have gone on for hours. She rushed over to comfort him.

"Shhh, Thomas, it's okay, everything's going to be fine. Your brother's out to destroy me, but I love you."

"Mom, are we still going to the movies?" Thomas asked.

"Of course, Thomas, *we're* still going. What do you want to see? *Anything you want*," she cooed to him.

"What about Matthew? Is he coming too?" he asked.

"His name is Mud, so he can stay here," she said.

I heard the door slam. Finally, I looked up. I was alone in a hotel room. I picked up the phone and placed a collect call to my father.

"Dad, I told her," I said, my voice shaky.

"What did she say?"

"I don't want to talk about it."

He clucked his tongue. "I understand. Your mother can be difficult."

"Difficult? *Difficult?*"

"Okay, that's the understatement of the year," he said.

"Dad, that's the understatement of the *century*. How are Mom and Bethany?"

"They're fine."

"Tell them I miss them."

"I will."

"So now that I've told her, does this mean you're going to file the custody petition?"

"Yup. I'll have the lawyer get to work on it right away."

After we finished talking, I lay my head down on the bed.

Here Comes the Bride

I had a pounding headache no medicine could cure, and an ugly new name. But at least *I'd done it*.

* * *

That weekend was the most miserable of my life. My mother did not permit me to leave the hotel room, while she took Thomas anywhere he wanted: to the mall, to McDonald's, to a water park. I stayed in the hotel room, all by myself, and occasionally she brought me food. She alternated between giving me the silent treatment and loudly reminding me of my new name.

While she was gone, I wandered around the hotel, leaving the door propped open so I could get back in. I knew I wasn't supposed to leave the room, but I had to do something, *anything*, to combat the boredom and isolation. But the Sheraton got old fast. Usually my mother gave me quarters for video game machines, but this time she gave me none, so I couldn't play. Instead, I stood in front of the game machines for hours, and as they ran their demo mode in an infinite loop, I pretended to play the game. I memorized the movement patterns of the game characters and moved the joystick as if I were controlling them.

Bored out of my mind, I walked around the hotel lobby in endless circles. I didn't feel like swimming, and just dipped my toe into the pool. I looked down into the blue water and saw a sad, haunted, familiar face gaze back at me with dark circles under the eyes. For a split second I wondered: *Is that my face or my mother's?*

Back in the hotel room, I flipped on HBO, and stumbled across *Kramer vs. Kramer*. It was hard to feel badly for the characters in the movie when all I could think was: *Is this for real?*

Love Wars

The parents aren't putting their son in the middle of their fighting. Why isn't my parents' divorce more like the Kramers'? And the Hollywood ending was *so* cheesy. I wished my mother would take a hint from Meryl Streep and let me go live with my dad.

My mother walked in just as it ended. I almost said, "Mom, you should watch this movie sometime," but one look at her angry face and I kept my mouth shut. She announced that she had to go to her conference, so she deposited Thomas into the hotel room with me, and handed him a stack of quarters.

"Now don't share with your brother," she said. "He's not allowed to leave the room, but you can go down and play video games in the lobby if you want."

After Mom left, we both went down to the lobby to play.

"Aren't you supposed to be in the room?" Thomas asked.

"Are you going to tattle on me?" I asked, clenching my hand into a fist.

"No," he said. Thomas played some games and offered me a few quarters without me having to ask. After we were done, I asked Thomas something I'd wanted to ask for weeks.

"Thomas, who do you want to live with?"

"I want to live with both of them! How could you ask me something like that?"

"What do you mean?"

"You want me to choose between my mommy and my daddy? Are you crazy?"

"Crazy? Thomas, you see the way Mom acts. She's the crazy one!"

"I don't like it when you talk bad about Mommy."

"But, Thomas, she's a lunatic! Look at what happened with

Here Comes the Bride

Bob Trapp. Remember when she went to the beach . . ."

I trailed off as I looked into Thomas's wide, vacant eyes, and I had a sudden flash of insight about my seven-year-old brother. Thomas didn't understand what she had been planning to do at the beach. Either he didn't get it, or *he didn't want to get it*. It was the same either way. It was useless to try to talk to him about the whole mess. I stared at the *Donkey Kong* demo and watched it loop around and around.

"Matthew, if you want to live with just Daddy, you can do whatever you want, but leave me out of it. If you don't like Mommy, that's your deal, but I'm not taking sides. I don't want to be in the middle. Let's just play video games and stop talking about it."

I felt annoyed and resentful, like Thomas was taking sides with our mother against me. Was he completely ignoring what she was doing to me? Didn't he get that she'd do it to him too someday? I wanted us to stick together. I wanted him to be my wingman in my mission to blow up the Divorce War Death Star.

I thought of his enormous collection of more than one hundred stuffed bunnies, a warren straight out of *Watership Down*. I wished, *Why can't my brother be Bigwig the fierce rabbit instead of Pipkin the timid?*

I was on the verge of saying something more, but my little brother gave me a look I'd never seen from him before. He was *almost angry* at me. His eyes said, "I'm always nice to you, but you're pushing me to my limit." I sighed, and dropped it.

"Okay, Thomas, we can stop talking about it. Do you have any more quarters?"

"Nope, all out," he said.

"Well, we can just pretend to play. That's what I did all day

Here Comes the Bride

yesterday while you were out with Mom at the water park."

"Uhhh, okay." Thomas looked up to me and would do virtually anything I suggested . . . anything, that is, except fight for his freedom. So the two of us pretended to play games stuck in demo mode.

Finally, it was time to go home. On the long flight, I finished reading *The Hobbit*. Near the end, a strong warrior named Bard finds the dragon's weak point and shoots an arrow right into his gut, sending the beast crashing to the ground and ending the reign of Smaug the fearsome.

I wasn't Bard. I didn't want to destroy the dragon, nor could I. I was more like Bilbo. I wanted to escape before the dragon destroyed me.

* * *

Back in Chapel Hill, life with my mother took a turn for the worse—much worse. The way she'd treated me after the Hebrew Lesson Lawsuit was rough, but that was nothing compared to her attitude toward me now. She made it perfectly clear that I was the *bad son*. We barely spoke to each other.

My mother set about enlisting the rest of the family into her little army. Gordon joined her in giving me the silent treatment. I was the house reject, the bastard, the ugly duckling. Lisa and Cindy talked to me sometimes, but it was clear that they had changed their opinion of me. Even Thomas, the brother who had always taken my cruelty with a smile, who would do my chores for me and almost never complain, turned a cold shoulder to me.

Interacting with my mother for any reason at all became a

Love Wars

nightmare. Whenever I asked her for anything, her replies were short and acidic. I would ask for an explanation and she would say things like, "Just because," "That's the way it is," or, "I don't have to explain myself to you." If she'd pick me up from school and I'd ask her, "Where are we going?" she'd reply, "You'll find out when you get there." What insanity is going to happen next? You'll find out when you get there.

One day Gordon knocked on my door, and when I let him in, I could tell from the cold look in his eyes that he didn't want to shoot hoops.

"Son, you got a minute?"

"Sure," I said, looking down at my shoelaces.

"Matthew, I'm worried about you. I know you're close with your dad, but why are you taking sides with him against your mom? Wouldn't it be easier not to get in the middle and just let them deal with all the adult stuff?"

Even though Gordon's voice was calm—unlike my mother's—I heard the faint sound of battle sirens. I wanted to say, *Don't you think I wanted to stay out of their fighting?* But instead I just said, "Uhh, what do you mean?"

"Son, here's the thing. I know you need your father—Lord knows my daughters need me—but you need your mother too. A healthy kid's gotta have both. Why are you so angry at her? Divorce happens because two people don't get along, and that's no reason to make your mother the target. Why are you blaming her for everything?"

How could I possibly describe the past four years of my crazy life to him? How could I convince my mother's live-in boyfriend that she was a hateful basket case and I was right to want to leave? Maybe if I reasoned with him, he'd understand, but the

Here Comes the Bride

whole thing was so mixed up and backwards and upside down, I couldn't even explain it to myself.

I sputtered, grasping for what to say, and finally I spit it out: "Gordon, my mother's been putting me in the middle of her stupid war for years! She sued me to force me to take Hebrew lessons!"

Gordon interrupted before I could say any more.

"Son, it's typical that a primary custodian makes decisions about her child's religious education. I decided to send my daughters to Catholic school and their alcoholic, absentee mother had no say in it whatsoever. It was a fluke that your father managed to convince the judge not to enforce the custody agreement."

My mother had outflanked me. I couldn't believe she'd brainwashed an adult so effectively. I was about to say something more, but I shut my mouth tight. It was pointless. Gordon was *never* going to take my side over my mother's.

"Look, son, I'm not involved in your parents' fighting, so you can trust me. I'm a neutral party in all this. I'm just looking at it from the outside, and it rips me up to see all this drama. I know your father probably hates your mother, and your mother's not too fond of him either, but why don't you just cut yourself a break and stay out of it? It would make your life a lot happier and easier," Gordon said.

My eyes glazed over, and I nodded. "Uh huh."

He ruffled my hair. "That's a good kid. Let's go shoot some hoops," he said.

"Some other time. I was about to go ride my bike."

As I sped away from the posh house in the country club, I replayed the conversation. Gordon hadn't listened to anything I'd said, nor did he care. All he wanted to do was change my

Love Wars

mind about living with my father. He was just following his marching orders, like a newly hired shrink.

* * *

As the weeks went on, Gordon approached me more often and pressed harder and harder. I resisted, and our relationship degenerated. Gordon didn't ask me to play basketball anymore, and he stopped giving me high fives. *Fine, Gordon, you want to be that way? Go ahead. Someday you'll regret being on my mother's team.*

I knew my mother was telling Gordon terrible things about me, and I wanted to know exactly what she was saying. It was time for more spying.

On Christmas Eve, four years to the day after my mother kidnapped my brother and me, I waited until the other kids were fast asleep, dreaming what might await them under the tree. I crept up to the top of the stairs, stood a few feet from the master bedroom door and listened. I'd gone on fishing expeditions for juicy info many times in the past, and sometimes come away empty-handed as I heard the two of them discuss nothing important. But this time, I struck gold.

". . . and that's why we have to get married," I heard my mother's voice float through the door.

"Are you sure it will make that much of a difference?" Gordon asked.

"Definitely. My lawyer says that having a stable nuclear family makes a world of difference in a custody hearing. My bastard ex-husband married some floozy he met at his laboratory, and now they have a daughter. But you have *two* daughters. When

Here Comes the Bride

the judge looks at us, he'll see a model family. Just like the Brady Bunch!"

"I don't know, Vanessa. You said when we moved in together you wanted to wait at least a year before we get married. It's only been four months."

"I know, but what's to wait for? Everything's going great. And I can't lose Matthew. My ex is poisoning him against me. My son's losing his mind; he doesn't know black from white. He's so confused. What kind of a father would do that to his son, turn him against his own mother?"

"That boy is turning into a little rebel without a cause. I feel sorry for Matthew. I've done my best, but it's hard to get through to him."

"Thanks for trying. He needs a real man in his life."

"So if I marry you, you think it will help you rescue Matthew from his father's brainwashing?"

"That's exactly right. We can save him, you and me."

Yikes. This was bad. *Very bad.*

"Are you still planning to convert to Catholicism?" Gordon asked. "You know I can't marry outside my faith."

"*Of course,* Gordon. I told you I'll gladly accept Jesus Christ as Lord and Savior before we tie the knot."

"Let me think about it. But I'm not saying no."

"That's wonderful! I love you so much, Gordon."

All that followed were the sounds of kissing and adult noises. I crept back downstairs, desperate to get away. Did she *really* say she was planning to convert to Catholicism less than a year after suing me over Hebrew lessons? What next? Would she file a lawsuit to force me to get baptized?

Downstairs I found Cindy in her pajamas, watching the movie *WarGames* on TV. Guess she wasn't asleep after all.

Love Wars

Saying nothing about what I'd overheard, I collapsed on the couch and watched as the genius kids desperately tried to stop the idiot grown-ups from blowing up the planet. The grown-ups seemed to have no clue how completely *insane* they were to even have nuclear weapons in the first place, much less use them!

As I watched the countdown to doomsday, I thought about my mother's "stable nuclear family"—about as stable as a ticking bomb.

What the hell is wrong with this world? Why do nuclear weapons exist? Why do nuclear divorces exist? If kids were in charge, we'd stop all the wars, get rid of the nukes, and then maybe we'd all have a chance to survive.

* * *

The next day, I phoned home, just like E.T.: The Extra-Terrestrial.

"Dad, it's me. Can we talk?"

"Sure. Merry Christmas. Is your mother on the line?"

"Nope, coast is clear."

My mother wouldn't allow me to call my father while I was at her house without supervision. I had to ask permission, and I had to have a very good reason to call. Last time I called him, I had an allowable reason: I needed him to bring my soccer ball to my next game. But she picked up the other phone and listened in on our conversation. Once I started talking with him about things beyond the scope of the soccer ball, she rushed into my room, ripped the phone out of my hands, and berated me for disobeying her in her own home. So this time I called my father in secret.

Here Comes the Bride

"I think my mother and Gordon are getting married."

"Are you sure?"

"I overheard them talking about it."

"How do you feel about the idea of your mother getting married again?"

"It's ridiculous. I think they shouldn't be planning the wedding, they should start planning the divorce."

He laughed.

"Matthew, you are without a doubt the smartest ten-year-old I've ever met."

"There's something else you should know. I think they're getting married because she's trying to figure out how to stop you from winning custody."

"How'd you figure that one out?"

"Well, I over—"

Suddenly, I heard footsteps. I whispered, "Sorry, Dad, gotta go!" I hung up the phone and quickly slid it under my bed. Just then the door opened.

"MATTHEW! WHO WERE YOU TALKING TO?"

"No one. I'm playing with my Transformers." I set about changing Optimus Prime from a big rig truck into a giant robot.

"If I catch you talking to your father on my time, you're going to be punished. You got that, you impudent brat?"

"Yeah, I got it," I replied.

She stormed out.

The phone calls became another war. I got so proud of my ability to outwit my mother and call my father, I made a card for him that said "M.T. Phone Home" in the same typeface as the *E.T.* movie logo. I was a terrible artist, but I drew me on one end of the phone and Dad on the other, both of us smiling.

Here Comes the Bride

The phone became my emotional lifeline, a way for me to escape from my mother's repulsive world.

* * *

Just before the end of the winter holidays, my mother and Gordon gathered all the kids together in the living room to announce the big news.

"We're getting married!" my mother said. Gordon nodded his head.

Lisa acted surprised. "Really? Wow, congratulations."

"You're getting married? That's great," Thomas said, doing his best to fake surprise.

I'd told all the kids about the impending nuptials. The house spy couldn't keep it to himself.

As the wedding drew closer, I felt a gnawing sense of responsibility in my heart. Despite everything, I still liked Gordon and his daughters, and I mostly didn't hold it against the weak-minded fools that they'd fallen victim to my mother's black magic. I wanted to save them from the grief and destruction that I predicted would ravage their lives on the other side of the wedding bells. I knew what I was going to say would make Gordon despise me, but so what? I had nothing left to lose.

A few days after the big announcement, when I got home from school, I ran into Gordon in the hallway.

"Gordon, I need to talk with you. Can we go somewhere private?"

"Everything's out in the open in this household, Matthew. We don't keep secrets. Whatever you need to say to me, say it, I don't care who listens."

Love Wars

I looked around. No one else was within earshot. Oh well, here goes nothing.

"Please don't marry my mom."

"Excuse me?"

"Please don't marry my mom."

"Matthew, I'm sorry, but my marriage plans are *none of your damn business!*" Gordon looked *very* angry. He'd never been like this with me.

"Umm, I know. It's just that... you're a nice guy, and I really like Cindy and Lisa. And I don't want to see your lives ruined." I paused, stared at the ground, at my little sneakers, then at his shiny black dress shoes.

Gordon was six-foot-two and towered over me like a skyscraper. I looked up at him, sucked up all my courage, and said, "My mother's going to destroy you."

"Son, what *on earth* are you talking about?"

"My mother will turn on you. She *hates men*. She hates her father, she hates my father, she hates her ex-fiancé Bob Trapp..." I almost added, *and she hates me.*

"Matthew, listen to yourself. How could you say such mean things about your mother?"

"Because I've lived with her antics my whole life. Someday you two will get divorced, and she'll sue you and take all your money. Just take your daughters and *run*. Get out of here before it's too late!"

"Look, Matthew, I've had just about enough out of you! Your mother told me what your father's doing to you, brainwashing you, turning you against her. You have no right to disrespect her this way. On top of everything else, now you're trying to break up our relationship. You should go to your room and think

Here Comes the Bride

about all the terrible things you're saying. Show some respect. This conversation is over!"

Gordon stormed off.

I understood him getting mad at me... it must have been a shock to hear that from his fiancée's son. Still, I felt sad for him, even pitied him. I wished he'd come to his senses, but I knew it was hopeless.

After that, my relationship with Gordon got *much* worse. He rarely said anything nice to me. Whenever he was around me, his face changed. Instead of being his bright, jovial, happy self, all I saw was a mask of contempt and judgment. When he came home, he hugged his daughters and Thomas and ignored me.

Whatever, Gordon! Someday, you'll see you were wrong. Someday, you'll admit a fifth grader knew better than you did.

Gordon must have told my mother about the warning I'd given him. She seemed to despise me more than ever. I was jittery, on edge, constantly worried about what would happen. I thought she might explode. Being alone with her was terrifying, and I tried to avoid that at all costs.

* * *

One Wednesday, when my father showed up, my mother said we couldn't go see him because he'd violated The Contract and lost his rights to see us for the day. Dad waited in the driveway, and when she wouldn't release us, he left.

On Friday, I was afraid she would try to keep me from Dad again, so I decided that I was going to get what I wanted. And I knew there was one surefire, never-fail way to get anything I wanted from Mom: pretend to be nice to her. Using all my well-honed acting skills, I approached her early in the afternoon

Love Wars

with a glass of soda and a Hostess cupcake in hand.

"Mom, *how are you?* You've been working *so hard* and I appreciate what you do for Thomas and me *so much*. You deserve a treat." I flashed her my fakest of fake smiles. Over the years, I'd become an expert at fake-smiling when grown-ups expected me to.

She accepted the offering with the grin of a little girl who'd just been handed a surprise ticket to a pony ride.

"Oh, Matthew, I'm so happy to have a son who loves me so much. You're the greatest. I love you." It was the first nice thing she'd said to me in months.

"*Of course*, Mom. Wow, you look *really tired*, I bet you could use a nap. I'll stand guard and make sure no one wakes you."

"How did you know I needed a nap? Matthew, you know me so well."

She hugged me. *Ick!* But I was careful not to pull away. She went straight up to her bedroom and laid down in her bed. I crept up to her door and pressed my ear against the wood until I could hear her faintly snoring.

Satisfied, I crept back downstairs, went to my room, and called Dad. I told him to come get me, but not to pull into the driveway, and instead to wait at the neighbor's house down the street. I told him I didn't want to bring Thomas with me because I didn't want him to get in trouble with our biological mother. Dad agreed, and said he was on his way. It would take him a half-hour to get there, and I waited by the clock, staring at it, willing the hands to move. My stomach clenched. I farted like a racehorse and felt so nervous. What if she woke up? What if she busted me? What if she heard Dad's car drive up?

Finally, after precisely thirty minutes had passed, I carefully

Here Comes the Bride

opened the door, closed it gently behind me, and started walking across the lawn. At first I padded lightly, but then I realized I was out of the house. If the door opened, it was possible Mom could catch me, but if I started running, no one, no way, no how was going to stop me. I took off at top speed, dashed across the lawn, down the driveway, and down the street, until I reached Dad's red Chrysler station wagon. Breathlessly, I jumped in and yelled, "Go go go!"

I had done it! Freedom! I got to be with Dad and my new mom and my sister, and there was nothing my mother could do to stop me. I felt like a hero.

When we got home, Holly let me hold my baby sister. I nuzzled and kissed Bethany while my stepmother cooked up a Friday night dinner storm of casserole, cornbread, and Kool-Aid. "How's it going at your biological mother's house?" she asked.

"You mean Vanessa's Foul Den of Yelling and Screaming? Umm, okay I guess. I'm counting the days 'til I'm out of there." We both laughed, which helped me not feel bad that Thomas had been left behind for the weekend, poor kid.

The afterglow of my mini-victory didn't last long. The following Monday, my mother was furious, and wouldn't speak to me or answer any of my questions. I was nobody. I didn't exist. She made a big show of being extra kind and considerate to Thomas, while she spurned me as if I were some wretched, worthless creature she'd found in the street and was simply carting around until she could drop it off at the animal shelter.

One day my best friend Johnny Callaghan from our old Lark Lane neighborhood came over to visit. By this time, the silent treatment had given way to renewed bouts of apocalyptic screaming. As I'd learned many times before, one of the only

Here Comes the Bride

things that would get my mother to be nice—or at least, pretend to be nice—was the arrival of a visitor.

"MATTHEW, YOU'RE THE CRUMMIEST SON *EVER!* YOU'RE TRYING TO BREAK UP MY FAMILY AND—" The doorbell rang. *Thank God.* My mother walked over to the door, still screaming, "—DESTROY MY MARRIAGE BEFORE I'VE EVEN WALKED DOWN THE AISLE! WHY ARE YOU ALWAYS MAKING ME THE TARGET? WHY IS IT THAT—"

And just like that, she opened the door and smoothly transitioned from rabid hyena to a *Leave It To Beaver* portrait of maternal sweetness.

"Hi, Johnny! It's *so* good to see you," Vanessa Cleaver cooed. "I'm so glad you're here to keep Matthew company. He needs good influences like you in his life. From what your mother tells me about how well-behaved you are, I bet you could teach him a thing or two about how to be a good son."

"Aw, shucks, Dr. Tower, you're always so nice to me," Johnny replied.

On one hand, I wanted to barf. On the other, I thanked God that Johnny was there to give me a few hours of reprieve.

After an afternoon of basketball, video games, soda, and pizza—our usual Saturday agenda—Johnny's mother arrived to pick up her son. My mother stood in the doorway and waved goodbye, but the moment the car pulled away, the hyena ripped off her sitcom mask and slammed the door shut. The onslaught continued right where it had left off.

"YOU AND YOUR FATHER ALWAYS MAKE ME THE TARGET! YOU TWO ARE OUT TO DESTROY ME!"

I slunk back into my bedroom and tried to read a *Dragonlance* book.

Love Wars

M.T. Phone Home took on a new level of desperation. Every time I asked my father when he'd be going to court to get custody, all he could reply was, "The court calendar is backed up. I'll let you know when I know." It dragged on forever.

Finally, Dad told me a date had been set for the end of summer.

* * *

Late that spring, my mother and Gordon's wedding day arrived like an Easter egg filled with rotten cockroaches.

A knock at the door.

"Matthew, we're leaving in twenty minutes!" Cindy said.

The happy couple was already at the church, and Cindy was in charge of driving the kids. I started to put on my suit pants, then stopped. I held my head in my hands and cried. *No. I'm not going. This isn't my family. No way in hell am I going to pretend to be part of this madhouse and go to a stupid, meaningless wedding between two people who are destined for divorce.*

The custody hearing was only two and a half months away, and I knew liberation was just around the corner. I'd successfully refused when my mother had tried to drag me to her baptism, so perhaps I could get out of this one too.

Twenty minutes later, another knock on the door.

"Matthew, it's time to go. We need to be down at the church in half an hour."

I didn't answer. Cindy popped her head in and saw me sitting there with my pants half pulled on and tears in my eyes.

"I know you don't want to, but you *have to go*."

"NO!" I yelled at her.

Here Comes the Bride

She grabbed me by one arm.

"LEAVE ME ALONE! LEAVE ME ALONE! LEAVE ME ALONE!" I screamed with all the viciousness I could summon. Five-and-a-half years older, Cindy was quite a bit taller and stronger than me. She didn't try to fight me, though. She just stared down at me, then threw her hands up, walked out of the room, and drove off with the rest of the kids.

I sat down on my bed. I was alone in the house for over an hour, waiting. I was pretty sure I knew what was coming, but I hoped against hope that I was wrong.

As it turned out, I was right. *Here comes the bride.* My mother stormed into my room in her white wedding dress and laid into me.

"*Get dressed right now, young man! You are coming to our wedding.*"

Suddenly, I lost *all* inhibition. Usually, if I got mad at her, I held back out of fear, but this time I cut everything loose and ripped into her.

"*What's the point?* You're going to get divorced from Gordon pretty soon anyway. Why don't you just invite me to that? It would save a lot of time and trouble."

"SHUT UP! SHUT UP, SHUT UP, SHUT UP, AND *SHUT UP!* GET DRESSED YOUNG MAN OR YOU'LL BE SORRY!"

"NO! NO, NO, NO, AND *NO!*" I screamed back at her.

"DON'T MAKE ME MAKE YOU! YOU'RE MY SON AND YOU'LL DO AS I SAY!"

I crossed my arms over my chest and looked away, out the window. Then I looked back at her and screamed, "*YOU'RE NOT MY MOTHER! HOLLY IS MY MOTHER!*"

"*YOU MISERABLE TRAITOR!*"

Love Wars

She grabbed me, held me down on the floor, and forced me into my clothes. I struggled briefly, but then gave up. I went limp like Jell-O and let her finish dressing me as my mind voyaged into a heated round of my favorite Apple II computer game, *Sneakers*. I was the little robot, blasting the other little robots. I was clearing stage after stage, playing better than I had ever played before. I was on my way to a record high score!

As we pulled out of the driveway, I stuck my mother's Paul Simon tape into the deck, searching for a song to fill the empty spaces between us. Just as I heard the opening strains of "Crazy Love" come out of the speakers, she pounded the eject button. The tape flew out of the deck, and a geyser of words shot out of her mouth: "You're making my wedding late! You're ruining my wedding day! You're embarrassing me in front of my family and friends! *This is all your fault!* Oh forget it . . ." She trailed off.

The rest of the drive to the wedding chapel was conducted in silence. With tears in her eyes and smeared makeup, my mother was not the picture of a happy bride.

When we arrived, we rushed into the chapel and soon the service started. I stood next to my little brother who was holding the ring. I was uncontrollably nervous. I looked at Gordon, at Vanessa, at everyone else, and something snapped in my mind. I felt so out of place, so disconnected. *This isn't real. This can't be happening. This is insane.* Before I knew what was happening, diarrhea was dribbling down my leg. I shifted from leg to leg, trying to adjust, trying to make the diarrhea stay put. No one seemed to notice.

The vows were exchanged. "'Til death do us part," they both said. *Or 'til my mother decides she hates you.*

Love Wars

After they were done with the meaningless vows, I whispered in Mom's ear that I had to go to the bathroom—bad.

"Well, go!" she whispered back.

"I need to go home," I said.

"Why?" she asked, raising her frustrated voice loud enough for others to hear.

"I have to go home and change because I crapped in my pants," I whispered, hoping she wouldn't repeat what I said in front of everyone.

She was silent, and for a moment I was afraid she'd make me stay at the church and tell me to go wash up in the bathroom. But I got lucky—she told Cindy to take me home. Neither of us said a word on the drive to the country club. Cindy dropped me off, and I cleaned up and changed my clothes. Cindy didn't even bother trying to force me to come back with her for the reception.

Grateful to miss out on the rest of the afternoon's madness, I went to the computer room and turned on *Sneakers* and played for hours, blocking out my tears. As I got deeper into the game and bested my old high score, I thought about how all the other kids were such suckers for playing along in Mom and Gordon's pathetic charade of a wedding. I wondered if they knew that the *real* reason our parents were getting married was to try to stop me from escaping to Dad's house.

Suddenly, all the rage and sadness melted away, replaced by a sense of calm as one truly happy thought crossed my mind: *If I'm brave and lucky, soon enough I'll be living with my dad and real mom and little sister and I'll be out of my biological mother's nightmare life forever.*

Chapter Thirteen
QUALITY TIME
Age 11 • 1985 • The Summer After Fifth Grade

As the custody hearing approached, my mother became increasingly desperate. I could see in her eyes that she knew she would lose me. *I'm going to live with Dad and there's nothing you can do.* I tried to ignore what he'd said about only a 50 percent chance of winning and the courts being biased against fathers. *If I believe I'm going to win, I will win*, I kept thinking to myself. *How could she possibly stop me?*

"You're going on vacation to upstate New York to stay with my parents," my mother said on my last day of fifth grade, snuffing out whatever joy I felt for finally graduating from George Armstrong Custer Elementary.

I felt a deep freeze chill my entire body. *No. Not that. Anything but that!* I'd underestimated my mother. She was calling in the big guns.

Grandpa Avi's powers of manipulation were legendary. My father called him the Master Manipulator, and said he had a mind like an iron vise. He told me that Avi had Mafia connections from his days as a slumlord and that he was a womanizing pig who'd cheated on Grandma Libby for years. Ever since the phone call in which Avi threatened to have my father's entire side of the family killed, I'd lived in mortal fear of him.

How could I hold out in the face of the Master Manipulator? Grandpa Avi would play a dark side mind trick on me and I'd come back from summer vacation having lost my resolve to live with my father. I'd say the wrong thing to the judge, and then the whole court case would fail. Too late, I'd realize the horrible mistake I'd made. I'd be stuck living with my mother for the rest of my childhood—*if* I even managed to survive to adulthood.

"I don't want to go to New York," I whined.

"Tough. This isn't your decision. My parents haven't seen you in two years and they want to spend some quality time with you."

What kind of quality time? Brainwashing time?

"Why can't I see them over Christmas break?" *After the custody hearing—that would be perfect.*

"Young man, it's settled. You are leaving next week for New York, and you'll show your grandparents some respect. Listen to what they have to say—they're very wise, unlike you. You're intelligent, but you're not *wise*. If you were wise, you'd love your mother. Listen to Grandpa Avi; he'll talk some sense into you."

My shoulders sagged. I wasn't going to get out of this one. If she had to, my mother would force me onto the plane. I had no choice but to go face-to-face with my grandfather and beat him—or at least not lose.

QUALITY TIME

* * *

For the first time in my life, I flew alone on an airplane, without even my little brother to keep me company. Apparently, my mother didn't think Thomas needed any "quality time" with his grandparents. When Grandpa Avi and Grandma Libby picked me up from La Guardia airport, I said very little. I wasn't happy to be there, and it seemed like they weren't too pleased, either. I was not expecting them to buy me toys or ice cream like they usually did. I was expecting a two-week-long tongue-lashing. So I decided to keep quiet and hope somehow I was wrong. We drove in silence toward their cabin in the foothills in upstate New York.

Not two minutes after I set my bags down in their vacation bungalow, Grandpa Avi fired his opening shot.

"So, I hear from your mother that you want to go live with your bastard father." *Here we go.* I raised my block-out shields and tried not to listen as the indictments of Nate came fast and furious.

That evening, over a dinner of stiff spaghetti and canned tomato sauce—Grandma Libby's cooking was as bad as my mother's—both of my grandparents ripped into me. They'd undoubtedly compared notes with my mother and had managed to encapsulate all of her most salient talking points, plus some brand-new material. The smells of *old people* mixed with oregano and garlic bread. Grandma Libby's ever-present ashtray overpowered my senses.

"Matthew, your father's so poor," Grandpa Avi said. "Do you know how wealthy your mother is? She'll be able to send you to the best college, any college you want, Harvard. If you live

Quality Time

with your *father*"—he punctuated the word "father" by stabbing the air with his butter knife, sending drops of tomato sauce flying—"you'll end up in a lousy state school, *at best.*"

"Your mother loves you so much," Grandma Libby piled on in her raspy voice. I could hear her two-packs-per-day smoking habit in her vocal cords. "She spent nine months pregnant with you, then endured excruciating pain to bring you into this world. How can you be so disrespectful *to your own mother!* I *never* treated my mother the way you treat yours."

"Your father's a sick man," Grandpa Avi interjected. "Believe me, I know the type. They rented apartments from me, and I'd see them in court all the time. Jerks like him are the dregs of society. Only a bastard would try to steal a son away from a mother."

The more they talked, the less I listened. The TV was on in the background, playing the cartoon version of *The Lord of the Rings: Return of the King*. I tried to watch Frodo, Samwise, and Gandalf on their epic journey to throw the ring of evil back into the fire and undo Sauron's dominating power once and for all.

"Matthew, listen to your grandfather when he talks to you," Grandma Libby said.

Grandpa Avi got up, turned the TV off, and sat back down to resume his assault on my mind. He stared into my eyes like he was sizing up an opposing lawyer.

"You need to learn respect for authority, respect for your elders. Plus, if you want to be successful in life and have a good career, a good wife, and children, your mother's in a much better position to financially support you. And I can support you too, but you'll lose *all* my support if you abandon my daughter."

Love Wars

I felt sick to my stomach, and it wasn't just because of Grandma Libby's cooking.

Finally, the lecture drew to a close, and Grandpa Avi promised me, "We'll talk more about this tomorrow."

That night, I tossed and turned, afraid somehow I'd screw it all up and succumb to my grandfather's mind games. I drifted off into a Darth Nightmare . . .

I was facing off against my nemesis Darth Avi in a desperate attempt to win my freedom and save my brother, Thomas Rabbit, from being frozen in carbonite. But Darth Avi was too big, too powerful. His cane turned into a lightsaber, moving faster than mine. I turned this way and that, desperately trying to deflect his blows.

"Impressive . . . most impressive. Matthew, your rhetorical talents are the best of any Padawan lawyer I've ever seen. Your tongue's even sharper than your cousin Wendy's."

Suddenly Darth Avi overpowered me and sliced off my hand!

I screamed in pain, clutching the railing as the vicious wind threatened to pull me down a dark shaft into the underbelly of Cloud City.

Darth Avi sized me up with a cold, calculating stare.

"Join me and I will complete your training. With our combined strength, we can operate the most powerful grandfather and grandson law firm in all of New York."

"I'LL NEVER JOIN YOU!"

"If you only knew the power of the dark side of the Law. Do you know how many wealthy families get divorced every year in Queens alone?"

"LEAVE ME ALONE!"

Love Wars

"Come, my grandson. Live with your mother. Go to the best law school in the country. I'll pay for everything. It is your *destiny!*"

"NO!"

"You insolent brat. What in the hell do I need to do to get you to turn to the dark side already? Turn, goddammit, *turn!* Okay, *fine*, I'll throw in a sports car. What was that thing your cousin wanted? A BMW convertible? Yours will come with leather seats!"

As the dark menace stared back at me, I did the only thing I could do: I let go. Falling, falling, falling into the void . . .

Awakening in terror, I rolled over to hold my right hand up to the moonlight peeking through the window and flexed my fingers. *Whew*, still intact—unlike my heart.

For two solid weeks, Grandpa Avi and Grandma Libby lectured me and guilt-tripped me, grasping at any argument they could dream up to dissuade me from wanting to live with my father.

But I held fast. Their rantings had less effect on me than I'd feared. Perhaps all the years of enduring my mother's tirades had prepared me to take on the Master Manipulator and his sidekick. The more they lectured me, the more my resolve grew.

Interspersed between the hate therapy sessions were a few moments of fun. On my eleventh birthday, Grandma took me to play miniature golf and to the dollar theater to see *Return of the Jedi*. I never tired of the *Star Wars* finale, despite having seen it countless times since its release two years before.

In the end, I won. They couldn't manipulate me. They couldn't change my mind. I was going to go live with Dad and there was nothing they could do to stop me. I was Luke Skywalker, and I'd resisted Darth Avi's call to turn to the dark side. I was ready to be a Jedi.

Love Wars

* * *

It was a huge relief to get back to my father's family. Dad's parents came into town, and since Dad had to work most of the time, Grandpa Stanley and Grandma Miriam took Thomas and me to the nearby Waters and Courts rec club to wile away the sweltering, humid days.

"So, sport, are you ready for your big day in court?" Grandpa Stanley asked during a break in one of our tennis matches. Even though he and Grandma Miriam were much better shots than I was, my young legs could run circles around them, so I had challenged them to a game of one-on-two while my eight-year-old brother took a diving lesson.

"Yup, all set. I can't wait for this nightmare to end." I wiped a quarter-cup of sweat off my brow. They were cleaning my clock in straight sets, but I refused to admit that two sixty-somethings were superior to me in tennis, or anything. I was hoping if I beat them, or somehow stole a set, I'd make Holly and Bethany my permanent fan club. They were watching from the shade under an umbrella. Even if I didn't stand a chance against my grandparents, the running around came with a side benefit: a lot of my baby fat disappeared that summer.

"Are you scared?" Grandma Miriam asked. "Having to talk privately to a judge is a heavy burden for an eleven-year-old."

"Scared? No way! Besides, I'm undefeated in court so far." I laughed to hide my nervousness. "Unlike on this court."

They both chuckled.

"Don't get cocky, Matthew. Your mother's got a lot more money than Nate, and her father's willing to go to the mat for her. This isn't going to be as easy as getting out of Hebrew lessons."

Love Wars

"Yeah, tell me about it," I mumbled, wondering if "going to the mat" meant Avi thumbing through his Rolodex of hit men.

After two hours and three sets of demolition derby tennis, courtesy of the dynamic geriatric duo, we called it a game. Done with his diving lesson, Thomas joined us for lunch, and Holly set out a picnic of fried chicken, deviled eggs, fudge brownies, and frosty lemonade she'd brought in a red thermos.

I loved my family.

* * *

All summer long, I daydreamed about the court date, which was set for late August, right before the start of the new school year. With only a few weeks left to go, Dad gave me some shocking news: I had to see a shrink. Not "a" shrink, *two shrinks!* And this time, Thomas wasn't getting a hall pass.

"I'm taking you two to see Dr. Wallaby, the court-appointed child therapist, on Thursday. Your mother's attorney has hired a therapist to help her with her case, Dr. Leeks. You'll have to see her on Friday."

"*What?* Dad, you know I hate shrinks. *Hate 'em!*" I exploded. Thomas kept quiet. I wasn't sure if he didn't care or just didn't know what was coming. He was so agreeable.

"Matthew, you've got no choice. Look, the court's doing the right thing by asking you to see a neutral therapist, and if you decide you don't want to speak to your mother's therapist, that's fine, all you have to do is show up. It's only an hour with each of them."

"But Grandpa and Grandma said they'd take us to Waters and Courts all this week."

Quality Time

"Too bad. You want to come live with your stepmother and me? Then you've got no choice. I'm under court's orders to take you, and if you fail to show up, my case could be in jeopardy."

That got through to me. I shut my mouth tight, pouted for another few seconds, and then got a mischievous twinkle in my eyes.

"Dad, what do you call a hundred shrinks at the bottom of the ocean?"

"Let me guess: a good start?"

We both cracked up. My father always made that joke about divorce lawyers.

Surprisingly, I liked Dr. Wallaby. A rotund Australian with a Crocodile Dundee accent, he seemed more like a shopping mall Santa in a dress shirt and khaki slacks than an evil shrink. Plus, I almost trusted him a little because Dad said the court had appointed him and he wasn't on my mother's payroll.

At first the conversation was light and easy, and we even cracked some jokes.

"Don't worry, this won't hurt a bit, unlike a visit to the dentist. I promise," he told me.

"You mean you're not going to clean my head out with a high-powered toothbrush?" I shot back.

He laughed. "Nope, just a few questions about your relationship with your parents."

"Okay, go for it." I felt a cold fear grip my stomach, but tried to stay calm. What if he gave the judge the wrong advice? I had to make sure Dr. Kangaroo heard the message loud and clear.

"How do you feel about your mother?" he asked.

"I despise her with every bone in my body," I responded, looking him right in the eyes.

Love Wars

"Why?"

"'Cause she's a lunatic who tries to brainwash me against my father. She screams at me, dumps on me, even sued me to force me to take Hebrew lessons. But I beat her sorry butt in court," I bragged.

He scribbled some notes, then paused to peer at me.

"It's unfortunate that you have so much animosity for your mother. What's it like to feel that kind of rage?"

I grimaced. "What's it like? I don't know, you should ask her. She hates me a thousand times more than I hate her," I said.

Dr. Wallaby sighed. "Matthew, I spoke with your mother, and she told me she loves you. Do you believe that?"

I squinted at the fat dude in the black leather swivel chair, then turned away and gazed out the window for long moments. I'd heard that from my mother plenty of times before—after she said goodbye while dropping me off at soccer practice, when she gave me quarters to play video games, or at the end of a tearful, makeup-smearing tirade about whether or not she was a good mother. Of course, I hadn't heard it recently, not since I'd tricked her with the soda and cupcake to escape for the weekend with my father.

I remembered her screaming that she wished she'd never given birth to me. I thought to myself, *Golly gee willikers, Dr. Kangaroo, my mother sure has a special way of showing her eldest son that she loves him. Hallmark should make a series of greeting cards featuring my mother's face and her best lines.*

I wondered what he wanted to hear. Finally, I told him, "Yeah, right. Whatever she says. I still want to live with my father and stepmother."

Quality Time

* * *

The next morning, a white Toyota Camry pulled up in front of my father's driveway. I started to freak out, thinking it was my mother's car, but then I remembered she had no business being there when it was my father's visitation time. Who in our neighborhood had the bad taste to drive a car identical to my mother's?

As I stared out the window, trying to make out the license plate, my father announced to Thomas and me: "Sorry, boys, you'll have to endure your mother for a few hours."

"*What?*" How could he betray me like this?

"While your mother has the legal right to have you evaluated by her psychologist, I don't have to be the one to bring you. I had my lawyer tell her lawyer that she's responsible for the transportation. Don't worry, you'll be back in time for lunch—just go straight to the pool to meet Holly and your grandparents."

"How do you know she won't kidnap us?"

"With the court date coming up, she won't take any chances on blowing her case. Off you go," he said, opening the door.

I trudged out of the house, staring at the ground. Each footstep felt like I was marching into Sauron's lair with the One Ring around my neck, turning myself over to The Enemy. If Thomas had an opinion about this, which I doubted, he kept it to himself.

My hand rested on the Camry's door handle, and I fingered the smooth metal for long moments. Finally, I pulled the door open, and my nemesis and I locked eyes. We glared at each other and declared an unspoken truce: neither of us would say a single word to each other the entire time.

Love Wars

And we didn't. She and my eight-year-old brother prattled on about nothing—his diving lessons, her summer vacation with Gordon and the girls. I kept my lips firmly zipped.

We arrived at a brick building I hadn't seen for four years, but I recognized it instantly. I almost asked, "Are we going to see Dr. McCrackpot?" but then remembered my vow of silence.

On the eighth floor, down the hall from Shrink Number 1's office, my mother led us to see Shrink Number 3: Gretchen Leeks. This time Thomas went first, and I entertained myself reading some old copies of *Boys' Life* I found piled up on the tables in the waiting room. Fifty minutes later, it was my turn, and Thomas and I traded places.

Unlike the young, attractive Shrink Number 1, Dr. Leeks was a decrepit fossil. Even from all the way across the room, I could smell her nasty old-lady perfume. Her face puffed out with layers of makeup so thick a bird could have used it as a landing pad. Her forced smile only sharpened the wrinkles and caverns on her face.

She sized me up for a second before starting in with her questions, to which I responded by sticking my tongue out and putting my fingers in my ears. The silent treatment was working quite well, thank you very much, and I was going to keep it up.

"Matthew, I'm here to help you. I know your parents' divorce has been messy and confusing, and I want you to know I'm your friend..."

She rambled on as I tried to block out her voice completely. I imagined that if I waggled my fingers fast enough, I could make myself fly out of her office.

"You know a son needs both of his parents. I realize that

Quality Time

boys like you feel close with their fathers, but your entire world cannot be defined solely by masculinity..."

I remembered *Charlie Brown* TV specials, in which the teachers spoke but the only words that came out were "Mwah mwah mwaaah mwaaaaah."

Unaware that her words sounded like foreign gibberish through my *Peanuts* garbage filter, she charged right ahead. "How can you expect to have a girlfriend someday if you can't love your mother? It's good training to learn..."

Ouch. She'd found a soft spot and hit me where it hurt. I wanted a girlfriend, and felt jealous of friends like Johnny who got lots of attention from cute girls at school. Suddenly, I burst out laughing at the thought that time spent with my mother could teach me to be a good boyfriend. I made a *pffft* sound with my tongue, and a little glob of spittle flew across the room and landed on the carpet just in front of Dr. Reeks's black flats.

She paused in mid-lecture and stared at me wide-eyed. Then she grabbed her clipboard and moved her pen rapidly across the page. I hoped she'd just keep writing for the rest of the session. But eventually, she looked up at me again.

"You're beyond help, aren't you?"

For the first time since I'd walked into her office, I relaxed. Then I grinned again, like a jack-o-lantern.

"And you're *proud* of it, aren't you?"

I nodded my head, *yes*.

The session over, I skipped out of the room, only to run into my mother as she marched past me into Dr. Reeks's office for her debrief. Just as I'd done four years before on my last visit with Shrink Number 1, I left the door cracked just a bit on my way out. I shot Thomas a don't-you-even-*think*-about-tattling glare. I needn't have worried. Thomas loved reaping the rewards of my masterful eavesdropping, so long as he didn't have to share the risk.

As I listened to Dr. Reeks's clucking tongue, I imagined the *Mission Impossible* theme song playing faintly in the background.

"Dr. Tower, I must tell you, in my entire career I've never encountered two siblings of such polar opposite personalities. Are you sure one of them wasn't adopted? Your younger son is well-adjusted, gentle, and easygoing. He's bonded to both you and your ex-husband, and he loves and respects his older brother. Matthew, on the other hand, seems quite disturbed. He's hostile, domineering, and disrespectful. His father appears to have executed a masterful act of parental alienation. Turning him against you was all the easier because of the preadolescent's tendency to identify with the same-sex parent. You're facing an uphill custody battle."

Peeking through the door, I saw my mother nod her head.

"I know, Dr. Leeks. Thanks for trying," she replied.

"I will of course testify on your behalf in court as we discussed. Dr. Tower, one last thing. Matthew's stubborn, rebellious attitude indicates he's well on his way to a full-blown case of oppositional defiant disorder. Kids with that affliction have a hard time experiencing happiness and success. In extreme cases, they spend their lives in futile, blind, and ultimately self-destructive struggles against authority figures. Especially as he moves into his teenage years, keep in mind this risk and monitor his behavior. Consider seeing a psychiatrist for a prescription if he doesn't grow out of it."

"I will, Dr. Leeks, thank you. I'm glad to have a name for his illness."

Love Wars

When my mother emerged from Dr. Reeks's office, all she saw was two docile sons, quietly reading magazines. As she drove us back to my father's house in silence, I pressed my face against the window and looked forward to spilling my ill-gotten secrets to anyone in my father's family who wanted to hear.

* * *

With one week to go until the court date, my father took me to The Men's Wearhouse to outfit me in a new suit.

"Matthew, I want you to look your best for the trial," Dad said as the clerk measured and tucked and pinched and stuck pins into the navy blue fabric.

The trial. It sounded frightening. "Is this going to be like *L.A. Law*?"

He laughed. "Better. Much better, if it goes well. But it's probably going to be crazy, too. Maybe even crazier than the TV show."

"What are our chances of winning?" I asked for the millionth time.

"My new guess is 80 percent. Our case is excellent. But I'm more optimistic than the lawyer," Dad said.

"What does the lawyer say?"

"Don't ask questions you don't want to hear the answer to." He shook his head.

"No, Dad, I want to know. I'm a big kid. What does he say?"

My father sighed. "He says that outcomes of custody hearings like these are about as predictable as the weather."

That might be true, but I was used to weathering storms—and now the sun was finally about to come out.

Love Wars

Or was it?

The night before the trial began, I had a dream that I was on a mission to blow up the Death Star...

As I flew my X-wing across the gray trenches, turbolasers narrowly missed me left and right, and I saw my wingmen get picked off one by one.

"Stay on target! Stay on target!"

I focused on the exhaust port just twenty-three thousand meters ahead, twenty-two thousand, twenty-one thousand...

Suddenly from behind, Darth Avi flew up hot on my heels, his wife Libby and their daughter Vanessa flying their TIE fighters together in tight formation.

Obi-Wan's voice calmed me. "Use the Force, Matthew. Let go, Matthew."

"The Force is strong with this one," the Dark Lord of the Sith mumbled grudgingly as he twisted his knobs and tried to lock me in his sights.

"Matthew, trust me," Obi-Wan implored.

A call came in from home base. "Matthew, you switched off your targeting computer. What's wrong?" Holly asked.

"Nothing. I'm all right."

All I have to do is tell the judge. All I have to do is tell the judge.

Just as Darth Avi pressed the button to activate his tractor beam and suck me into his extended family's black hole of madness, I jerked awake in a cold sweat, my fingers aching to fire the most important shot of my young life.

Chapter Fourteen
THE TRIAL
Age 11 • 1985 • On the Eve of Sixth Grade

Bright and early the next morning, Dad and Holly drove us down to the courthouse. When we arrived, I couldn't believe my eyes.

Everyone was there, dressed up in their best clothes like they were ready for a wedding—or a funeral. Every grown-up who was even vaguely important in my life—or thought they were important—had flown in for the Trial of the Century: grandparents, aunts, uncles, cousins, my stepsisters, Gordon, my friends' parents, neighbors, the rabbi from the synagogue, school teachers, Dr. Kangaroo, Dr. Reeks . . . and even Dr. McCrackpot! *What the hell is she doing here? I haven't seen her in four years*, I thought. *Oh God, three shrinks and you're out!*

Love Wars

Holly whispered in my ear, "Looks like your mother's subpoenaed half of Chapel Hill." Apparently most of the townies were there at her attorney's behest.

My mother had an army on her side, my father had an army of his own—a much smaller one—and they were heading into the biggest battle of The War yet.

As confident as I'd been when I woke up that morning, my energy quickly went down the drain once the trial started. A steady stream of relatives, acquaintances, and mental health professionals traipsed in and out of the closed doors of the courtroom to testify about me, and I wasn't even allowed to listen. There was nothing I could do but sit and wait. I'd forgotten to bring a book—big mistake. Nothing happened for hours. As the day wore on, I just sat in the corner of the hallway, bored out of my mind.

During breaks, everyone came out of the courtroom and clustered into two groups. I walked back and forth between them, but mostly stayed on my father's side of the hallway. I went to my mother's side briefly, and Gordon stiffly said, "Hi Matthew, how are you doing?" *Wow. That's more than you said to me the last time you saw me*, I thought. When Grandma Libby greeted me, her face was all smiles. "Matthew, darling, how are you? Give your grandmother a kiss." *Yuck*, I thought as I gave her a perfunctory peck on the cheek. *Where was this version of my grandma in upstate New York?* Speaking of which, where was Grandpa Avi? He was the *only* relative I hadn't seen all day.

My mother was in the courtroom with her lawyer for hours, but at one point she walked out and caught sight of me. She *glared* at me. As her barely concealed rage washed over me, I had a sudden thought that had never occurred to me before.

The Trial

Why the hell do you want to hang onto me? LET GO! You hate me, I hate you, so why on earth do you want to keep me?

It made no sense. But then, somehow it did: For some crazy reason, *she needed me*. It didn't matter whether I needed her. What I wanted wasn't relevant in the slightest. She'd brought her army with her not to save me, but to save herself from the pain of losing me.

Whatever pain you're going to feel when I'm gone, tough. Life isn't fair; deal with it. Go pick on someone your own size.

My mother turned away from me, caught sight of her new husband and plastered a smile on her face. Then she disappeared back into the courtroom.

Full of drive to win my freedom, but with nothing to do, I wandered outside the courthouse and touched the smooth stone statues I'd first met nearly two years ago when I'd won the Hebrew Lesson Lawsuit. In the center of the courtyard, a sixteen-foot-tall soldier erected by the Daughters of the Confederacy commanded the entire platoon. I pondered the words chiseled below his boots:

> Soldiers:
> In your duty,
> your devotion,
> your sacrifice,
> you teach us
> how to endure
> in silence
> and strength.

As I gazed into the warrior's unyielding face, I wondered

Love Wars

if someday someone would erect a monument to my parents' war—maybe even right here, at the primary battlefield.

As the shadows in the courthouse grew longer, Holly gave Bethany a pacifier to keep her quiet. I asked my new mom if I was ever going to talk to the judge. She frowned and said we'd have to come back tomorrow.

A second day dragged into a third. The hearing seemed to go on forever. I slumped against the smooth marble wall of the hallway and daydreamed about my against-all-odds mission to blow up the Death Star . . .

"The rest of Matthew's childhood is now in range," my mother's attorney announced to all the ominous men in masks who just follow orders and push buttons. "You may fire when ready."

As the Divorce War Death Star commenced primary ignition to annihilate my future, I saw the exhaust port straight ahead.

Darth Avi locked me into his sights. "I have you now!" Just as he was about to press the button, out of nowhere the *Millennium Falcon* flew in to save the day!

"*What?*" Darth Avi cried as a hail of turbolasers knocked him and his wingmen off course. They careened helplessly into distant space.

"You're all clear, kid! Now let's blow this thing and go home," Dad's voice crackled over the radio, accompanied by a big throaty grunt from his seven-foot-tall walking carpet of a lawyer.

Home. That sounds great.

I reached forward to grasp the trigger for my proton torpedoes. It was time to use the Force. *All I have to do is tell the judge . . . All I have to do is tell the judge . . .*

"Matthew, it's time to see the judge," Holly said, bringing me back to reality.

Love Wars

* * *

The bailiff led me in through the closed doors. As I entered, I sized up the two opposing armies seated on opposite sides of the courtroom. No less than thirty grown-up heads turned, and sixty eyes bored into my soul, analyzing my every move. I rubbernecked to take it all in, and suddenly realized, *Oh my God, all these people are here because of me. Don't these people have anything better to do with their lives than try to convince the judge who I should live with? Shouldn't I get to choose?*

For the second time in less than two years, I walked into Judge Handelman's private chambers. We went through the same routine. He asked me a few simple questions about my friends, my favorite sports, and my schoolwork.

"Are you still an aspiring public speaker?"

"Yeah," I told him. He had a good memory.

"What did you last speak about?" he asked.

"Henri Marie Raymond de Toulouse-Lautrec-Monfa, the famous painter," I replied.

"The Impressionist? Son, you're quite precocious," the judge said.

In fifth grade, Mrs. Kaputnik had made all the kids draw names out of a hat. I got an eccentric French artist who was obsessed with scantily clad dancing girls. This time I wrote my own speech and didn't just copy *National Geographic*. Mrs. Kaputnik loved my speech so much, she suggested I perform it in the end-of-year talent show.

"How did the speech go?" the judge asked.

"Uh . . . pretty well, I guess," I lied.

The talent show was a day I would have preferred to forget.

Love Wars

I had dressed in a top hat and a long black trench coat and walked with a cane, just like Lautrec. I started the speech perfectly, and read the notecards off without hesitation. I felt so confident that I stopped using the notecards, looked up at the audience in order to make eye contact, and spoke from memory.

Midway through my speech, I looked out at the sea of kids all gazing intently at me, and I lost my nerve and my place. *Where was I?* Frantically, I flipped through my notecards, trying to find the spot. My hands sweated, and I dropped the cards all over the stage. It was hopeless: they were a mess, scattered everywhere. I ran off the stage as fast as I could, sobbing. It was the most humiliating moment of my elementary school career.

But I said nothing about this to the judge.

"Who do you want to live with?" the judge asked, cutting to the chase.

"My father and my stepmother. I'm 100 percent certain. Actually, 110 percent," I added for good measure. And I meant it. I may have blown my speech, but there was no way I was going to screw this one up.

"You sound certain," the judge said.

"Yes," I responded.

"Okay, we're done. You are excused. Good luck with your public speaking career. I'm sure you'll go quite far."

That's it? This meeting had been even shorter than our last one.

I walked out of the judge's chambers, half my heart still buried in shame under stacks of flubbed notecards, the other half set free. I'd launched my proton torpedoes, and now all I could do was wait to see if they caused the anticipated chain reaction that

The Trial

would destroy my mother's fearsome battle station—or at least, her toxic grip on my life.

As I walked into the hallway, my father was waiting for me. "How'd it go with the judge?" he asked.

"I told him. Proton torpedoes down the hatch."

"Great shot, kid. That was one in a million!" he grinned.

Then the bailiff appeared, and called out in a redneck drawl: "Thomas . . . Thomas Tower?"

I turned to my brother, and he looked down at his shoes. He had about as much enthusiasm to go off with the big police officer as a prisoner on his way to the gallows.

I wanted to say, *Please, Thomas, just tell the judge you want to live with Dad.* But I knew it was hopeless. I could almost see the ghosts of his stuffed bunnies clutched close to his chest. Thomas Rabbit would sooner hop off a bridge than betray either of his parents.

* * *

The rest of the day, I asked Holly every four minutes or so, "When will it be over?" She kept saying, "Soon, soon."

When Dad emerged from the courtroom, I asked him the same question.

"Matthew, be patient. Remember the words of Mark Twain: 'The peach was once a bitter almond. Cauliflower is nothing but cabbage with a college education.'" I had no idea what this meant—what did cabbage have to do with cauliflower? He disappeared back into the courtroom.

Out of the corner of my eye, I saw Grandpa Avi push his way through the courtroom door. He'd finally made it. *Where had*

Love Wars

he been? I felt my stomach sink. Dad had mentioned how glad he was that my mother's trial-lawyer-of-a-father was nowhere in sight. Avi strode swiftly, his cane pounding the floor with purpose.

A half hour later, my father exited the courtroom with a frown on his face.

"Holly, Matthew, it looks like we're going to have to come back next week. Vanessa requested a continuance."

"*What? What does that mean?*" I almost yelled at my father.

"Matthew, keep your voice down," Holly hissed. "This is a courthouse."

"I don't know what it means," Dad said. "I'm guessing your mother knows she's not doing too well, so she's probably taking a time-out to regroup. Apparently her father's here to help dig her out of her hole. In any case, we won't get a decision until next week."

"But Dad, next week is *the first week of school!* I don't want to go to sixth grade in my mother's school district."

"Looks like you have no choice. I can't take you home with me or I'll get accused of kidnapping you. You have to go home with your mother now, but if all goes well, you'll be with me and Holly by the end of next week and then you can start at the right school."

"But I don't want to start school late. That will put me behind all the other kids!"

"Matthew, we have to play by the rules. We don't want to risk the entire case over a few days of school. You can call me from your mother's house if you want to talk," he said.

"Fine," I said stiffly. I stormed out and Holly followed me. When we got outside, she put her hand on my shoulder.

The Trial

I looked into her kind face, and my anger melted into a stream of tears. She hugged me, and then I cried out, "I'M NOT GOING TO STAY WITH HER! I DON'T CARE WHAT THE JUDGE SAYS! IF THE JUDGE MAKES ME LIVE WITH HER, I'M RUNNING AWAY!"

"Shhh, Matthew, I think it's going to be okay, I really do . . . I think the court case is going well, and there's little chance the judge is going to force you to stay with your mother. He didn't force you to take Hebrew lessons, remember?"

I cried a little more, but then she kissed my forehead and I started to feel better.

"Really, Mom? You think we're going to win?"

"Yes, I think so. We can only hope the judge will do the right thing. Now off you go to your mother's. We'll see you soon."

As I trod off to rejoin the fake Brady Bunch for what I hoped was the last time, my brain spun around in a dizzying circle. *What happened in there? What did Grandpa Avi do? Why did my mother take a time-out?*

* * *

As I got ready for school that weekend, an enormous swarm of belly-eating gray moths descended onto the big country club house, flew in through the chimney, hooked a right turn down the hallway into my bedroom, and dove directly down my throat and into my gut. As nervousness consumed me, all I could think about was the courtroom—and what Grandpa Avi was up to.

Grandpa Avi and Grandma Libby were staying on the pullout couch in the living room, and part of me wanted to go

The Trial

ask them. But the Master Manipulator scared me to my bones, so I avoided them completely.

On Monday, I rode the bus to Andrew Jackson Middle School. I prayed that it would be my one and only week in that building, and then I'd start over in a new school near my father's house. I told all my old friends from elementary school, "It's been nice going to school with you, but next week, I'm outta here." I bragged about how I wasn't going to touch any of my homework, because there was no point.

Please let me win. Please let me win. Please let me win.

After I got home from school, I secretly called my father for an update.

"Dad, what's happening? When will there be a decision?"

"I don't know, Matthew. Your mother's got a new lawyer, and they're re-arguing the entire case. It could go on for another week."

"*Another week? I can't wait that long!*"

"Tough, kiddo. You think I like it? Anyway, I don't want to say any more. I can't trust that this is a secure phone line."

"Okay, Dad, I'll talk to you tomorrow."

That night after dinner, Grandma Libby went outside by herself for a smoke. At least she wasn't sneaking cigarettes in the bathroom like she used to when I was younger. I'd been avoiding her, but now that she was outside by herself I realized: *Now's my chance. Go!* I walked outside into the dark North Carolina night. The moon was waning, and it was hard to see the stars because the streetlamps blocked them out.

Grandma furiously puffed away like she was trying to suck in a divine elixir of eternal life. When she saw me, her face lit up brighter than the tip of her cigarette.

Love Wars

"Matthew, darling! Come here and give Grandma a kiss."

I did as she asked, and stifled a gag. If I wanted to get anything out of her, I'd need my best fake-out moves.

"Oh, my dear sweet grandson, how I love you so. I know you're angry at your mother, but I don't blame you at all. I know your sick father has been brainwashing you, and you're under his thrall. Someday—*someday!*—you'll wake up and realize how good you have it with Vanessa. She loves you *so much!*"

I smiled. "Grandma, what was Grandpa Avi doing in the courtroom on Friday? Was it something important?"

Grandma Libby let loose the most outrageous, witchy cackle I'd ever heard.

"Oh Matthew, you're *so* smart. Did you figure out that Grandpa Avi rode in at the eleventh hour to save the day?"

"Save the day? What do you mean, Grandma?"

I needn't have worried that it would be hard to extract this information from her. She *bragged* about her husband's cunning plan.

"You know where you get your smarts from? Your Grandpa Avi, that's who! He didn't set foot in the courthouse the whole week for a reason. He was just biding his time. When your father didn't see Avi's car, he thought for sure he was going to win the case! But Avi was just waiting for the right time to make his move.

"On the third day of The Trial, your mother thought she was going to lose. You see, the judge is a relative of your father's lawyer. They're pals! It's so outrageous! Not to mention that Judge Handelman officiated at your father's second wedding. Vanessa was an *idiot* to agree to waive her right to challenge that conflict of interest. Actually, her Podunk lawyer was the idiot.

The Trial

"Avi and I took your mother out to lunch, and she was wailing. She was so upset, Matthew. She said she'd kill herself if she lost custody of you and Thomas! So Avi realized we'd need to bring in some heavy firepower if we were going to defeat that kind of nepotism. He asked the judge for a continuance, and got one. Your father almost fainted, honest to God. He never expected a continuance."

The belly-eating moths that'd taken up residence in my stomach went ballistic, as if someone had shaken them up like snowflakes in a snowglobe.

Grandma gazed off into the distance, starstruck by her husband's heroism, all the while dragging on her cigarette. She continued: "Avi picked up the phone and called your aunt Ellen, who found a Big-Shot Lawyer in Washington, DC, Mr. Ira Schneiderman. Now he's here and we're paying for his hotel and all his food. We kept Vanessa's local lawyer, and made him 'of counsel,' and paid him twelve thousand. But we're paying the Big-Shot Lawyer *fifty thousand*. When Schneiderman walked into the courtroom today, Nate's lawyer almost dropped dead. These little guys don't stand a chance against Big-Shot Lawyers from DC and New York."

Was I doomed? Would Avi's new lawyer wreck everything? I could run away to Dad's house, but then the police would come after me, arrest me, and send me back to my mother's jail. I'd rot in country club prison as I served out a seven-year sentence without possibility of parole, until I somehow managed to escape to college—or kill myself.

I wondered if someone would write a newspaper story about me after I was swinging from a rope. What would the obituary say? Would anyone know what *really* happened to me?

Love Wars

I imagined the news reports and interviews with my family members... "Oh but he was such a good son, he played soccer and wrote great book reports and gave amazing speeches about Impressionist painters at school. No one had any idea this could happen," my mother would coo to the reporter, adjusting her hair to make sure she looked good on TV. Gordon, his daughters, and my brother would stand behind her, the perfect suburban family, nodding their heads in unison to her every word. Pretty soon I'd be forgotten. Just another typical and utterly inexplicable teenage suicide, whose true story would be buried with his body like all the rest.

Grandma Libby snapped me back to reality, which was getting worse all the time.

"Matthew, do you think we're going to just stand by and watch while you become your father's minion? While your mother's life goes down the tubes? Do you know how much your Grandpa Avi loves you, and his daughter? You mean the world to him! He just dropped *sixty-two thousand dollars*. Grandpa Avi is going to save you, Matthew. He's going to save you, and save his daughter. *That's what being a responsible father looks like!*"

"Uh, gee whiz, thanks, Grandma," was all I could think to say as the wind shifted and blew clouds of cigarette smoke up my nostrils. I coughed, and my stomach heaved.

"Now *don't tell any of this to your father!* I don't want this getting back to him."

"Of course not, Grandma," I said with a big, watery-eyed smile.

Suddenly, her face changed into a beady-eyed scowl. I worried that I hadn't fooled her a bit. Then she burst out laughing, and relaxed.

The Trial

"Oh fine, go ahead, tell your father whatever you want. It doesn't matter, he can't use anything I just said to you in court. It's all hearsay. It wouldn't help him anyway; he's going to lose. Lose, lose, lose, *lose,* I tell you! There's *nothing* he can do against the Big-Shot Lawyer," she bragged as she flicked cigarette ash onto the lawn.

I was about to turn and go back into the house, to find the closest toilet in which to vomit up my guts, but Grandma Libby grabbed me tightly by the shoulder.

"Matthew, there's something else you should know."

"Uhhh, okay," I said feebly.

"There's a problem with Gordon," she said with a grimace of disgust. "You wouldn't *believe* what I found out about him. It's too adult for you anyway, but when I tell your grandfather about it, he's *not* going to be pleased."

Somehow I wasn't surprised that Libby had dug up some dirt on her new son-in-law. My grandparents hadn't been exactly thrilled about my mother marrying a Catholic, to say nothing of her surprise baptism.

"I'm going to talk with your mother about it after The Trial and she's not going to like it. When the dust settles and we rescue you and your brother from your father's vile clutches, we'll have to see about Gordon."

Great. Mom and Dad's War wasn't even over and already I heard the horns blaring a call to arms for my mother's next crusade. *Please God . . . get me out of here!*

"Uh, okay," I responded. I didn't know what else to say. Doubled over, I pulled away from her grip and dashed across the lawn, hoping I'd make it to the bathroom in time.

Love Wars

* * *

That night and every day after, I called my father to ask him for updates. My mother didn't bother to try to stop the phone calls. It seemed she was too busy worrying about the court case. Dad had little to no news. "We'll know by the end of the week," was a comment I was getting tired of hearing. When I saw him on Wednesday, I repeated Grandma Libby's little speech about Gordon to him, but he told me I shouldn't believe everything Libby said, and besides it was too vague to use as evidence.

Finally, Friday came. Dad picked Thomas and me up from my mother's house after school. When I heard his car roll up, I looked around my bedroom in the big Chapel Hill Country Club house and decided: *I don't care what the verdict is, I'm never coming back.*

But I did care. I wanted to win. I worried that my plot to never come back to my mother's house would be foiled if the judge ruled against me. Even if I was ready to defy the judge's orders, I feared my father never would. *Please let this be good news.*

"What's the decision, Dad?" I asked as soon as Thomas and I got into the car.

"I don't know yet. We're going down to the courthouse, and we'll find out when we get there."

When we arrived, I saw Grandpa Avi, Grandma Libby, Gordon, Lisa, and Cindy waiting on one side of the hallway, and Holly, with a sleeping Bethany cradled in her arms, on the other side. Thomas walked over to stand in the middle of the hallway, turned toward both sides, and then froze, not knowing which side he was supposed to be on, not wanting to choose. Without hesitation, I joined Holly and Bethany.

The Trial

My father walked through the closed doors into the courtroom to find out what the judge had decided, as did my mother, one step behind him.

I looked over at my so-called family assembled on the other side of the hall, and, for the first time since I'd been forced to spend quality time with him in upstate New York, made direct eye contact with my grandfather. He stared at me, his head nodding in a slow, rhythmic motion. But I didn't back down. I stared right back, and imagined laser beams shooting out of my eyes.

Twenty minutes later, Dad emerged from the courtroom. He did *not* look happy. His eyes were haunted. *Oh NO. CRAP! CRAP CRAP CRAP CRAP CRAP! What went wrong? Did the Master Manipulator and the Big-Shot Lawyer ruin everything?*

My mother walked out of the courtroom a step behind my father, and she looked pissed off, too. *Why are they both upset? Could the judge have decided they are BOTH unfit parents? Will Thomas and I end up in foster care?*

As Dad walked over to Holly and me, I saw my mother whisper something into Gordon's ear. The only words I could make out were "I can't believe it!" *I liked the sound of that.* After he'd absorbed the news, Gordon glared at me and said in a loud, haughty voice, "Don't worry, Vanessa, one day *he'll be back.*"

My heart leapt. Maybe the sun was ready to come out after all!

But then my mother grabbed Thomas by the hand and said, "Come on, we're going," and just like that the entire Brady Bunch—minus me—exited the scene. As they left, my grandfather's cane thudded on the marble floor and he looked back at me one last time. His eyes felt less intimidating. The old man's powers seemed to falter.

Love Wars

But where were they taking my brother?

"What happened, Dad?"

My father was silent for long moments, leaning his head against the wall. I could see tears in his eyes. Finally, he turned to face me.

"I have good news and bad news," my father announced in a choked voice.

It was one of my father's favorite expressions, like: "The bad news is you can't stay up past ten o'clock watching television. The good news is I picked up a pint of ice cream."

I knew the drill. "All right, give me the bad news first."

"The bad news is you aren't going to see your brother very much anymore."

"What? Why not?"

"The good news is you're free."

"Wait, what happened, Dad? Tell me exactly!"

"The judge awarded me custody over you and your mother custody over your brother. It's a split decision."

He sighed, and then his sadness turned into anger.

"I can't believe I lost Thomas. *Dammit!*"

Then he looked at me and softened his voice a little.

"It hurts like hell that I lost your brother. But as hard as it is for me, this is worse for you. A brother is your truest, best friend for your whole life. What the judge did is criminal."

"Will I ever see him again?"

"Under the new orders, you see your mother every other weekend. The rest of the time, you're with me. Likewise, I get to see Thomas every other weekend. So that means you'll see him on weekends, but not on weekdays."

I felt a lump in my throat. I couldn't believe what the judge

The Trial

had done. My father was right: it was criminal. I felt awful for Thomas that he had to spend so much time with our crazy mother. I felt bad that saving me cost Dad so much.

But it wasn't *my fault*. I'd tried to persuade Thomas to choose. By not choosing, he'd let the judge choose for him.

Still reeling from the shock, my mind wandered back through everything Thomas and I had been through together. The fighting had started when I was six and Thomas was three, and I was the one my parents both tried to draft as their soldier. They hadn't involved my brother in their war because he was "too little to understand." And he'd done all he could to stay on the sidelines, whereas I had no choice.

He and I were opposites. First I was Encyclopedia Brown, trying to figure out the fighting, and then I was Mafatu, the Polynesian warrior, struggling to conquer the sea and escape its wrath in order to get the heck out of my mother's life. And finally, I was Luke Skywalker, bravely confronting a parent—and grandparents—who'd turned to the dark side.

During all of our parents' fighting, Thomas had imitated his favorite stuffed animal: the rabbit. He'd curled up into a little ball and tried his best to ignore it all. Thomas Rabbit, the meek little child, had avoided The War by disappearing down his rabbit hole. Even when he was older, and I'd asked him to join me in my rebellion, he acted like a frightened Ewok, running to hide under a tree stump while the battle raged around him.

Angry at my parents for putting me in the middle, but most of all angry at my mother for trying to keep me away from my father, I'd taken all my rage out on my little brother and beat the stuffing out of him. As much as I hated the kids at school who bullied me, I'd bullied Thomas just as badly, if not worse.

The Trial

Thomas absorbed all the negativity around him like a happy sponge. He was kind to all those who had been mean to him—including and especially me. My cute little brother loved everyone, and never said a bad word against me, or my mother, or my father, or *anyone*.

The only time Thomas had ever spoken up about the way I treated him was when he'd written a Sunday school essay about his relationship with his family members. He wrote that he hated it when his big brother picked on him and he wished I would stop. The teacher had showed the letter to my mother, and she showed it to me and scolded me. After that, I'd felt ashamed and I dialed down my bullying a bit. But later it escalated again, and Thomas went right back to putting up with my crap with a smile on his face.

As much as I picked on him, I wished with all my heart that things had turned out differently. Bewildered, my eyes watery, I stared up at Dad.

"Why would the judge do such a thing?" I asked.

"I think I know what happened," Holly said, walking up. She'd been talking to my father's lawyer.

"The judge was sick of this whole custody battle," she said to Dad. "He'd seen you and Vanessa in court too many times, and he wanted to put an end to the fighting."

Then she turned to address me. "Apparently, the judge told your father's lawyer off the record that if either parent tries to alter the custody arrangement again, he'll be highly inclined to award custody over both sons to the non-complaining parent. Splitting the kids is the judge's way of putting an end to The War. It's crazy, but that's what he did."

I remembered the story of King Solomon.

Love Wars

"And by the way, it seems your grandfather's investment paid off. Apparently, that DC lawyer he brought in after the continuance knew you were a lost cause, so he focused all his energy on convincing the judge that Thomas would die of a broken heart if he didn't live with his mother."

As soon as Holly mentioned my mother, a new feeling flooded through me: relief. Horrid as it was to lose Thomas, I felt grateful to *finally* be out of my mother's madhouse.

"So I'm free?"

For the first time since he'd delivered the verdict, my father smiled.

"Free at last, free at last, thank God almighty, Matthew, *you are free at last!*"

"I love you, Dad. Thank you for saving me."

I reached up for a hug.

"I love you too, kiddo." He embraced me in a big bear hug.

We all hugged, me, Dad, and Mom, who cradled my sleeping one-year-old sister.

As we walked out of the courthouse, I wondered: *What will life be like with my new family? Will Mom and Dad love each other forever? Will I finally have a normal childhood?*

I imagined the coming years stretching out before me like an open road leading to fantastically fun destinations. Mom and Dad would take my little sister and me fishing, and we'd have picnics with deviled eggs and Pompadour Pudding. We'd go to the beach, play games on the boardwalk, and bury each other in the sand. I'd make new friends at middle school. By high school, I'd be super popular, have a pretty girlfriend, and get voted most likely to succeed on my way to being senior class valedictorian.

Love Wars

I was so happy, I felt like my face would burst.

On our way to the parking lot, I took one last glance over my shoulder at the courthouse, praying that we'd left the wreckage of The War behind us forever. I hoped I'd never again have to face my lunatic mother in a court battle.

"Dad, are the Love Wars over?"

"They better be, Matthew Skywalker. I can't afford another round! Let's go home."

As we walked out, he held my little hand in his big hand, and I returned to the final scenes of my movie . . .

As I flew my X-wing to safety, I heard my mother's attorney announce over the Imperial loudspeaker, "Standby . . . Standby . . ."

I looked behind and saw an image projected onto the doomed battle station's gray surface: my parents, pulling me apart when I was six years old.

And then the Divorce War Death Star exploded into a billion pieces!

As I guided my ship back to the rebel base, a familiar voice from beyond this mortal world told me something I'd cherish for the rest of my days: "Remember, the Force will be with you. Always."

I landed on the planet Yavin for a hero's welcome. To the sound of trumpets, the entire Rebel Alliance assembled to witness Princess Bethany place a golden medallion around Han Solo's neck, and then around mine . . .

Suddenly, I felt my father's grip clamp down, interrupting my victory ceremony. I noticed his other hand clench and unclench, his pink fingernails turning white as he made a big fist.

LOVE WARS

Dad scowled, his jaw tightened, and a red fire burned inside the pupils of his eyes. His face seemed to disappear behind a dark mask, and I heard heavy breathing. Although he didn't say it out loud, I watched him silently mouth the words: *I can't believe I lost Thomas. I can't believe I lost Thomas. I can't believe I lost . . .*

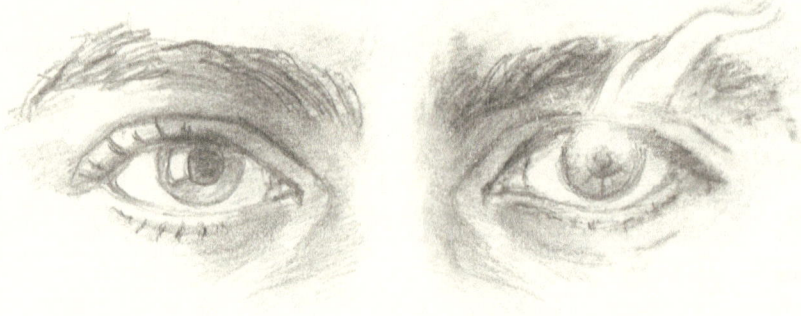

What happened in my teenage years is another story.

Epilogue

A Conversation with Grandma Libby

After The Trial, I became estranged from my grandparents Libby and Avi. In my mid-twenties, I began writing this memoir as a way to heal from the past. I came to see how much I wanted to reconnect with family members who had been adversaries during the custody battle.

Sadly, I missed my chance to reconcile with Grandpa Avi when he passed away in 2002. However, in April 2010, at the age of thirty-five, I finally got some quality time with my grandmother. When I met Grandma Libby for forkfuls of spaghetti at an Italian restaurant in Manhattan, I had my first heart-to-heart conversation with anyone on my mother's side of the family.

Matthew: Grandma, remembering back to when I was a little kid, how do you think the divorce affected me?

Grandma Libby: I never even thought of it. Now that you're asking me, it must have been devastating. But at the time, I only thought of my daughter.

M: You only thought of Vanessa?

GL: Vanessa was everything, everything. I was completely involved with Vanessa, all the time. She was always in trouble, and we had to get her out. I'll tell you the truth—only at this moment do I realize that I was thinking about my child and not about you. I tried for her to get custody of both of you. That's when we hired the Big-Shot Lawyer.

Love Wars

M: So when you went to hire the lawyer, you were thinking about my mom, not about how it would affect Thomas or me?

GL: No. I'll be very honest. But now you're telling me, and I realize, *Oh my God*. But at that time, all I could think about was that my child might lose her babies, so I have to help her. It must have had a terrible effect on you. You probably suffered. Maybe you had nightmares; I don't know. You were a child who was isolated. Terrible. Now that I think back, am I right? Is that how you felt?

M: That was some of it.

GL: And I apologize now that I wasn't aware.

M: (crying) Thank you, thank you, thank you, Grandma. You're the first adult to genuinely apologize to me. No one else in this entire drama has ever given me any kind of real apology or acknowledgment for what they did.

GL: Of course, I apologize, and I always loved you. And I tried to do my best. But, don't cry.

M: Grandma, I know your generation was told that crying is bad, but crying is okay.

GL: (sighing) You know what, Matthew? When I was a parent, everyone thought that children didn't really have feelings. They were taken care of, they were fed, they were bathed, and they had no feelings. And if children have feelings, they should keep them to themselves. When I was a child, I didn't like my mother, but I would

A Conversation with Grandma Libby

never express it. I felt she was stupid. I was smart enough to see she made wrong decisions, but I never told her.

M: So you never expressed yourself?

GL: Oh no. Never.

M: Would it surprise you to hear that in my childhood I frequently expressed myself?

GL: Well, good! It's a different generation. Don't regret it.

M: Grandma, I don't regret standing up for myself. Also, I am sad about things I did that hurt others, especially what I did to hurt my little brother. I wish I'd never bullied him. Yet, I don't blame myself. I don't hold myself responsible. I was a kid and I was acting out. I didn't know any better.

GL: Your parents probably didn't know any better either.

M: True, they didn't know any better, and still they had the space and possibility to see something different. Oppressed children should not be blamed for acting out. It is the grown-ups who are responsible, who have access to the resources they need to change their behavior.

GL: I didn't take you into consideration, you as a human being. I was ignorant of what your needs were; ignorant, but not malicious and knowing and doing something wrong. But you know, you can't turn back the clock.

Love Wars

M: Grandma, all we have is now. And right now I feel seen. I feel that you see who I am, and you care about my feelings.

GL: In my dislike of your father, I overlooked you. Terrible. You're your own person.

M: But now we've heard each other. I forgive you. I thank you, and I love you.

GL: I love you too. I've always loved you. I'm so glad we finally had this conversation. Such drama all around me, and I was so dumb and I didn't even know. But the marriage from the beginning was so incongruous, so wrong. I mean not just for Vanessa, but for your father too.

M: But they were in love at one point.

GL: I imagine they were.

M: (pointing to pictures) Just look at their wedding photos, Grandma! What do you think?

GL: Absolutely! You're right. They did love each other.

M: I also brought some pictures from when Thomas and I were little kids. Do you want to see?

GL: Of course, I do. By the way, Matthew, why did you say you're recording our conversation? Are you writing a book about your life?

A Conversation with Grandma Libby

M: How'd you guess?

GL: You know, everyone's crazy in our family. There's so much great material. You *should* write about it, and it'll be a bestseller, guaranteed! Just change all the names.

M: Of course, Grandma, I plan to change all the names.

GL: I can't wait to read it. Now let's look at those beautiful photos of my darling grandsons.

Last Dance

Finding healing and closure with my mother proved to be more difficult than with Grandma Libby. When Vanessa was diagnosed with Alzheimer's disease in 2008, she rapidly began losing her memories and vocabulary. However, a miracle occurred—no, two miracles—when I was forty and visited my mother in August 2014 in her nursing home.

"I love you," my mother said the moment she saw me, immediately recognizing me despite her dementia.

Turning away from her caregiver, she walked over and reached out to me. I embraced her and felt a wave of relief. I hadn't seen her for six months and I had feared she wouldn't know who I was anymore.

It's easy to take for granted those three little words. To hear them from my mother, who had mostly lost her ability to speak, was amazing. For the next two hours, she didn't say anything else comprehensible. Her vocalizations were a jumble of scattered mumblings and half-formed words. But her hugs, her kisses, the warm look in her eyes communicated everything she could no longer say. She loved me, she had missed me, she was grateful to see me.

Alzheimer's had been unkind to her. Although I was visiting on her sixty-eighth birthday, she looked more like an 88-year-old. Her graying skin hung loosely from her face and arms, her hair had thinned and splintered like the frayed ends of decayed twine, her eyes had sunk deep into dark sockets. In nine short years, the dementia had extinguished much of who she had been: her long-term memories, her rational mind, even her ability to take a shower without assistance.

Love Wars

Despite all she'd lost, a flame remained alight inside. Although she couldn't say much, she could understand quite a bit.

"Happy birthday, Mom. Do you know it's your birthday?" I asked, and she mumbled something incoherent. My girlfriend, Amber, and I sang "Happy Birthday" to her, and by the end of the song, she got it and smiled. She tried to sing along, but all that came out was, "appy . . . day . . . Mom, appy . . . you . . ."

I pulled out an iPod preloaded with some of her favorite music from her youth: Tchaikovsky's "The Nutcracker," the Beatles, Eurythmics, Pat Benatar, Gene Chandler, Paul Simon. My father had helped me pick out the tracks; he knew Vanessa's tastes better than I did. If I'd had a recording of my eight-year-old violin screechings, I would have added those to her playlist.

I turned on the iPod and played Carole King through a speaker. My mother's eyes lit up, and Amber and I stood up to dance for her.

"I feel the Earth move under my feet,
I feel the sky tumbling down,"
we sang along with Carole.

My mother reached her arms toward us. We pulled her up from her comfy chair and we all held hands and danced together. I remembered vowing as a seven-year-old never to dance with her again when she made me her date at the country hoedown. If ever there was a time to break that vow, this was it.

As she swayed and rocked back and forth with a big grin, I wondered if she was flashing back to the '70s, when she was a twenty-something medical student in love with my father.

It was such a relief to see her enjoying herself after the nightmare she'd endured during her move into the memory-care

Last Dance

facility. After three years of living with her boyfriend, Gustavo, he'd waved the flag of surrender when she could no longer use the toilet without help and let my brother move her into a skilled nursing home earlier in the summer while I was traveling overseas. Thomas said her first day in her new home went unexpectedly well. Photos of loved ones and a big-screen TV tuned to the Golf Channel seemed to placate her. But on day two, it took five burly sheriffs with a stretcher to subdue her after she flew into an unhinged rage, hitting the nurses and screaming. They transferred her to a psychiatric hospital for sedation and an adjustment in her meds.

When she was moved back into the memory-care facility seventy-two hours later, Vanessa seemed to give up on life. She stopped eating and drinking, apparently determined to fade away. However, a series of visits from Gustavo, Thomas, and her sister Ellen cheered her up, and she started drinking chocolate milkshakes and Gatorade. Apparently, a person can live a long time on milkshakes and Gatorade, the nurses told me. After returning from my travels, I'd visited her, grateful for a chance to help her celebrate her birthday.

After our little dance, it was time for dinner, and my mother slipped her frail arm into mine. We walked to the dining room, her steps slow and uncertain. Her fingernails dug into my sleeve. The only strength in her body seemed to come from her love and trust in me.

I'd brought a home-cooked spinach-and-coconut-milk soup, hoping to entice her to eat real food. She ate a little, although not as much as I wanted. During the entire dinner, her eyes never left mine. I held her hand. I told her again and again how much I loved her.

Love Wars

After dinner, we walked outside and she sat on a bench for a while, the warm California sun bathing her face. She leaned back toward me, and I massaged her shoulders to work out some of the stress she'd been carrying for so many years. Soon she was tired, and Amber and I walked her back to her room, helped her get into bed for a nap, and put on some of her favorite classical music as a lullaby.

* * *

I visited my mother several more times over the following weeks. Each time, she seemed weaker, less responsive, less able to connect. She was once again refusing to eat or drink.

By early September, it was clear that she wasn't going to last much longer. I began visiting daily. When I walked in, her eyes opened partway. I wasn't sure if she could see me through the narrow slits. She moaned, no longer able to speak or to even mumble.

The nurses had told me that hearing is the last sense to go. Presumably, she could still hear me—and, perhaps, understand. This was my last chance to say what I needed to say to get complete with her.

"Mom, it's Matthew. I love you a lot," I said, squeezing her hand. I felt her squeeze back.

"I'm so grateful you brought me into this world. You worked hard in your medical practice and you always found ways to support me. You supported me when I was a kid playing soccer, you supported me when I started my publishing company, you've always been there for me.

"I know you experienced a lot of pain in your life, as a child

Last Dance

and as an adult. I know you didn't want to have borderline personality disorder. I feel compassion and empathy for all you've been through. You didn't want to be so angry; you wanted peace in your life. It's such a blessing that you finally found the peace you craved in your relationship with Gustavo.

"I know we come from a long line of trauma, both in our family and in what our Jewish ancestors experienced in the Russian pogroms. I know you did not want to pass that trauma on to me. I'm sad about the negative things you did to me, and I forgive you. I know it wasn't intentional; you didn't want to hurt me. You wanted to take care of me."

I squeezed her hand again and felt her squeeze back.

"Mom, I'm so grateful for the opportunity I have to work in the world to change the trauma that people experience. I want to help people break those generational cycles of trauma. I'm going to help change things. Isn't that beautiful, Mom? You were a doctor and you helped so many people. I'm going to help people, too.

"It's nice to feel close to you," I said, softly stroking her head. "It's nice to forgive you and let go of the past. Remember our little Hebrew-lesson court adventure? I became empowered, I became a strong man in part because of you. We had our hard times and conflicts, didn't we? I'm sorry it took me so long to recognize your love for me. Thank you for helping me to recognize it now.

"I'm going to say goodbye, because I don't know if I'm going to see you again. Goodbye, Mom, I love you. I hope you have a safe journey. Do you know how much I love you? I love you, Mom."

I now felt complete in my relationship with my mother. But I realized that not everyone who had been close to her was complete.

Love Wars

I tiptoed out of the room and called my father.

"Hi, Dad, it's Matthew."

"Matthew! What can I do for you?"

"Dad, I'm sad to have to tell you this . . . I'm with my mother at the memory-care home, and I don't think she's going to last much longer."

"That's a real shame, Matthew. I'm sorry you're going to lose her," he said.

"Dad, I want to ask you to do something, and I realize this is going to be an unexpected request. I want you to speak to her and say something nice. You haven't spoken to her in more than a decade, and I know that all the difficulties the two of you had still weigh on her. It would be a real gift to her if you can help her release the burden of her past before she departs. And," I said, choking up, feeling tears coming, "it would be a gift for me too."

"I don't know, Matthew. I don't want to cause her any upset, especially now," he said.

"Trust me, Dad, she isn't angry at you anymore, and I suspect hearing from you would help her find some peace."

"All right, Matthew, if you're sure . . . What do you think she'd want to hear?"

"Just say something nice to her. That's all I'm asking."

"Okay, put me on speakerphone."

I tapped the phone's screen and ducked back into the room. I took my mother's hand and held the phone close to her.

"Vanessa, this is Nate," my father said. She moved her head a little and seemed to recognize his voice.

"Listen, we had eleven good years together. We were an amazing couple, and all of our friends said so. I know things became emotionally difficult between us at the end. The

Last Dance

only reason it became so difficult is because we both love our children unconditionally. I know how much you love Matthew and Thomas, and I love them just as much. Whatever difficulties happened between us are in the past and don't matter anymore. I'm proud of our children, and I know you are too.

"I also want you to know I still hear from your former patients about what a fantastic physician you were. You built an extraordinary medical practice and left a profound legacy. I'm so sorry that you've succumbed to this damn illness. It's not fair, and you deserve better. I wish things were different and you didn't have to face this right now.

"Vanessa? I hope the sound of my voice isn't causing you distress after all these years. Matthew, are you sure she's okay hearing from me?" he asked.

I squeezed her hand. She squeezed back.

"Dad, I think she appreciates your call. A few years ago, Mom and I looked through some of her family photo albums, and she didn't have any negative reactions when she saw you in her wedding photos. She had even saved photos from your courtship and the early years of your marriage, before I was born, and she smiled when we looked at them. You two were quite an attractive couple."

"Vanessa, you were a gorgeous woman. I still remember your beautiful long hair," my father said.

"You know, I saw photos of the two of you on vacation with your brother and her sisters. You were traveling in Greece, lying on the beach, hiking through forests . . ."

My father interrupted me. "Vanessa, I'm glad I'm finally in touch with you again after all these years. And I hope you are finding some solace and comfort."

Love Wars

I choked up. "Dad, I'm grateful for what you just said. I've fantasized about a moment like this since I was six years old. I wanted for the two of you to be able to move past the pain of your divorce and arrive at a sense of mutual respect. You just did that," I said, now on the verge of tears. "This is one of the greatest gifts you could ever have given me."

"Matthew, I am glad you asked me to speak with your mother. I feel a lot better now, and I hope she does as well."

"I know she does." I felt my mother's hand squeeze back as I squeezed hers. "I'll talk to you later, Dad. Goodbye."

I put the phone back in my pocket and sat next to the bed, listening to my mother breathe.

The next day, Vanessa passed away in her sleep.

* * *

Ever since I first met Luke Skywalker on the silver screen at age three, I fantasized about being a Jedi. But what does it mean to be a Jedi in real life? I think of Yoda's words: "Adventure . . . Excitement . . . A Jedi craves not these things." And, "Wars not make one great."

The moment in my life that I am most proud of—when I most embodied true Jedi principles—was when I convinced my father to make peace with my mother.

Where Are They Now?

An Internet search indicates that **Ira Schneiderman**, dubbed the Big-Shot Lawyer by Grandma Libby, acquired a well-deserved reputation as one of the most aggressive and expensive family law practitioners in Washington, DC, charging $875 per hour. However, when he sued one of his own divorce clients in 2013 for half a million dollars—and lost—his practice went into a tailspin. By 2014, he'd filed for bankruptcy.

Judge Handelman passed away in 2009 before I had a chance to track him down and ask him to elaborate on his rationale for splitting up Thomas and me. He's remembered in Chapel Hill as a "model judge."

When **Grandpa Avi** was on his deathbed in 2002, my mother arrived to say goodbye, only to learn that Avi had written her (and the rest of her siblings) out of The Will and left everything to Grandma Libby. According to Aunt Ellen, my mother threw the most dramatic screaming fit of her life and stormed out less than an hour before her father passed away.

Grandma Libby passed in 2020, aged 96. Her legacy was love, and that was my inheritance, for which I am eternally grateful.

Aunt Ellen owns a prominent corporate litigation firm headquartered in Manhattan. When I saw her for brunch, Ellen bragged that she's worth tens of millions and implored me to go to law school because "there's no money in writing."

Love Wars

My cousin **Wendy,** Ellen's daughter and winner of the Passover *Afikomen* contest, is vice president of her mother's law firm.

Years later, I found out why **Aunt Kendra,** my mother's twin sister, had been confined in a Bethesda hospital when I was nine years old. She had been diagnosed with bipolar disorder. Refusing treatment, within a few years she divorced her husband, Rod; abandoned her children; and gave up her career as a schoolteacher. Living in isolation, she developed a fantasy alter ego as the world's greatest cancer researcher, submitting hundreds of articles to medical journals worldwide. None were published.

My cousins **Joshua** and **Rachel**, Kendra's children, are both married with kids. When Josh learned that Aunt Ellen told Grandma Libby to spend every last penny of Avi's estate on housing and health care, ensuring Josh would never inherit anything from his grandparents, he stopped speaking to Ellen.

Nate retired from his position as Professor of Genetic Engineering at the University of North Carolina in Chapel Hill. Although he never fulfilled his ambition to cure every bloodborne disease known to mankind, he takes delight in simple things, like his non-genetically modified vegetable garden.

Holly retired after working as a nanny in Chapel Hill. She read the entirety of this memoir prior to publication and called it accurate and fair to all parties.

Thomas lives with his wife in Lake Geneva, Wisconsin, and

Where Are They Now?

works as a national park ranger. When we were in our twenties, I apologized for bullying him as a child.

Bethany lives with her husband in New York and works in Broadway theater production.

Gordon is still a Professor of Mathematics at the University of North Carolina. When I sat him down for coffee in 2009, at the end of a moving conversation about the past, we exchanged high fives for the first time in more than twenty years.

Gordon's daughters, **Cindy** and **Lisa**, are both full-time moms raising children and live near their father.

Johnny Callaghan married his crush from fifth grade. They live near his mother in Chapel Hill, where he runs a sporting goods shop.

My father's mother, **Grandma Miriam**, passed away in October 2009. A few days before she died, I asked her if she remembered the summers she and Grandpa Stanley spent playing tennis with me during my childhood. Her last words to me were, "Let's do it again."

Although he was forlorn after Miriam passed, **Grandpa Stanley** continued his habit of working out seven days per week. He died on a treadmill at age 101. The gym in Chapel Hill hung his photo in memoriam at their front desk.

Bob Trapp was never seen nor heard from again.

Illustrations

Parent Labyrinth 4
Edge of Destiny 5
Family 7
Before 12
The Nuclear Divorce 14
Goodbye to My Hundred Acre Wood 17
Tug-of-War 19
I Had to Be a Jedi 26
My Hundred Acre Wood Shatters 33
Charred to Cinders 34
How the Divorce Stole Christmas 35
Stormtrooper Moving Services 37
It's All His Fault 41
Someday You'll Be a Lawyer 50
Child Soldier 54
When Do I See Daddy? 55
A Galaxy Far, Far Away 63
Johnny's Hammer 75
Mommy Mental Patient and Daddy Hitler 78
Divorce War Death Star 80
The Shrink 81
Shrunk 83
Sugar High 92
Obey the Contract 95
Sandbox 98
Cut the Child 99
Invisible 102

Love Wars

Arrested	107
Encyclopedia Tower Takes the Case	109
Messenger Boy	110
Holly's Knitting	114
Driven	115
Please God, Let This Work	119
Bob Trapp	122
Pitcher's Mound	128
Haunting Thomas	133
We're in the Money	139
Dumping Session	144
The Monsters	145
Cocoon	146
Trainspotting	153
Ally	157
The Rebellion Against the Divorce War	158
Tuning the Violin	161
A Shattering Performance	163
Lost Dogs	179
Another Red Fern	180
Call It Courage	187
Failure	189
The Wise Adult	195
Darth Avi	199
Wendy Takes All	201
My First Lawsuit	205
No One Can Hear Her Scream	210
Love Wars or: Someday, They'll Make a Movie	215
Judgment	225

Illustrations

School's Out	226
The Beach	227
Where's My Hero?	231
Freedom?	241
Make a Wish	249
Slim Pickings or: How Vanessa and Nate Learned to Stop Worrying	254
The Nuclear Bride	255
Everybody Wants to Rule Our World	257
Medusa	260
Brothers	266
M.T. Phone Home	274
Lost Boy	280
'Til Death Do Us Part	285
Quality Time	287
Listen to Your Grandfather	290
Save Thomas Rabbit	293
Intact?	295
Training	297
Diagnosis	305
Suiting Up	307
Please	309
Standby	313
Grown-ups Watch Me	315
Attack of the Moths	320
Splitting	330
It Doesn't Get Any Better Than This	333
The Love Wars Better Be Over	335
What Happened in My Teenage Years	336

Love Wars

Grandma Libby	338
Old Photos	343
Last Dance	344
Peace	353
Where Are They Now?	354
Keep Your Eye on the Ball	358
Untitled	362
Marcelo's Perpetual Journey	370

Artist's Afterword

The author's passion inspired me to create the LOVE WARS illustrations.

Star Wars brought Matthew and me together. He discovered my artwork in an official *Star Wars Illustration* book and contacted me. He came all the way to Japan to meet me for the first time in a restaurant, and requested I work on his project. I was moved by his passion and accepted the job, which was the LOVE WARS cover illustration.

Once I had completed the cover, Matthew asked that I also work on interior illustrations. I never intended to do interior illustrations for books published where the culture and customs were different. I thought it would be hard for me to understand the everyday problems of a different culture and draw illustrations based on them.

Matthew was persistent, but I turned him down. After that, he found several other artists, commissioned sample interior illustrations from them, and asked me for my feedback. Although the illustrations were well done, I thought they were imitating the text and not helping readers ignite their imaginations.

After that, he asked me to art direct the interior illustration project. I responded to his request with sketches instead of writing an email. Once I did that, I felt I couldn't say no to him any longer and decided to do the interior illustrations myself.

At first, he asked me to create 25 illustrations, which wasn't an awful lot of work. However, I'm amazed that we ended up with more than 90 illustrations.

Love Wars

In the beginning, I was drawing more objectively, but as I kept going, I found myself caught deeply in the story, understanding the main character's feelings more and more. Matthew was bombarded with adults' egos and suffered emotionally. I was confident that I could depict things through his eyes and had a good experience with this project.

This story shows that fights caused by differences in values between parents can affect a child's feelings over time and take away their right to be happy. I hope many people, especially parents and children, will read LOVE WARS and learn some important lessons.

I would like to thank my good friend and the author, Matthew, for giving me this fantastic opportunity. Also, I would like to thank Michiru for providing us great assistance with translations.

- Tsuneo Sanda
Tokyo, Japan
SandaWorld.com

Acknowledgments

The author would like to acknowledge:

Bill Eddy, whose groundbreaking book *Splitting* helped me to understand my parents' divorce. His resources for parents and professionals navigating high conflict dynamics, such as the New Ways for Families program, the BIFF Response method, and many books, videos and free articles are found at highconflictinstitute.com.

Chelsea Page, developmental editor extraordinaire, and this memoir's primary champion.

Tsuneo Sanda, master artist and dear friend, whose brilliant illustrations I will cherish forever. Delve into his works of wonder at SandaWorld.com. Arigatou so much, Sanda-san!

Regina Brooks with Serendipity Literary Agency, for her exceptional dedication, wisdom, and faith.

Marcelo Anciano, whose visionary design and art direction transformed our raw material into a compelling synthesis of words and images.

E.B. Lewis, Artistrator and art director, who guided the illustration development process. View E.B.'s award-winning portfolio at eblewis.com.

Director Garrick Hagon and Producer Liza Ross with The Story Circle, who alchemized LOVE WARS into a dramatized, full-cast audiobook. Find the audiobook at LoveWars.com.

Linda Sivertsen, publishing coach, for always believing. She offers writing retreats to help authors discover their magic. Check out Linda's full range of literary resources at bookmama.com.

Love Wars

Penny M., who encouraged me to start writing when the wilderness of my memories seemed impassable; Miss Pamela, who knows a thing or two about memoirs; my stepmother, whose real name is not Holly but whose love for me is; Mary Jane N., who did for me what a hairstylist does best, other than cutting hair; and TMC, especially Andrew J. D., for supporting me in living my purpose.

Kathy Skaggs, brilliant managing editor; publishing coach Nicole Geiger, who helped me to navigate the default publishing world; Brandon Hamilton, whose phenomenal contributions helped to evolve the cover's direction; Nick Des Barres, who threw down the jams; Daniel "Dabu" Burwen and Sergio Paez for additional artistic input; Lisa Callif, Victoria Rosales, Dean Cheley, Seema Tilak, and Erez Rosenberg at Donaldson Callif Perez and Katherine Bond at Cislo & Thomas, for peace of mind on intellectual property; Michiru Tabuchi, for her ace translations; Laura Yorke for challenging me to uncover this book's primary audience; and additional editorial contributions from Samantha Clark, Ann Howard Creel, Laurel Roberts-Meese, Brooke Warner, Lisa Henson, and Joanne Farness.

Cheryl and Mark Pozzi, proprietors of Whispering Spirit Ranch, where I lived for a glorious summer of rewriting surrounded by horses in New Mexico's Sandia Mountains.

Philip Halpern and Marty Steiger, Bay Area English teachers who made one of my dreams come true.

The Society of Children's Book Writers and Illustrators (scbwi.org) and the National Association of Memoir Writers (namw.org).

Alexis, who was there for me; Molly, whose cover sketch rocked; and Kirsten, who told me that the first draft of this book sucked.

Mom and Dad, for the gifts of life and fantastic material.

Acknowledgments

During the course of revision, I stumbled upon the power of beta readers. Superstar reader Isaac K., then age ten, told me an early version of this book was a "D−" because it contained no dialogue. Thanks, Isaac! Also thanks to: Ashley A., Joan A., Shatonya A., Erica B., Josh B., Joshua B., Khadija B., Marvion B., Tatayana B., Jason C., Kim C., Laurel C., Peter C., Terra C., Frances D., Miranda D., Ryen D., Solomon D., Zachary D., Aleeca F., Alexandria F., Jaynie F., Karen E., Sherry F., Amparo G., Amri G., Andre G., Celestine G., SaraKay G., Sheyna G., Danny H., Jenafir H., Max H., Brittney J., Hiroshi J., Oren J., Wendy K., Jeffrey L., Miki L., Margot L., Philippe L., Carrie M., Kirk M., Liz M., Michael M., Morgan M., Xeno M., Sophia O-H., Allana P., Cheryl P., Gabe P., Gaya P., Laura P., Mark P., Collette Q., Alyana R., Linda R., Tom R., Esther R-A., April S., Bar S., Barbara S., Bob S., Brian S., Colleen S., Damian S., Dan S., Darrell S., Laura S., Lori S., Sam S., Sherry S., Angus T., Maurice T., Tim T., Adriana V., Faith V., Michael V., Phil W., and William W.

With so many beta readers, I undoubtedly omitted a few. If you read a preliminary version of this book and your name doesn't appear above, please know that I appreciate your feedback.

To learn more about the Dramatized Audiobook and eBook editions, and to stay up to date on future projects, visit LoveWars.com.

Love Wars

About the Author and Illustrator

MATTHEW A. TOWER is an author, art director, audiobook narrator, and entrepreneur. He first saw *Star Wars* in theaters at age three. LOVE WARS is his debut work of literature. For Q&A with the author, visit LoveWars.com.

TSUNEO SANDA is an award-winning artist who lives in Japan. He is celebrated for his *Star Wars*, *Star Trek*, and Disney illustrations. George Lucas owns many of his original paintings. Explore his creations at SandaWorld.com.

Review Call to Action

Please kindly review LOVE WARS on your favorite bookseller's website and at GoodReads.com. Help others discover this book! Here's one we received just prior to publication.

"**Takeaway**: Powerful, expressive rendering of divorce from a child's perspective.

Tower's debut is obviously written from the heart. What makes it resonate is the palpable emotion Matthew feels: fear, resentment, grief—and a burning desperation to somehow just be a kid while his world fractures into pieces . . . Illustrations by Tsuneo Sanda give powerful voice to Matthew's distress, depicting the weight of his parents' anger and his youthful hope that, with a little inspiration from his childhood heroes, he can right their sinking ship . . . Though it looks different than expected, Tower closes with his long-sought-after peaceful ending, recognizing his years of pain eventually give way to empowerment, closure, and purpose.

Production grades
Cover: **A**
Design and typography: **A**
Illustrations: **A**
Editing: **A**"

LOVEWARS.com

Your source for:

The Full-Cast Dramatized Audiobook

The Illustrated eBook

T-Shirts • Posters

Guides and Resources for Readers,

Educators, Parents, & Professionals

and Future Books

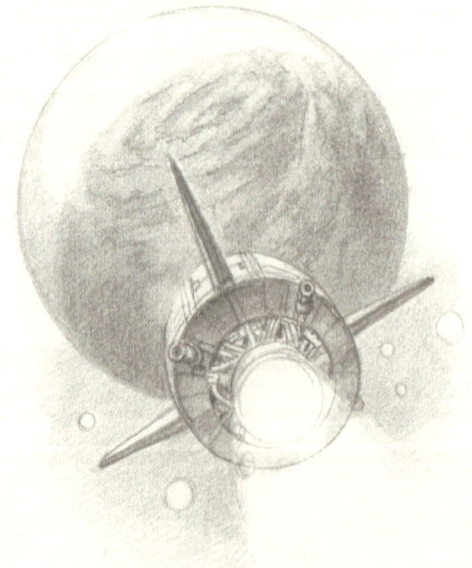

www.ingramcontent.com/pod-product-compliance
Lightning Source LLC
Chambersburg PA
CBHW030447100526
44580CB00001B/12